Anonymous

Official Record of the Tasmanian International Exhibition, Held at Launceston, 1891-92

Anonymous

Official Record of the Tasmanian International Exhibition, Held at Launceston, 1891-92

ISBN/EAN: 9783337272180

Printed in Europe, USA, Canada, Australia, Japan

Cover: Foto ©ninafisch / pixelio.de

More available books at **www.hansebooks.com**

OFFICIAL RECORD

OF THE

TASMANIAN

INTERNATIONAL

EXHIBITION

HELD AT LAUNCESTON, 1891-92.

TASMANIA:
PRINTED FOR THE COMMISSIONERS AT THE "LAUNCESTON EXAMINER"
OFFICE.

MDCCCXCIII.

PREFACE.

In compiling the Official Record of the Tasmanian International Exhibition I have to offer my thanks to Mr. Fenton (author of the "History of Tasmania") and Mr. R. M. Johnston, Government Statist, for much of the information contained in this volume, and to acknowledge the assistance which the excellent reports published in the "Launceston Examiner" have afforded me. From Mr. Jules Joubert I have had ready and willing help in the compilation of the work.

RONALD W. SMITH.

INDEX.

	PAGE
PREFACE	iii.
LIST OF OFFICIALS	vii.
HISTORICAL SKETCH OF TASMANIA	1
PHYSICAL FEATURES, NATURAL PRODUCTS, ETC.	8
REPORT OF THE EXECUTIVE COMMISSIONER	16
THE OPENING CEREMONIES	19
THE PROCESSION	22
WITHIN THE ALBERT HALL	25
THE LUNCHEON	29
THE EVENING'S PROCEEDINGS	37
INAUGURAL CANTATA	39
A BIRD'S-EYE VIEW OF THE INTERIOR	42
DEATH OF THE DUKE OF CLARENCE	46
THE MINERAL ARCH	48
THE FERNERY	49
THE MODEL DAIRY	50
LIST OF JURORS	51
AWARDS	58
REPORT OF THE SPECIAL JURY	111
REPORT OF CHAIRMAN OF JURORS	114
THE CLOSING CEREMONY	115
THE BRITISH "AT HOME"	119
THE MAYORAL PICNIC	120
AGRICULTURAL AND HORTICULTURAL SHOW	126
BALANCE SHEET AND STATEMENT OF ACCOUNTS	135

LIST OF OFFICIALS.

PATRON:
HIS EXCELLENCY THE GOVERNOR, SIR ROBERT GEORGE CROOKSHANK HAMILTON, K.C.B.

VICE-PATRONS:
The hon P. O. Fysh, Premier and Chief Secretary; the hon. A. I. Clark, Attorney-General; the hon. W. Moore, President of the Legislative Council; the hon. B. S. Bird, Treasurer; the hon. A. T. Pillinger, Minister of Lands and Works; the hon. N. J. Brown, Speaker of the House of Assembly.

PRESIDENT:
The hon. Wm. Hart, M.L.C.

VICE-PRESIDENTS:
The hon. G. P. Fitzgerald, M.H.A.; J. G. Davies, Esq.; the Mayor of Hobart; Richard Green, Esq.; the Mayor of Launceston; W. H. D. Archer, Esq.; William Gibson, Esq.; the hon. Adye Douglas, M L.C.; the Members of both Houses of Parliament; the Aldermen of Launceston—Messrs. H. J. Dean, R. H. Price, S. J. Sutton, H. Edgell, David Scott, E. H. Panton, P. Barrett, W. I. Thrower.

EXECUTIVE COMMISSIONER:
S. J. Sutton, Esq., M.H.A.

COMMISSIONERS:
Hon. Adye Douglas, M.L.C., Chairman; Messrs. Alex. Webster, J Brickhill, W. H. Knight, J Gunn, F. G. Duff, J. Campbell, W. R. Marsh, R. H. Price, M. E. Robinson, W. W. Stewart, S. J. Sutton, B. P. Farrelly, Jules Joubert, C.M.G.

GENERAL COMMITTEE:
Hon. W. Hart, M.L.C., President; S. J. Sutton, Esq., Executive Commissioner; Alex. Webster, Esq., Treasurer; Messrs. A. W Birchall, J. Brickhill, Henry Button, J. Campbell, Jos E. Clarke, D. H. Connolly, C. Dodgshun, F. Gee Duff, H. Edgell, J. C. Ferguson, J. T. Farmilo, B. P. Farrelly, J. Galvin, H. Gatenby, Richard Green, J. Gunn, F. Hart, jun., A. Haywood, W Horne, J. S. Kerr, W. H. Knight, A. E. Luttrell, W. R. Marsh, T. W. Monds, G. Paton, W. F. Petterd, R. H. Price, M. E. Robinson, C. W. Rocher, Aug. Simson, W. W. Stewart, J. B. Waldron, J. Wallace, C. Dempster, P. O. Fysh, jun., W. L. Stokes.

HOBART COMMITTEE:
Hon. G. P. Fitzgerald, Chairman; Hon. N. J. Brown, M.H.A.; Messrs. W. H. Burgess, J. Baily, J. Maughan-Barnett, J. Cooke, Alfred Crisp, M.H.A., J. G. Davies, M.H.A., D. Johnson, R. M. Johnstone, J. C. Paton, C. A. J. Piesse, J. W. Syme, J. B. Walker, C. E. Walch, H. Wright.

Hon. Secretary—Alex. Morton, Esq., F.L.S.

LONDON COMMITTEE

Chairman—The hon. Sir Edward Braddon, K.C.M.G., Agent-General.
Members—Sir Philip Cunliffe Owen, K.C.B., K.C.M.G., C.S.I.; Sir Douglas Galton, K.C.B., D.C.L., F.R.S.; Colonel Sir Herbert Bruce Sandford, K.C.M.G., R.A.; Sir Frederick Young, K.C.M.G.; Sir James Youl, K.C.M.G.; Sir Henry Trueman Wood; Prof. W. C. Roberts-Austen, C.B., F.R.S.; A. J. R. Trendell, Esq., C.M.G.; Prof. C. LeNeve Foster, D.Sc.; James Dredge, Esq.; D. Larnach, Esq.; W. J. Last, Esq., M.I.C.E.; James Paxton, Esq.

Secretary—R. Hewlett, Esq.

OFFICIAL REPRESENTATIVES:

New South Wales—W. H. Vivian, Esq., Executive Commissioner; Louis Saber Esq., Official Agent.
Great Britain—Arthur Day, Esq.; Austria and Germany—Herr Bossomaier; France—M. Victor Laruelle; Victoria—D. Fergus Scott, Esq.; South Australia—H. J. Scott, Esq.; Queensland—H. C. Luck, Esq.; Western Australia—H. J. Scott, Esq.; New Zealand—D. H. Hastings, Esq.

GENERAL MANAGER:

Jules Joubert.

SECRETARY:

Herbert A. Percy.

STAFF:

Superintendent, Mr. E. H. Sutton, jun.; Comptroller of Admissions, Mr. Louis Saber; Clerk and Accountant, Mr. W. H. Twelvetrees; Official Photographer, Mr. R. J. Nicholas; Architect, Mr. A. E. Luttrell.

HISTORICAL SKETCH OF TASMANIA.

THE history of Tasmania is an oft told tale. Its past is full of stirring and pathetic events from which it emerged under a more fantastic name than which it had previously borne to be regarded as the Cinderella of the colonies—endowed with great natural beauty and attractions, but for some unexplained reason kept in the background in the race for progress. The events of the last twenty years, however, have effected a marvellous change, and the display of mineral and other products made at the exhibition just closed affords ample proof that the future of the colony is great with promise of abundant prosperity. In days to come, and not far distant days either, it will attract attention rather by its commercial status, mineral output, and fruitful fields, than for its lovely scenery and superb climate.

The discovery of the island was made by Tasman in 1642, and he named it Van Diemen's Land in honour of Anthony Van Diemen, Governor of Batavia, under whose directions the expedition was formed. Tasman first sailed from Batavia to Mauritius, thus for some unexplained reason forsaking the object of his voyage, and on the 8th October, 1642, he left Mauritius in the *Heemskirk* with his brother Gerritt Tasman in the fly-boat *Zeehaan* in company, and steered in a south-easterly direction in search of the "Great South Land." Travelling over an unknown sea to an unknown port Tasman decided that that course was the most likely one to enable him to ascertain how far the land extended to the south which had already been followed by the pioneer Dutch navigators along the west and south-west coasts of Western Australia. At four o'clock on the 24th November, 1642, in about $42\frac{1}{2}°$ south latitude Tasman sighted the island which years afterwards was named after him. The land sighted was a spot not far distant from Macquarie Harbour. As the vessels approached the coast the outlines of lofty mountains rising in majestic stateliness discovered themselves in the back-ground. Two of these were in 1798 named by Flinders Mounts Heemskirk and Zeehan, after Tasman's ships, and it is beneath their shadow that the most extensive mining operations which have yet been undertaken in the colony are now being conducted. On December 1 Tasman's ships anchored in a bay on the East Coast, now marked on the maps as Marion Bay, north of Forestier's Peninsula. On the following day the explorers proceeded on shore, but saw no natives. "I fancied I heard the sound of people upon the shore," wrote Tasman, "but I saw none. . . . I observed smoke in several places; however, we did nothing more than set up a post on which everyone cut his name or his mark, and upon which I hoisted a flag." The voyager did not further explore the land he had discovered, but proceeded along the coast and steered in the direction of New Zealand, which he discovered and named Nova Zeelanda, after which he returned to Batavia.

For more than a century after this no white man set foot on Tasmania, but one hundred and thirty years after Tasman's discovery Marion du Fresne, a French captain, arrived with two discovery ships, and anchored in Marion Bay on the 4th March, 1772. The natives were then seen for the first time. They proceeded with confidence to meet the boats, and with their children and wives remained close to the strangers. Some misunderstanding, however, took place, and the result was that the natives retired and threw a volley of stones at the Frenchmen, who repelled the attack by a discharge of firearms, killing and wounding some of the blacks. Marion du Fresne was afterwards killed by the more warlike natives of New Zealand.

In the following year (1773) the island was visited by Captain Furneaux, in the *Adventure*, who was accompanying Captain Cook, of the *Resolution*, into more southerly latitudes in search of what was then supposed to be an unknown continent. The vessels separated in a fog, and Furneaux entered Storm Bay, anchoring in Adventure Bay, which he called after his ship. This occurred during Cook's second voyage. On his third and last voyage, in January, 1777, Captain Cook called in to Adventure Bay with the *Resolution* and *Discovery*. He had friendly interviews with the natives while he remainded.

Twelve years elapsed before Van Diemen's Land attracted other visitors, and at that time the infant colony of New South Wales had been established. In July, 1789, Captain Cox, in the brig *Mercury*, sailed inside Schouten and Maria Islands, and discovered Oyster Bay. Later on in the same year Lieutenant Bligh, in the *Bounty*, spent twelve days at Adventure Bay, Brown, the botanist, accompanying him. Bligh returned to England, and on his second voyage (1792) again called, and planted several trees on the south side of the island.

At this time the French displayed some anxiety to become better acquainted with the "Great South Land," and fully intended forming colonies there. Instructions were given in 1785 to La Perouse to explore the extreme southern point of New Holland, which at that time was supposed to extend to the land discovered by Tasman. It is unknown whether the navigator carried out his instructions, for he lost his ship in Vanikoro, in the Santa Cruz Group, and no tidings of the disaster reached France for nearly forty years. In 1791 the National Assembly of France sent out another expedition under command of Admiral Brune D'Entrecasteaux, to search for Count de la Perouse, and continue his explorations. D'Entrecasteaux spent four weeks in 1792, and five weeks in the following year, making the most minute surveys of the bays, rivers, and harbours on the south side of Van Diemen's Land, several of which still bear the names of the explorers and their ships. Again, in 1802, when Napoleon was ruler of France, Commodore Baudin sent two ships and a corvette to execute further surveys, which were carried out, and extended to the East Coast. These expeditions were happily conducted in a manner which materially assisted scientific research. The most cordial relations existed between the natives and the French, but a variety of causes prevented the Government of France from carrying out its original intention of founding colonies to the south.

The ships of both expeditions were singularly unfortunate. Out of 219 men who sailed with D'Entrecasteaux 89 died before they returned to Mauritius. The Admiral himself died at sea, off the Admiralty Isles, and his second in command, Huon Kermadec, at New Caledonia. Baudin, commander of the second expedition, died at Mauritius on the voyage home. There were twenty-three scientific men on board his ships, of whom only three returned home. There was not one in either vessel free from scurvy in its most malignant form; not more than twelve men were capable of doing duty. Added to those disasters France was involved in internecine troubles both at home and abroad. The nation groaned beneath the burden of Buonaparte's ambitious designs; there was no leisure for the furtherance of peaceful conquests in the south. To these circumstances may be ascribed the dominancy of the British flag in Australasia.

The existence of a strait dividing Tasmania from the mainland was discovered by Lieutenant Flinders and Mr. George Bass, a surgeon in the Royal Navy, in 1798, six years after D'Entrecasteaux's visit, and two years prior to that of Commander Baudin. Flinders and Bass sailed through that channel, and circumnavigated the island in a little sloop of 25 tons, called the *Norfolk*. In the afternoon of November 3, 1798, they discovered the estuary of the Tamar, and sailing up the river remained sixteen days. They named many places in the river and along the coast, rounded Cape Grim, and entered the Derwent on the 18th December.

The immense value of such an important marine highway as Bass Strait did not fail to arrest the attention of Governor King, of New South Wales. He had observed the proceedings of the French in Van Diemen's Land, now that it was found to be a separate island: he feared that unless prompt action were taken it would be occupied by France, and thus lost to the British Crown. Accordingly King communicated to the Home authorities, strongly recommending settlements to be formed in various parts, in order to secure the right of Great Britain to the country on either side of Bass Strait.

COLONISATION.

The prompt action taken by Governor King led to the despatch of Lieutenant-Colonel David Collins in order to found a settlement on the newly discovered shores of Port Phillip. On the 24th April, 1803, he sailed from Spithead with H.M.S. *Calcutta*, and the transport ship *Ocean*, 481 tons. The former ship carried the Lieutenant Governor, Rev. R. Knopwood, Mr. L'Anson, principal surgeon, Lieutenant Sladden, 307 male convicts, and a military guard. The *Ocean* carried seven officers of the civil establishment, two officers of marines, 13 free settlers and their families, and stores to the value of £10,000. When Governor Collins arrived at Port Phillip, near the present township of Sorrento, it was found that the natives were hostile, water scarce, the soil barren and sandy, and snakes and insects innumerable. Altogether fate seemed to be averse to the foundation of a settlement in that country, which is now so famous for its wealth and continued progress. Collins searched both sides of the bay without finding what appeared to him the neccessary elements of colonisation. He appealed to Governor King, who had authority to sanction a change of locality, with the result that Port Phillip was abandoned, and Collins and his party removed to the Derwent, in Van Diemen's Land.

In the meantime Governor King, with admirable foresight, had sent a small party, under Lieutenant John Bowen, to occupy a position at the Derwent, on or in the neighbourhood of Risdon Creek, a place which was so named by Captain Hayes in 1794, and was again visited by Flinders and Bass in 1798. Dr. Bass wrote favourably of Risdon Creek as a future settlement—"preferable to any other place on the banks of the Derwent." Bowen arrived at Risdon with a small party of convicts and military, in the *Albion* and *Lady Nelson*, on 12th September, 1803, one month before Collins landed at Port Phillip. "Lieutenant-Governor" Bowen's salary was 5s. a day! His short term of office was most unsatisfactory. On one occasion he abandoned his post and sailed for Sydney (9th January, 1804) with a prisoner in charge to have him tried for a robbery. The settlement was in a highly disorganised state, and during his absence a large party of natives were cruelly massacred.

This state of affairs was terminated by the timely arrival of Lieutenant-Governor Collins on the 15th February, 1804. Collins was eminently fitted from his ability and experience to found a new colony. He had been Judge Advocate in Sydney for eight years, and was one of the passengers to New South Wales by the first fleet. On returning to England, and before his appointment as Lieutenant-Governor, he wrote "An account of the English colony in New South Wales," which was favourably received in England. Collins spent a few days examining sites for a town on the river Derwent, and finally decided to establish his head-quarters on the spot which is now the City of Hobart. It was named Hobart Town by Collins, but Bowen had already, at Governor King's request, named the Risdon settlement Hobart, in honour of Lord Hobart, who was then Secretary of State for the Colonies. The population of the Australian colonies at this period (1803) was as follows:—

New South Wales	7134
Norfolk Island	1200
Van Diemen's Land	49
Total	8383

In July, 1804, a return of the inhabitants at the Derwent River, Van Diemen's Land, was published. It does not include the people belonging to Bowen's Risdon Creek Settlement, who had been sent back to Sydney by the *Ocean*.

	Men.	Women.	Children.
Civil Department	18	5	9
Military Department	48	9	3
Prisoners	279	2	—
Prisoners' wives and children	—	16	8
Settlers	13	7	16
Total			433

A few months only elapsed between the founding of the Hobart Town settlement, and the occupation of another in the northern portion of the colony. King was determined to keep the French out of Van Diemen's Land, and acting with the approval of Lord Hobart appointed Lieutenant-Colonel W. Paterson, of the New South Wales Corps, Lieutenant-Govenor of a new colony at Port Dalrymple (River Tamar). The armed colonial cutter *Integrity*, 56 tons, was fitted for sea, and a small vessel of 25 tons, called the *Contest*, was chartered to assist in conveying Paterson and his party from Sydney to the new settlement. They were to take 20 convicts and a force of 34 soldiers—in all 56 persons. On the morning of the 7th June, 1804, the New South Wales Corps was drawn up on the Government Wharf, at Sydney, as a guard of honour, and Lieutenant-Governor Paterson proceeded on board his vessel; the battery fired a salute, and according to the *Sydney Gazette*, "the most animated acclamations issued from the shore." But the wisest schemes of man are often frustrated. It was midwinter. The *Integrity* battled in vain against head winds, and in a fortnight's time returned to Sydney, whilst the *Contest*, after beating about for a month, was obliged to follow her consort's example. It was not until the end of September that arrangements were again made for the conveyance of Paterson to the Tamar. H.M.S. *Buffalo* was fitted out for sea; the armed tender *Lady Nelson*, and the colonial schooners *Francis* and *Integrity*, were to accompany her to assist in carrying the people and stores. The Governor's salary was fixed at £250 per annum. There were 74 convicts, 64 non-commissioned officers and privates of the New South Wales Corps, besides a few civil and military officers, and one free settler—in all 146 persons. The troops embarked on 3rd October, "The music of the band being only interrupted by the reiterated peals of acclamation from the spectators" (*Sydney Gazette*). On the 14th the Lieutenant-Governor embarked under a salute of 11 guns. On this occasion, as in the former attempts, heavy gales were experienced. Most of the live stock died. A fortnight after leaving Port Jackson the *Buffalo* anchored at Kent's Group, where she found the *Francis*. Remaing there for six days while it was blowing a strong gale, the vessels then sailed for Port Dalrymple. On the following day the *Buffalo* entered Tamar Heads, and came to anchor below Green Island. It blew hard during the night, and harder in the morning, until the ship was driven ashore on the eastern shoals. She lay there in a helpless condition for three days, when at length the *Integrity* came in, lightened the ship of part of her cargo, and got her off on the fourth day without much damage. The *Buffalo* then came to anchor in Outer Cove (George Town), where the military, prisoners, and stores were landed, tents were pitched, and on the 11th November possession was formally taken by hoisting His Majesty's colours under a royal salute from the man-of-war, and three volleys from the troops. The two other vessels did not arrive until the 21st. The *Lady Nelson* suffered much damage by the storm, having her decks swept, and having lost all her live stock. Thus, after a long chapter of accidents and misfortunes, the first settlement in northern Tasmania was established.

Paterson made his head-quarters at York Town, a most unsuitable spot up a western arm of the river, difficult of approach, and without any advantages for settlement. He soon discovered the mistake he had made. On the 28th November, 1804, he sailed up the Tamar in the *Lady Nelson*, and anchored at the junction of the two rivers which now form part of Launceston. The Governor and his party proceeded up the North Esk in two boats as far as they could go at high tide, and made excursions on foot several miles into the country. On returning they visited the Cataract Gorge, and were delighted with all that they saw. Paterson named the South Esk and the Tamar. He wrote enthusiastically about the park-like scenery, the rich plains, the beautiful rising ground covered with wattles, and the verdant hills in the vicinity of Launceston. This city he founded, and moved his head-quarters there in March, 1806, Government House being for many years situated in a portion of what is now the City Park, in which the exhibition buildings are erected.

The history of the colony for the first forty years of its existence is a sad, dark tale of hardship, privation, guerilla warfare, cold-blooded retaliation, and murder. The blacks smarting under a sense of cruel illusage became the white man's enemy. The convict bushrangers were a terror to the country. Savages and outlaws were often masters of the situation. Not until the natives were exterminated, and the miserable remnant removed to Flinders Island in 1833-5, together with the abolition of transportation in 1852, did Tasmanian colonists breathe the air of freedom. There is no room here to describe the heartrending scenes that transpired during the early days of the colony. The governors had the power of despots, and too often used that power freely. The first settlers received grants of land in proportion to the capital they possessed, the maximum area being 2560 acres (four square miles), but this rule was subject to the will of the Governor. In this manner the fine grass-covered pastures of the midland districts were alienated prior to 1830, when the system of free grants ceased. Responsible Government was introduced in 1856, and since that period the progress of the colony has been more rapid.

Launceston itself stands on the River Tamar, about 40 miles from its mouth, at the conflux of the North and South Esk rivers. The Tamar is navigable for vessels of 4000 tons the whole distance at high tide. The city lies in a valley enclosed by hills, known as the Windmill and Cataract hills, and derives its name from Launceston in Cornwall, England. It is distant 120 miles (133 by rail) from Hobart. The buildings and lands assessed number 4272. The annual value of rateable property is £135,168. Extent of roads and streets, 45 miles. Area of town, 3440 acres. The town is well laid out, is lighted with gas, and has a good supply of water (derived from St. Patrick's river, 15 miles east of the city), with streets of ample width, in which are numerous fine public buildings as well as substantial theatres, stores, public halls, etc. The City Council has decided to light the city with electricity, there being ample water supply for the motive power, and the work is likely to be advanced during the current year. The principal ecclesiastical edifices are St. John's (foundation stone laid on December 28, 1824), Trinity, and St. Paul's (Episcopal), St. Andrew's and Chalmers' Church (Presbyterian), two Wesleyan churches in Patterson and Margaret streets, the Roman Catholic Church of the Apostles, two Congregational churches, Christ Church in Prince's Square, another in Tamar street, the new Baptist Tabernacle in Cimitiere street, and a Christian Mission church in Wellington street. The Salvation Army has a large wooden building in Elizabeth street west, which is used as a hall for meetings. It has accommodation for about 1500 persons. There is also a Primitive Methodist Church in Frederick street. The General Hospital has accommodation for 92 patients. The building has cost £25,000. The Invalid Depot has an average of 150 inmates. The Mechanics' Institute is well patronised, and has a library of 17,000 volumes. The Town Hall is an elegant and spacious building. The

Albert Hall newly erected in the City Park has cost £14,000, and will seat 2500 people. The Government buildings in St. John street are also above the average order. There are a Grammar School (Church of England), Wesleyan Ladies' College, numerous private schools, two public schools under the Board of Education, and a convent of the Presentation Order, with day school attached. The banks are the Commercial, National, Union, and the Bank of Australasia. There are also the Launceston Bank for Savings and the Post Office Savings Bank; the new Post and Telegraph Office has been erected, at a cost of £20,000, also a Custom House erected at a cost of £10,000. These buildings form a group worthy of remark. The Academy of Music, a newly-built theatre, is the best and most commodious building of the kind in the colony. The Mechanics' Institute has a hall suited for festive gatherings or minor entertainments. The Market is in Lower Charles street. A handsome Fire Brigade Station with tower is in Brisbane street. The city was incorporated November 1, 1858, and is governed by a mayor and eight aldermen. The City Park, extending over an area of nine acres, is much frequented. The Prince's Square is permanently improved as a recreation ground or public garden. A new park has been opened in Inveresk, and is the largest in the city. The Racecourse is at Mowbrary, about two miles from the city. The land under cultivation in the district is principally for wheat, oats, peas, and potatoes. Fruit also is grown in yearly increasing quantities. Corra Linn, about six miles from the city, is much visited for its romantic scenery, being a deep gorge, through which the North Esk rushes. The Punch Bowl and the Cataract Gorge are also favourite places of resort, the latter being within five minutes walk of the city, and so called from the falls of the South Esk immediately above its junction with the North Esk. The City and Suburban Improvement Association has constructed a new and picturesque walk along the gorge, from which a splendid view of its beauties can be obtained. Invermay, a village on the east bank of the Tamar, Distillery Creek, and Clarke's Ford, are also favourite picnic places. The population, including suburbs, is 20,358. The newspapers published at Launceston are the *Launceston Examiner* and the *Telegraph*, daily; and *The Tasmanian* and *Democrat*, weekly; and the *Tasmanian Catholic Standard*, monthly.

PHYSICAL FEATURES, NATURAL PRODUCTS, ETC.

On the north coast of Tasmania are several rivers, falling into Bass Strait. The principal one is the Tamar, navigable for 40 miles inland to the city of Launceston, where it is fed by two considerable freshwater streams, the North and South Esks. The former takes its rise (as also a large tributary, the St. Patrick) in the broken, mountainous country to the east of Launceston; the South Esk and some of its tributaries rise within four or five miles from the East Coast at St. Patrick's Head, and father to the north. In its winding course it receives the Macquarie and Lake Rivers from the South, and the Meander from the west, thus draining a considerable area of the midland districts as far as the vicinity of Oatlands and the Western Tiers, when it at length falls into the Tamar at the Cataract Gorge. The Mersey, a good port for large steamships, Forth, Leven, Emu, Inglis, Detention, Black, Duck, and Montague, all with bar harbours, are considerable streams falling into Bass Strait on the west side of the Tamar; the Piper, Forester, and Ringarooma on the east side. The western side of the island abounds with rivers of considerable size, but they are all bar harbours, fit only for the reception of vessels of light draft. On the south side the noble Derwent takes its rise from Lake St. Clair, receiving in its course, the Nive, Dee, Ouse, Clyde, Russell Falls, Styx, Jordan, and numerous smaller streams, when it empties itself into Storm Bay, below the City of Hobart. The Huon is also a river of large size in the South. There are no rivers of importance on the East Coast, but the country in that direction is well watered by small streams.

The Lakes form a peculiar feature in the hydrography of Tasmania, as a glance at the accompanying map will show. Unlike such reservoirs in other parts, where they mostly lie in the valleys, the Tasmanian lakes occupy the mountain tops! The Great Lake, in Westmoreland, covers an area of 28,000 acres; Arthur's Lake, 8000 acres; Lake Sorell (County of Somerset), 12,300 acres; and Lake Crescent, 4400; Lake Echo (Cumberland), 8500 acres; and Lake St. Clair, 9400 acres. Altogether the lakes occupy 82,500 acres, or 129 square miles. The Great Lake stands at an elevation of 3822 feet from the sea level; Lake St. Clair, 3230 feet; Lake Arthur, 3388 feet.

Mountains of moderate height rise from the valleys in several parts of the island, chiefly the western side. Only a few of these attain an altitude exceeding 5000 feet. Extensive caves of very beautiful formation exist in the Western mountains near Chudleigh, which can be reached by railway to within a short distance of the entrance.

The geological features of the island are largely diversified and somewhat eccentric. Basaltic rocks occur mostly in Devon, Wellington, and Russell, where they are covered (as a rule) with a rich chocolate soil, suitable for agricultural purposes. Other igneous formations (greenstone, etc.) are found on the banks of the Tamar, in Glamorgan, round the lakes to a large extent, running down to Franklin, Bruny Island, and Tasman's Peninsula. Granite occurs in places along the East Coast, at Cape Barren Island, Gould's Country, Scottsdale, Hunter Islands, Meredith Range, and a few small spots in the Western Districts, on either side of Mount Zeehan. Stratified rocks, including metamorphic schists, clay slates, quartzites, sandstones, and Silurian limestone occupy nearly the whole of the Western Districts, from South Cape to Woolnorth. The upper and lower coal measures, including the associated greywackes, fossiliferous mudstones, sandstones, and limestones of Palœozoic and possibly Mesozoic Age, exist at Port Frederick (Lower Mersey), and through to the Tamar *via* Franklin Rivulet; again along the Western Mountains, Bothwell, Apsley, Oatlands, and down to Brighton, Richmond, Hobart, and Sorell; also in the Huon District, and part of Glamorgan. The Tertiary formations extend along the watersheds of the South Esk River and its tributaries, as far west as Deloraine and Chudleigh; also along parts of the Nort-East and North-West Coasts, and Macquarie Harbour.

The flora and fauna of Tasmania are, with little exception, synonymous with the vegetable and animal products of Australia. The eucalyptus is monarch of the forests. There are no less than eighteen varieties of the eucalyptus, and twelve varieties of the acacia family. The following list of indigenous forest trees, tree-ferns, etc., was compiled by Mr T. C. Just for the Tasmanian Committee of the Imperial Institute, and published recently by order of Parliament. It contains the names of most of the larger vegetation :—

Acacia melanoxylon } Blackwood*
    ,,   ,, } Lightwood
    ,,   ,, } Pencil Cedar
  ,, dealbata—Silver Wattle
  ,, mollissima—Black wattle
  ,, verticillata—Prickly Mimosa
  ,, decurrens
  ,, sophora—Boobyalla
  ,, maritama—Boobyalla or discolor (Benth)
  ,, sp.—Rosewood of Norfolk Island
  ,, saligna (Wendl) — Weeping Acacia
  ,, salicina (Lindley) — Willow Acacia
Anopterus glandulosa—Native Laurel*
Alsophila Australis—Prickly Fern Tree
Anodopetalum biglandulosum — Horizontal Scrub
Athrotaxis cupressoides—King William Pine
  ,, sulaginoides—Red Pine
  ,, ,, sp. — Cedar or Pencil Wood

Alyxia buxfolia—Scentwood
Aster argophylla--Musk-wood*
Atherosperma moschatum—Sassafras
Bursaria spinosa—Native Box
Banksia Australis—Honeysuckle
Bedfordia salicina—Dogwood
Beyeria viscosa (*see* Croton)—Pinkwood
Callitris cupressiformis or Australis or Frenella rhomboidea (Endl.) — Oyster Bay Pine
Casuarina quadrivalvis—She-oak*
Casuarina suberosa—He-oak*
Cibotium Billardieri—Fern-tree
Croton viscosum—Pinkwood
Darcrydium Franklinii—Huon Pine*
Eucalyptus globulus—Blue Gum
  ,, obliqua—Stringy-bark Gum
  ,, leucoxylon—Iron Bark
  ,, gigantea—Stringy-bark var.
  ,, Gunnii—Swamp Gum
  ,, Stuartiana —Apple-scented Gum
  ,, viminalis—White Gum or Manna Tree

---

* Ornamental, suitable for veneering.

Eucalyptus amygdalina — Peppermint Gum*
„ hæmastoma — Gum-topped Stringy-bark
„ Sieberiana—var. Iron-bark
„ pauciflora—Weeping Gum
„ Muelleri—Mueller's Gum
„ resinifera—sp. White Gum
Eucalyptus coccifera—Dwarf Gum-tree
„ cordata—Gum-tree
„ urnigera—ditto
„ vernicosa—ditto
„ Risdoni—ditto
Exocarpus cupressiformis — Native Cherry
Eucryphia Billardieri—Pinkwood var.
Eurybia argophylla—sp. Muskwood
Fagus Cunninghamii—Myrtle, Red and White

Hakea lissosperma—Native Pear
Lyonsia straminea — Creeper with fibrous bark
Lagunæa—White Oak of Norfolk Island
Lepidosperma squamatum — Tea-tree with fibrous leaves
Lepidosperma gladiatum—ditto
Melaleuco ericæfolia—Swamp Tea-tree
Notelæa ligustrina—Ironwood
Olea apetela—Ironwood of Norfolk Island
Phyllocladus (rhomboidailis—Rich—asplenifolia)—Celery-topped Pine
Pittosporum bicolor—Whitewood
Plagianthus sidoides — Currajong (shrub)
Zieria Smithii—vul. Stinkwood

There are many interesting bush animals in Tasmania, including 19 varieties of mice, of which 10 are marsupial or pouched—not including the opossum mouse (*Dromicia nana*). The following are marsupials: —Tiger or Hyena (*Thylacinus cynocephalus*); Native Devil (*Sarcophilus ursinus*); Native Cat (*Dasyurus vivirrimus*); Tiger Cat (*Dasyurus maculatus*); Ring-tailed Opossum (*Phalangista Cookii*); Common Opossum (*Pha. vulpina*); Bandicoot (*Perameles obesula*); Striped Bandicoot (*Per. Gunnii*); Wombat (*Phascolomys wombat*); Red Kangaroo Rat (*Potorous rufus*); Forester Kangaroo (*Macropus major*); Brush Kangaroo (*Halmaturus Bennettii*); Wallaby (*Hal. Billardieri*); Jerboa Kangaroo (*Bettongia cuniculus*). Platypus (*Ornithorynchus anatinus*) is an exceeding curious specimen of the freaks of Nature. This little creature is about 23 inches long including bill and tail. Besides the characteristics of the *Monotremata* the Platypus exhibits other anatomical pecularities which resemble those of birds, and some which even resemble those of saurian reptiles. The young are produced in a very imperfect state. The fœtus receives no nutriment from the parent before birth, except what it derives from the ovum, which, however, is hatched within the body of the parent; but the young are suckled, the mouth being curiously adapted to this method of sustaining infant life by the shortness of the bill and the greater length of the tongue at this period of its life. The Flying Fox (*Pteropus foliocephalus*) is found occasionally on the banks of the Tamar, and along the North Coast; but there is reason to believe that it was imported from Australia, and is not indigenous to Tasmania. Mr. R. M. Johnston, in his valuable "Tasmania Official Record, 1891," says that the Flying Fox inhabits Kent's Group, and probably King's Island.

The mineral deposits are only in course of development. Gold was found in many parts of the island between the years 1852 and 1869; but there was not much done before the latter date, when the quartz reefs of Fingal and Waterhouse came into notice. The Lefroy and Cabbage Tree Hill (Beaconsfield) goldfields were discovered in the early part of 1870. Large yields were obtained from these mines. Gold also exists over a large extent of country at the Pieman River and its

---

* Ornamental, suitable for veneering.

tributary streams, near the West Coast. The celebrated "Tasmania" mine, at Beaconsfield, continues to give large returns. Mr. R. H. Price, the manager of this company, has kindly supplied the following information:—Crushed to the 5th October, 1891—232,163 tons of quartz, yielding 301,231oz. 2dwt. 14gr. retorted gold; net value, £1,082,596 3s. ½d.; total average per ton, 1oz. 5dwt. 20½grs.; amount paid in dividends, £574,625. Neighbouring mines are developing riches which had hitherto lain dormant. The auriferous country round Lefroy, Lisle, the Denison, and Golconda, from which considerable quantities of gold were taken in past years, is again showing sings of vitality, and many of the mines are yielding ore which, for richness and value, cannot be surpassed in any country. The largest nuggets of gold yet unearthed in Tasmania were found at the Whyte River—a stream falling into the Pieman. In 1883 a party of three found, within a few weeks, one lump of pure gold weighing 243oz. 1dwt., another 39oz. 10dwt., and a third 9oz. 10dwt., besides a number of smaller nuggets, varying from two to three ounces each, and aggregating about 60 ounces. In the same district two men obtained nuggets weighing altogether 144oz., and also 50 oz. of alluvial gold. Since that time quantities of coarse gold have been obtained, but, on account of the inaccessible nature of the Western districts, little more than crude surface work has yet been done.

The first discovery of tin in Tasmania was made by Mr. James Smith, of West Devon. On Monday, 4th December, 1871, he came upon the rich deposits at Mount Bischoff, aptly described as "the mountain of tin," and "the richest tin mine in the world." This fortunate discovery, after much toil and perseverance on the part of the explorer, had a sensible effect on the fortunes of Tasmania. A large area of stanniferous country was discovered shortly afterwards at George's Bay (East Coast), Mount Cameron, the upper branches of the Ringarooma River, and other places. In 1875 several companies were engaged in working stream tin in the N.E. quarter of the Island. Again, in 1876 tin was found to exist over a large area at Mount Heemskirk, near the West Coast, but the claims were abandoned without, perhaps, having been fairly tested, owing to the place being so remote and uninhabited at that time. The Mount Bischoff mine still produces a most extraordinary yield of tin. The following interesting particulars are supplied by the manager, H. Ritchie, Esq.:—"Ore raised to 30th June, 1891, 37,087 tons; 174 dividends declared to September 26, 1891, amounting to the sum of £1,159,500, equal to £96 7s. 6d. per share.

The wonderful richness and extent of the Western silverfields are attracting considerable attention both in the Home Country and in the Colonies. They are believed to be the richest argentiferous deposits in the world, but the difficulty of access to this remote region has greatly retarded the progress of the works. The Government have let a contract for the construction of a railway from Zeehan to Macquarie Harbour. Half the line is completed, and a temporary tramroad has been laid down on the other half, which has just been opened for traffic. Ore, passengers, etc., can now go by rail to the port, which is an incalculable advantage to the miners, who hitherto had to use roads that were almost impassable. A railway is also being constructed by a private company from Zeehan to Dundas. Acts of Parliament have been passed to enable certain persons to form companies for the construction of railways from the Ouse (Derwent Valley) to Zeehan, from Mole Creek (Chudleigh terminus) to Zeehan, and from Waratah to Zeehan. Whatever may be the ultimate fate of the first two of these large undertakings, it is certain that the latter from Waratah to Zeehan, will be carried out under the able direction of the local agent, W. J. Norton Smith, Esq., with the least possible delay.

In evidence of the magnitude of the mining industry in Tasmania the following information is copied from the Report of the Secretary of Mines, just published:—During the year ending 1st July, 1891, 488 leases for 25,000 acres of land have been issued, and 1830 applications for 97,000 acres are in process of being dealt with, besides a large number of grants of waterights and mining easements.

The areas leased and applied for are as follows:—

	Acres.
For Gold	7,700
Silver	119,000
Tin	32,000
Coal*	13,000
Other Minerals	4,000
Total	175,700

Against 70,795 acres on 1st July, 1890. The revenue for the year for rents, licences, etc., amounted to £35,942, or an increase of £16,745 for the year.

The past success and still more brilliant prospects of the mining industry have temporarily diverted the attention of the people from other sources of wealth; slower in their return, perhaps, but not less certain. The agricultural and pastoral industries have a great future before them; but the population is too limited to admit of the available capital and labour being largely employed in either tillage or stock-growing, while the attraction of the mines offer rich rewards. In the course of time these matters will be rectified, and Tasmania will rank high as a land capable of maintaining a very large population by means of rural industries.

PROGRESS.

It must not, however, be inferred that Tasmania is slumbering in other industries apart from mining. The occupation of the land, chiefly for pastoral and agricultural purposes, has been steadily advancing. Of 16,778,000 acres of land, comprising the whole of Tasmania, about 4,647,988 acres were either granted or sold at the commencement of 1890—more than a quarter of the whole area of the island, including lakes and mountains. Of the land alienated, 2,098,763 acres were given away, and 2,549,225 acres were sold at various prices from 5s. upwards. In 1889, there were 50,566 acres of country land sold, which realised £68,319, equal to £1 7s. 2d. per acre; and 884 acres of town and suburban land at the average of £15 17s. 6d. per acre. This gives a fair average of the area and value of Crown lands sold in one year.

---

*About 50,000 tons of coal are produced annually, chiefly from the Fingal mines.

The total population of the colony, when the census was taken in April 1891, numbered 146,667, of whom 24,905 persons were in Hobart; 17,208 in Launceston; 14,788 in Devon; 7,814 in Wellington, and the remainder in 20 rural districts. The following will show the increase of population each decade since 1821:—

YEAR.	POPULATION.	YEAR.	POPULATION.
1821	5,827	1861	89,977
1831	26,640	1871	101,785
1841	57,420	1881	115,705
1851	69,187	1891	146,667

The last decade shows an increase of 26·73 per cent.—an increase which has seldom been exceeded in the annals of any country.

The imports for 1890 were valued at £1,897,517. These consisted principally of wines, spirits, tobacco, tea, sugar, rice, cotton, wool, and silk goods, boots and shoes, ironmongery. Unfortunately the farmers fail to produce sufficient meat, bread, and butter for the use of the inhabitants. Consequently a considerable sum is sent out of the Colony for the necessary supply of articles that should be produced at home. The following table shows the value for the year 1889 thus lost to Tasmania through non-production:—

Beef and mutton	£9,843
Cattle and sheep	89,738
Wheat and flour	36,513
Butter, cheese, and lard	14,149
	£150,243

The total exports for 1890 were valued at £1,486,992, consisting chiefly of gold, tin, wool, fruit, potatoes, oats, stud sheep, bark, and timber.

The following is a statistical summary relating to finance; intellectual moral, and social progress; production, etc., etc., on the 1st January, 1890:—

REVENUE—
  From Customs ... £307,352
  Other Taxes ... 115,291
  Total Revenue ... 678,909

GENERAL EXPENDITURE—
  Interest on Loans ... £209,737
  Total Expenditure ... 681,674

LOANS EXPENDITURE—
  On Railways ... £173,548
  Other Public Works ... 193,491
  Total current year ... 367,039

PUBLIC DEBT, Dec. 31, 1889 £5,019,050

IMPORTS ... £1,611,035

EXPORTS—
  Wool ... £283,237
  Gold ... 123,486
  Tin ... 345,407
  Total Home Products ... 1,442,605

RAILWAYS—
  Miles open ... 375
  Cost of Construction ... £2,925,362
  Receipts ... 174,518
  Expenditure ... 152,172

TELEGRAPHS—
  Miles ... 1980
  Offices ... 178

POST OFFICE—	
Offices	293
Receipts	£39,536
Working Expenses	44,283
BANKS—	
Deposits	£3,958,848
Savings	497,492
PROPERTY—	
Assessed Annual Value	£1,102,397
AGRICULTURE—	
Cereals, acres	93,670
Potatoes, acres	17,015
Hay, acres	50,913
Land under cultivation, acres	488,354
LIVE STOCK—	
Horses	29,778
Cattle	150,004
Sheep	1,551,429
Pigs	58,632
SCHOOLS—	
State Schools	229
Number of Children on Roll	17,948
Private Schools	88
Number of Scholars	3,542
Technical Schools (newly established)	2
Attendance	153
Industrial and Ragged—attendance	471
Training—inmates	56
PUBLIC LIBRARIES	35
HOSPITALS	10
Total Expended in Charities	£55,602
FRIENDLY SOCIETIES	89
Number of Members	8,692
Capital	£59,523

Tasmania's favourable insular position in the Southern Hemisphere gives it nearly the same advantage, as regards immunity from extremes of temperature, as that enjoyed by Southern France and Northern Italy in northern latitudes. It is alike free from the extremes of heat, as in South Australia, Queensland, Western Australia, and New South Wales, and the extremes of boisterous cold weather, as in the more southerly portion of New Zealand.

The beauty of its mountain, lake, and woodland scenery, and its healthy clime, have combined to make the island a favourite resort for visitors from the neighbouring colonies in summer, as it affords to them a pleasant refuge from the hot winds and enervating influence of their sub-tropical climate.

The annual total death-rate per thousand of the mean population for 1890 is 14·74, and although undoubtedly low as compared with European countries, it differs very little from the average total death-rate of the Australasian Colonies as a whole. It has been demonstrated, however (see *Official Record*, 1891, pp. 196-212), that where the numbers living at particular age periods are rendered extremely abnormal by migration as in young colonies, the total death-rate is a most fallacious index of health conditions; and that the low death-rate in Australasia is as much determined by this cause as by its undoubtedly favourable health conditions. When, however, correction is made for disproportion in age groups, and especially for deaths from "old age" alone—which in Tasmania represents 14·82 per cent. of deaths from all causes, and where, unlike any other country, it is by far the greatest of all specific causes of death—it is evident that, next to New Zealand, the health conditions of Tasmania are superior to those of any other colony, and greatly superior to those of European countries.

The rapidity with which the population of young English colonies increases—for example, doubling in the space of 19·76 to 22·99 years—is marvellous when contrasted with the most vigorous of old densely populated centres. During the period 1875-1888 the United Kingdom only increased from 32,838,758 to 37,453,574, *i.e.*, an increase of

4,614,816 in 13 years, or 1·02 per cent. per year. This rate, if continuous, would take 68·52 years to double the existing population, that is, if other obstacles to growth did not arise.

The relatively more rapid progress of young countries is mainly due to the (1) large proportional influx of immigrants (relative to populatio) from older centres, and (2) to the favourable hygienic conditions of a thinly populated conntry, tending to prolong the average life, and to produce a much lower death-rate than is found common in unfavourably crowded centres of population.

It is more probable, therefore, that the progress of population in Australasia during the next hundred years will follow the curve exhibited in the United States progress between the years 1790 and 1890, rather than that the rate of the past 20 years shall continue to be maintained for such a long period. If the latter were possible, it would produce a population of 135,980,000 persons in the year 1990; but if the former and more probable curve of progress be maintained, the population in the same year would only reach 58,031,000, *i.e.*, a population nearly equal to that of the United States at the present time.

Perhaps, however, the higher stages of development in the United States in the coming century may specially favour the progress of the Australasian group.

An estimate, now prepared, based upon the experience of thirteen great countries—embracing a population of 314 millions, possessing an area of 6259 million acres—demonstrates that the present civilization requires the cultivation of 2·81 acres per head for food and raw products. International exchange disguises this fact as regards the experience of any one country. The present area of the United States is reckoned at about 2291 million acres. Allowing a need of the estimated requirement of cultivated land—viz., 2·81 acres per head—for supplying the whole round of wants of each person, and that three-fourths of her total area are capable of cultivation, then if her population increases only at the rate of 2 per cent. per year, the population woul l be so vast that the produce of every available acre 120 years hence would be wholly required for *home consumption*.

The checks to population, however, may be expected to increase. and this limit may be placed further back; but it is clear that the need to withdraw more and more her present enormous export of raw products from external markets will greatly operate in enhancing the value of the virgin soils of Australasia, and so give an additional spur to her development.

INCEPTION OF THE EXHIBITION.

It is well, I think, that I should place on record in this volume the events which led up to the consummation of the project for holding a "world's fair" in Launceston. The colony was represented at the Crystal Palace Exhibition of 1851, at most of the subsequent inter-colonial exhibitions, and at Calcutta in 1883, but prior to 1884 no attempt was made to hold one in Tasmania. The success of the Tasmanian Juvenile Exhibition held at Hobart in 1883, which took a wider scope than its promoters anticipated, was visited by over 5000 persons, and also proved a financial success, was an indication of what might be accomplished if properly undertaken. A public meeting was held in Launceston in 1883, at the instance of Mr S. J. Sutton, when a representative committee was formed, and it was decided to apply to Parliament for a grant of £5000 in aid of an Industrial Exhibition. In the House of Assembly the proposal met with strong opposition, and was refused by a majority of one. During 1884 no active steps were taken, but in the close of that year a project for a small miscellaneous exhibition by Mr. H. Haywood in the old Pavilion in the City Park was taken in hand by Mr F. G. Duff, and opening in 1885 was fairly successful, being visited by 14,000 persons, the financial results being satisfactory.

The success of this miniature exhibition resulted in a meeting of the committee formed in 1883, a public meeting being held in the Town Hall on July 7, 1885, when it was resolved that an Industrial Exhibition should be held at the close of the following year. The vice-presidents elected were Messrs. William Ritchie and Alexander Webster and the Hon. W. Hart, Mr. S. J. Sutton accepted the position of hon. secretary *pro tem.*, and strong general and working committees were formed. Resolutions were passed requesting the Government to place £5000 on the estimates and soliciting the co-operation of the Municipal Council. In a few days the Working Committee presented the Municipal Council with a memorial praying that £4500 of the Corporation funds should be appropriated in furtherance of the project (for a permanent building to be used for the purposes of the exhibition in the first instance), such sum to be expended under the joint supervision of the Council and the Exhibition Committee. The Council wisely decided to refer the matter to the citizens, and, accordingly, a poll was held on July 23, the result being—Yes, 1369; no, 142; informal papers, 16. At the next meeting of the Council resolutions were passed in favour of expending £4500 upon a permanent building, to be used as the main hall of the Exhibition, conditional upon the Government placing the sum of £5000 on the estimates, and a petition to that effect was forwarded to the Governor-in-Council. The situation and natural advantages of the City Park recommended it as the most suitable site, and the Parliamentary Committee of the Exhibition, with Mr. William Ritchie as chairman, worked vigorously to arouse public interest and support. Ministers, however, were still indisposed to render pecuniary assistance, and a motion for a grant of £5000 introduced by the late Mr H. E. Lette, one of the members for North Launceston, was negatived by a majority of two votes in the House of Assembly. The large measure of support, however, accorded by members of Parliament to the project induced Ministers in 1886 to offer a vote of £5000 for a Museum and Art Gallery in Launceston, and its acceptance seemed for a time to banish the Exhibition movement. At the close of 1887, however, it received a fresh impetus. Having aroused public attention Alderman S. J. Sutton invited those who were willing to co-operate in the scheme to a meeting, which was held at the Coffee Palace early in 1888, to arrange for a Juvenile and Industrial Exhibition. The suggestion met with approval, and a committee was appointed, which showed its earnestness by at once raising a guarantee fund of £450 to provide against any possible loss. *En passant* I may say that the promissory notes which formed this fund were never required, and at the close of the Exhibition Mr. Sutton had the pleasure of returning them to the citizens whose signatures they bore. Mr. Sutton resumed the position of hon. secretary, and to his unceasing energy the success achieved is mainly due, but when the work increased as the project expanded a paid secretary was engaged, and Mr. Sutton in May, 1890, became Executive Commissioner. The Committee found general support given to their modest scheme. The Municipal Council was prepared to erect a permanent building, and in view of the *bona fides* shown by the Committee and the Corporation the Government agreed to grant £500, which was subsequently increased to £1000. The promises of support which were so freely given led to the enlargement of the original programme, and the decision of the New Zealand Government to grant £500 towards the representation of that colony gave an intercolonial aspect to the project, and led to the co-operation of other colonies being sought. In July, 1890, the Hon. the Premier wrote to the Premiers of the other colonies inviting co-operation, and the Exhibition thus received the official patronage of the Government. The competitive design of Mr. J. Duncan was accepted for the Albert Hall, and its erection was completed by Mr. Farmilo in 1890. Subsequently the front was relieved by cement work, carried out by Messrs. J. and T. Gunn, contractors for the annexes, from designs by Mr. A. E. Luttrell, architect. The total cost of the hall has been nearly £12,000. Early in 1891 the large organ which stood in the Mechanics' Institute was removed to the new hall, to be held in trust for the citizens. In 1890 an Exhibition Choir was formed under the conductorship of Mr Alexander Wallace, Mr. J. A. James being musical director until his death, which took place shortly before the Exhibition opened. He was succeeded by Mr. E. H. Sutton, Miss Frost being organist. Owing to the rapid increase in the scope of the undertaking the co-operation of the residents at the capital was sought and obtained, in order to give the Exhibition a national character, and on May 14, 1890, at a meeting held in Hobart—when a working committee for the southern portion of the island was organised, Mr. G. P. Fitzgerald being chairman—the suggestion was made that the name be altered to the Tasmanian Exhibition. This was adopted, and it was decided to erect temporary annexes, giving a floor space of 25,000 ft., and to this another 50,000 ft. was subsequently added.

It had been arranged to open the Exhibition in December, 1890, but in consequence of the paralysing effect upon commerce and transport of the Australian shipping strike and the labour troubles in England, it was decided in September, 1890, to defer the opening for twelve months, and this proved to have been one of the most fortunate circumstances that could have happened. Shortly afterwards Sir E. N. C. Braddon, Agent-General for the colony in London, undertook to further the interests of the Exhibition, formed a committee in London, and secured promises of exhibits from Great Britain and the Continent. The scope of the Exhibition then assumed proportions too extended for local enterprise to cope with, the committee not having funds to provide for the display of the exhibits promised. Overtures were made to the Government to take over the control or appoint a Royal Committee to carry on the Exhibition, but these were refused by Ministers. The committee then offered to increase the guarantee to £1500 if the Government would grant £3000, and to this Ministers consented. Mr, Jules Joubert arrived in Launceston in April, 1891, and was appointed General Manager, a position he retained until the close of the Exhibition, which I have fully described in preceding pages.

THE ALBERT HALL.

In the preceding chapter I have narrated the events which culminated in the erection by the Launceston City Council of the magnificent pile of buildings known as the Albert Hall. The structure is situated in the City Park, fronting Tamar street, and it is consequently one of the first objects to attract the attention of visitors who come to the city by the railway. It was designed by Mr. John Duncan, and when finished cost £12,224 8s. 7d. It is in the classical style of architecture, the Corinthian order being employed above the ground floor. It comprises numerous roomy offices, a banquet hall, cloak and dressing-rooms, and lavatory. The main hall—150 feet in length, by 60 feet in width—for size and acoustic properties compares favourably with some of the largest halls in the world, its capacity, exclusive of platform and organ loft, placing it eleventh on the list of great apartments. At the rear of the spacious stage at the southern end of the hall, is erected the fine organ by Brindly, of Sheffield, which for some years stood in the Mechanics' Institute, the committee of which presented it to the Corporation in trust for the citizens. It is valued at £1000, and when removed to its new position was remodeled and placed in thorough repair. During the Exhibition, the Albert Hall was handed over to the commissioners, and added in a great measure to the success of the enterprise, the acoustic properties being excellent, and the building admirably adapted for concerts, oratorios, etc., when carried out on a large scale. The general offices were also contained in the building, and the opinion expressed by visitors was that it would do credit to a much larger and more important city than Launceston. The foundation stone was laid by the Mayor (Aldermon S. J. Sutton), on April 2, 1890; when Alderman Adye Douglas gave an interesting address, in which he narrated the progress of the city. The building, which was erected by Mr. J. T. Farmilo, was completed shortly before the opening of the Exhibition.

At the rear of the Albert Hall is the fernery, which reflects infinite credit upon Mr. McGowan, Superintendent of Municipal Reserves. It contains growing specimens of Tasmanian tree ferns — *Dicksonia, Alsophila*, and even the rare *Cyathea affinis*, besides tree ferns from New South Wales, New Zealand, and Queensland. Miniature waterfalls rush through the ferns, and the effect, altogether, is exceedingly fascinating.

EXHIBITION FESTIVITIES.

The social festivities in connection with the Exhibition were inaugurated by the luncheon given by Mayor Sutton on the opening day, when his Worship had for his guests the Governors of Tasmania and Victoria, the Premier and members of the Ministry, the Mayor of Hobart, naval and military officers, members of Parliament, and leading colonists. On November 26 the Mayoress gave a Juvenile Fancy Dress Ball in the Albert Hall. A large number of guests attended, and the sight presented was generally regarded as a most pleasing and fascinating one. Struan House having been placed at the Governor's disposal, his Excellency, Lady Hamilton, and suite took up their residence there for some time, and during their stay gave several dinner parties, and had as their guests Lord Hopetoun, Governor of Victoria; Sir Henry Norman, Governor of Queensland; Dr. Giffen, and other distinguished visitors. The Mayoress held a reception in the Albert Hall, which was largely attended. It should also be mentioned that the ladies of Launceston purchased a very handsome jewel case at the Austrian Court, and handed it to Lady Hamilton as a New Year's gift. A return ball was given to the Mayor and Mayoress on February 3.

In connection with the Exhibition itself there was a constant round of varied entertainments, and the Commissioners and General Manager were warmly complimented upon the manner in which this portion of the arrangements was carried out. The St. Joseph's and City Bands occupied the pavilion in the Avenue of Nations on alternate evenings, and gave enjoyable promenade concerts, whilst Miss Frost's organ recitals in the Albert Hall were keenly appreciated. The large hall was also occupied at various times by Mr. H. M. Stanley, the African explorer; Mr. Snazelle, with his delightful entertainment, " Music, Song, and Story;" Rice's Evangeline Company; and looked especially well upon the occasion of the Amateur Gardeners' Association's Show, which was affiliated with the Exhibition. The Exhibition Choir did effective service, producing "The Messish" at Christmas, and assisting at a number of popular concerts, as well as at the solemnly attractive requiem for the late Duke of Clarence. In addition to these festivities there were *al fresco* concerts in the South Australian reception room, Mr. Munnew's Pavilion, Dempsters' Court, and an exhibition of Living Chess, under the direction of Mr. Alexander Wallace, was a feature in the Exhibition not likely to be forgotten. Mr. Arthur Day, official agent for Great Britain, gave an "at home" in his Court on the closing night. It was largely attended, the guests including his Excellency the Governor, the Mayor, and leading citizens. Mr. Vivian, Executive Commissioner for New South Wales, gave a banquet on New Year's Eve, which was of a festive and enjoyable character. The Hon. R. H. L. White, of Sydney, who came to Tasmania in his yacht *The White Star*, was lavish in dispensing hospitality during his stay, and materially aided the social success of the

Exhibition. In the grounds, in addition to the side shows, costume cricket matches were played, a chopping and sawing match took place, there was a tug of war, won by a team from the local gasworks, Professor Hall lectured on "Astronomy," and the Australian Blondin performed on the tight rope. The Bochum portable railway added to the picturesque appearance of the grounds, which looked at their very best when thronged with school children, who were from time to time the guests of the Commissioners, special arrangements being made by the Railway Department to enable them to visit the Exhibition. I should mention that the crew of H.M.S. *Katoomba* were entertained by the Commissioners at Evandale, and that the men from H.M.S. *Rapid* gave an assault-at-arms in the Albert Hall. Of course I have said nothing of the impromptu entertainments that were arranged from time to time, but it is right that I should record that Mr. Scott, official agent for South Australia, was entertained at luncheon prior to his departure, and that at the close of the Exhibition presentations were made to Mr. S. J. Sutton (Executive Commissioner), Mr. Jules Joubert (General Manager), Mr. H. A. Percy (Secretary), Mr. E. H. Sutton (Superintendent), Mr. I. Morris (H.M. Customs), Mr. H. B. Hardt (Secretary to the New South Wales Commissioner), Mr. R. W. Smith (Press), and Constable Adams, of the Municipal Police Force.

TASMANIAN CITIES.

HOBART.

The city of Hobart, capital of the colony, which was known as Hobart Town until 1881, is situated upon the lower slopes of Mount Wellington, overlooking the broad expanse of the river Derwent, which forms one of the finest harbours in the world. It was founded as far back as 1803, and consequently possesses that which few Australian cities can boast of—the charm of comparative antiquity. Apart from this, however, the city has a natural beauty of its own. The broad river at its feet forms a huge land-locked lake with various bays and inlets. On the right are the white cliffs of Kangaroo Point and Rosny; further up the river is Mount Direction, and behind it again the sharp peak called Breakneck. On a lovely green promontory, between the river and the wharf, is Government House, a building of singular architectural beauty with picturesque surroundings. On the left side of the bay is Mount Nelson, above a beautiful beach called Sandy Bay; then comes Battery Point, and between the snugly ensconsed city gradually rising from the water's edge, with its shipping, and spreading up over its slopes, until instead of houses there are trees, and these keep carrying the vision still further skyward, and vegetation itself becomes lost, giving place to huge agglomerations of volcanic rock rising into an immense precipice, ranging in a sheer height of from 600 to 800 feet, and forming a natural walled barrier of magnificent proportions. Even still upward rises the crowning peak, surmounted with a small pinnacle, where, at the height of 4166 feet, earth kisses heaven. This is Mount Wellington, and so two mountains named after England's greatest naval and military heroes appear as though they kept constant watch and ward over the city. The town is well laid out, the broad streets running at right angles and being adorned with substantial and costly buildings. Hobart is the residence of the Anglican Bishop and Roman Catholic Archbishop, and the two cathedrals, though neither of them are complete, are creditable specimens of ecclesiastical architecture. There are five other Anglican churches in Hobart: St. Andrew's Church, erected in 1835; Chalmers and St. John's belong to the Presbyterian body, whilst the Memorial Church (Congregational) is one of the most imposing buildings in the city. The Houses of Parliament front the river, and though unpretentious in external appearance they afford ample accommodation and contain a magnificent library. The Public Buildings containing the Post and other Government offices, form a massive block of substantial masonry and front Franklin Square, in which are bronze statues of Sir John Franklin and the late Dr. W. L. Crowther. The Town Hall fronts the square on the opposite side. It contains, in addition to a commodious main hall, ample office accommodation, and a portion of it is devoted to the purpose of a public library. This is one of the most valuable institutions in the colony, much of its success being due to the untiring efforts of the Librarian, Mr. A. J. Taylor. It contains between 10,000 and 11,000 volumes, and the rooms, which are kept in excellent order and are well lighted in the evening, are open to the public daily free of charge. The Museum, of which Mr. Alexander Morton is Curator, is another institution of which Tasmanians are justly proud. It contains a superb collection of great value, comprising coins, birds, beasts, fishes, and geological specimens, whilst a picture gallery which has somewhat recently been added promises to become an additional attraction. The Queen's Domain, reserved for the use of the people, affords a magnificent vantage ground for obtaining a bird's-eye view of the city and its surroundings, and it is here that buildings are being erected for the forthcoming Tasmanian International Exhibition, which is to be held under the management of Messrs. T. C. Just and Joules Joubert. The Royal Society's Gardens are beautifully situated, and in addition to their natural beauty are rendered attractive by the fact that they contain flowers and plants from every part of the world—from the tropics to the South Pole. They compare favourably with the public gardens of the other Australian capitals. The charm of Hobart, however, rests not so much in its lovely harbour or well kept streets, with their handsome buildings, as in the fact that within easy access there are walks and drives of singular attractiveness. The Fern Tree Bower on the slope of the mountain is a veritable fairy scene, abounding in fern trees in their most beautiful form, whilst a stream of water, pure as heaven's dew, trickles through them. Grand views are obtained from Mount Nelson, and Mount Wellington possesses a charm for those who are strong enough to clamber over its "Ploughed Field." In addition to the places named, however, there are numerous quiet drives, all attractive, whilst the angler can obtain abundant fishing in the Derwent. There is an excellent racecourse at Elwick, and the new Cricket Ground, situated in the upper portion of the Domain, which is the result of the zeal and energy of Mr. J. G. Davies, M.H.A., is equal to any in the other colonies. The city is lighted with gas, and progress is being made with the preliminary work in connection with the introduction of tram-cars. The Municipal Police, under the control of Mr. F. Pedder, are a fine body of men, and the Volunteer movement meets with a fair measure of support.

LAUNCESTON.

Just as Hobart is the southern and official capital, so Launceston is the northern and commercial capital of Tasmania. Its settlement was first formed on the 15th October, 1804—just eight months after the foundation of Hobart Town. It was then a separate military command, and it was not until 1812 that the northern and southern sections of the island were united under one control. The River Tamar, upon which the city stands, was named by Lieutenant-Colonel Paterson, the first commandant, after the Cornish stream which flows through some of the most beautiful scenery of south-western England; whilst the city was named after the quaint old town on the banks of the English Tamar. The city, though having less majestic natural surroundings than the capital, possesses a charm of its own, and has been aptly termed a "city of gardens." The area of the city proper is 3400 acres, and the population only 17,600, so that there is ample room for expansion. It is the centre from which mining operations are directed, indeed it was the development of the mineral resources of the colony in the early seventies which gave the northern capital such an impetus that it was proclaimed a city in 1889. Very large sums of money have been spent upon harbour improvements, with the result that vessels of heavy tonnage can berth alongside the wharf, whilst the fact that it is the nearest port to Victoria makes it the terminus for the passenger traffic. The city possesses many imposing public buildings, notably the Post and Telegraph Offices (in the Queen Anne style of architecture), in which the arrangements for the convenience of the public are decidedly in advance of those in vogue in the other colonies. The Mechanics' Institute and Free Library contains some 15,000 volumes, and on its walls are hung the portraits of old colonists who have been identified with the progress of the island. The Town Hall is a sustantial building, erected at a cost of £6000, providing a large hall, Council Chamber, and the necessary municipal offices. Then there are the public offices, Bank of Australasia, Union and National Banks, Widows' Fund Insurance Company, A.M.P. offices, and other large mercantile buildings, which are well up to the requirements of the people, and will compare favourably with those to be found elsewhere. The Museum and Fine Art Gallery contains a very extensive collection, which are housed in a spacious building adjoining the Court House. The Albert Hall, which I have described at length elsewhere, is, of course, the building of the city, and constitutes a splendid memento of Mr. S. J. Sutton's thrice renewed term of office as Mayor. The ecclesiastical architecture of the city may be said to be represented by the Church of the Apostles, Christ Church, St. Andrew's Church, and the Patterson Street Wesleyan Church, whilst St. John's, fronting Prince's Square, was built more than half a century ago. Some of the buildings possess historic interest; for instance, the Cornwall Hotel, which is still tenanted, was once kept by John Pascoe Fawkner, one of the founders of Victoria. It is not so much with its buildings as with the surroundings of the northern city that I feel called upon to deal. Huge piles of bricks and mortar, excellent public buildings, hotels, and coffee palaces can be found throughout Australia generally, but such surroundings as those with which nature has endowed Launceston can rarely be met with elsewhere. In all directions charming and picturesque scenery is to be met with, and the silent influence of the beautiful enjoyed. Within half an hour's walk of the heart of the city is the Cataract Gorge, which is of the nature of one of those cañons of the Rocky Mountains of which we read so much in American literature. It is a collosal rift between cliffs of dark volcanic rock, and is evidently due to volcanic action; the First Basin, some three quarters of a mile up the stream, being regarded as the crater of an extinct volcano. The Gorge is shut in by basaltic rocks, in places columnar in form, to a height of some 300 feet. For half a mile above the handsome suspension bridge, which spans the river and gives us access to the Gorge, the water is deep; then a series of rapids over rocky barriers commences, called "the Cataract," leading to the

First Basin, a deep circular pool surrounded by hills. So deep is the First Basin that the whole stream of the river that comes foaming down a long stretch of rapids into it cannot make a current across the basin to where its rocky edge commences. Just above the lower end of the Cataract the stream has been roughly dammed, and on the southern bank commences a line of wooden shutes, carried down the side of the Gorge to Ritchie's flour mill. These ancient shutes (erected in 1836) clinging to the rocky sides of the Gorge, in places carried through the air on wooden or iron supports let into the solid rock and supplying a hundred miniature waterfalls from leakage and overflow, rather add to than detract from the romantic surroundings. It is doubtful whether a more picturesque spot can be found in the Australian colonies, and every facility has been afforded for viewing its beauties. In 1885 (during Mr. Henry Button's term of office as Mayor) the Municipal Council constructed what is known as the "Zig-zag," a winding pathway along the left side of the Gorge and over the hill to the First Basin, and from this pathway some lovely panoramic views of the surrounding country may be obtained. On the other side of the stream will be found what is known as the Gorge Track. The land here is private property, having been originally part of the Trevallyn estate, but in 1889 the City and Suburbs Improvement Association was formed, and a lease obtained upon nominal terms of a strip along the water's edge. Funds were readily subscribed, with the result that the Association has accomplished the Herculean task of constructing a pathway along the precipitous side of the Gorge to the First Basin. In places wooden bridges had to be constructed across clefts or round the face of a cliff; in other places thousands of tons of rock have been blasted away or thrown down, and the pathway is built upon walls of dry stone masonry. Nowhere is the edge of the path more than a few feet back from the side of the stream and in some places the bridges overhang the water. Every available gully and cleft has been planted with tree ferns; wherever practicable the banks have been sloped, made up with earth, and sown with grass seed. Ivy climbs up the gaunt old rocks, moss has been planted at their base, while the little nooks and terraces, and the hillside above, wherever there was soil enough, has been planted with native and European trees and shrubs. The Chinese residents, who have taken great interest in the work and materially assisted its furtherance, procured flowers from their own flowery land, whilst others have come from Japan and distant parts. The effect is very beautiful now, and Mr. H. N. Taylor, who has given his voluntary services as director, is proud of his work, but in a few years it will undoubtedly become one of the show places of the Australian colonies. At the entrance are two very handsome gates, whilst the caretaker's cottage, a pretty little Swiss chalet, is perched up on the rocks close by. Seats are provided along the path; a commodious band-stand has been erected; here and there we come across summer-houses, like eagle's nests, in the rocks. Overhead, indeed, as the visitor ascends the Gorge, winding in and out round rocky cliffs and blind gullies, the combination of water and mountain scenery is charmingly picturesque, and when the Cataract is reached and the river becomes one tumbling mass of seething breakers, churned into foam and roaring with the efforts made to surmount the rocky barriers that impede its course, while on the other side and in the background rise the grim silent hills, studded with massive basaltic pillars that seem tottering to their fall, it is difficult to realise that so much poetry and romantic solitude exist within a mile of the busy city. When the South Esk is in flood the view from the Gorge Track presents a scene of sublime grandeur. I have described the Gorge at length, not only because of its singular beauty, but because it will for ever form a memento of the success of the Tasmanian International Exhibition of 1891-92, the balance in hand, after having paid all demands, having been handed by the Commissioners to the City and Suburbs Improvement Association. The Association has purchased an area of land at the First Basin which will in days to come be provided with a concert hall and other accessories, and will be known as "Exhibition Park." But there are other lovely and picturesque outings to be had within a short distance of Launceston. Distillery Creek, the site of the Waverley Woollen Mills, Rosevears, on the Tamar, and the Denison Gorge, on the Scottsdale line of railway, are all well worth visiting, illustrating a charming scenery not to be met with on the mainland of Australia. The city prides itself upon its beautiful surroundings, but not less upon the excellent and successful administration of its municipal affairs, which has had the effect of establishing a record that cannot be surpassed, a fact owing in a great measure to the interest which the hon. Adye Douglas and other leading residents have taken in civic affairs. The city and suburbs possess an abundant supply of pure water, and are lit with gas, but the latter is to give place to the electric light, work in connection with its introduction having already been commenced.

REPORT OF THE EXECUTIVE COMMISSIONER.

Tasmanian International Exhibition Office,
Launceston, 31st March, 1892.

SIR,

1. I have the honour to forward my Official Report upon the Tasmanian International Exhibition recently brought to a successful close.

2. The proposal to hold a Tasmanian International Exhibition originated as far back as the year 1885, but it was not until the return of the Commissioners from the Melbourne Centennial Exhibition that a resolution was passed at a general meeting, "That it is desirable that an Exhibition should be held at Launceston." Following this, and with a view to the carrying out of the proposal, the City Council was induced to undertake the erection of the Albert Hall in the City Park, at a cost of £12,000.

3. The original proposal was to hold a Juvenile Industrial Exhibition, but, on the advice of the Government, the scope of the project was enlarged; it was resolved to hold an International Exhibition, and Government promised to assist in the erection of annexes conditional on a sum of £1500 being guaranteed by the citizens of Launceston, and that 20,000 superficial feet of space should be provided for a British Court, with a like area for each of the neighbouring Colonies and Tasmania; 15,000 feet for machinery, and suitable provision for Fine Art Gallery, Fernery, etc. On these conditions Parliament granted £4000.

4. As a preliminary step the Premier (Hon. P. O. Fysh) authorised the Agent-General in England—Sir Edward Braddon—to further the movement. That gentleman entered warmly into the scheme, and formed an influential committee of advice in London, through whose exertions the sympathies of exhibitors in Great Britain and the Continent of Europe were secured. To the Agent-General and the London Committee we are deeply indebted; their efforts contributed greatly to the success achieved.

5. In February, 1891, Mr. Jules Joubert was invited to advise the Tasmanian Commission, and was ultimately engaged as General Manager, taking the charge of operations in April. He at once revised the prize schedule, appointed official agents in various parts of the world, and proceeded with so much energy that applications for space came in freely, and the success of the Exhibition was assured.

6. The erection of the necessary annexes and buildings was entrusted to Messrs. J. and T. Gunn, who carried out their contract expeditiously and to the entire satisfaction of the Committee.

7. The Exhibition was opened by his Excellency the Governor, in presence of a brilliant assemblage, including his Excellency Lord Hopetoun, Governor of Victoria, and a number of distinguished visitors. The event was marked by an industrial procession, by an imposing ceremony within the Albert Hall, and by an inaugural luncheon in the Mechanics' Institute. The Exhibition was closed by a similar ceremony on the 22nd March, 1892.

8. An inaugural Cantata was composed by Mr. John Plummer, of Sydney, for the opening ceremony. The words of the Cantata will be found in Appendix A. to this report.

9. Arrangements were made to enable his Excellency the Governor to countenance the Exhibition as much as possible. Struan House, Cameron street, was secured, suitably furnished, and placed at the disposal of Sir Robert and Lady Hamilton. His Excellency Lord Hopetoun, and his Excellency General Sir Henry Norman, Governor of Queensland, were for a time guests at Struan House, and took a great interest in the Exhibition. H.M.S. *Katoomba* and H.M.S. *Rapid* also visited the Tamar during the season, the officers and men evincing great interest in the Exhibition.

10. Numerous visitors from the neighbouring Colonies and Europe have visited the Exhibition. The number registered as having passed the turnstiles is 262,059.

11. That the full educational value of the Exhibition might be realised, arrangements were made with the railway authorities under which the children of the State and other schools were conveyed to and from Launceston at nominal fares; the Exhibition was thrown open to them free, very large numbers attended, and it is believed the impressions produced on so many youthful minds will prove of lasting benefit.

12. The countries represented at the Exhibition were—Great Britain, France, Germany, Austria, Bohemia, Italy, Canada, New South Wales, Victoria, South Australia, and Queensland. There were 1372 Exhibitors, and the Exhibits numbered 6826. A plan of the Exhibition is attached (Appendix F).

13. Thanks are due to the gentlemen who accepted and carried out so thoroughly the work of the Juries; to the staff of the Exhibition, and more especially to my brother Commissioners, who devoted so much time and labour to the carrying out of so great an undertaking; to the City Council of Launceston and to the Government of Tasmania, to whom we are respectively indebted for the permanent building known as the "Albert Hall," and for the liberal subsidy which enabled us to erect the annexes in the City Park, grateful thanks are also tendered.

14. After the official closing of the Exhibition a produce show was held in the buildings and grounds, at which a magnificent display was made by the agriculturists and horticulturists of the Colony. The show was kept open for a week, and attracted an immense concourse of visitors.

15. In conclusion, I congratulate the Government and the Colony on the successful termination of our efforts, believing that the results of the International Exhibition will prove of great ultimate benefit, not only to the City of Launceston but to the Colony of Tasmania.

16. The following Appendices are attached :—

    APPENDIX A. Inaugural Cantata.
          ,, B. Report of Chairman of Juries.
          ,, C. Exhibition Statistics and Balance Sheets.
          ,, D. Plan of the Exhibition, showing the allotment of space.

I have the honour to be,
    Sir,
        Your obedient Servant,
            S. J. SUTTON, *Executive Commissioner.*

The Hon. the Premier of Tasmania.

THE OPENING CEREMONIES.

If a bright sun and a cloudless sky could be regarded as a good omen, the career of the Tasmanian International Exhibition was destined to be a successful one, for the day was warm and clear, and surrounding nature was adorned in her most attractive garment on Wednesday, the 25th day of November—the occasion of the opening of our long looked forward to international show. The morning broke most auspiciously, and in the early hours of daylight there were many astir making due preparation for the big holiday. There was much to be done, for those taking part in the procession had been summoned to assemble at 9.15 a.m., and punctuality was the watchword impressed upon all concerned. The city was therefore early astir, and the citizens with their families by eight o'clock were to be seen issuing into the streets dressed in their holiday attire, all ready to take their share in the celebrations which were soon to follow. Launceston wore her gala appearance, the main thoroughfares being rendered all the more festive looking by the bunting displayed from various of the residences and business establishments. Flags of all nations and all descriptions, from the "Union Jack" to the humble banner of nondescript pattern, were flying from various points of vantage throughout the city. The vessels in port also had an excellent show of bunting, and the wharfs looked especially gay with the numerous bright coloured ensigns floating in the breeze. By half-past eight a continuous flow of sightseers was to be noted, making in the direction of the Market Green, whence the procession was to start. The numbers ere long began to increase, and the main streets commenced to assume a crowded appearance, for as the morning wore on residents of the outlying suburbs and people from the country arrived to swell the ranks of the holiday-makers. The number of country visitors who arrived in Launceston by rail during the two days was estimated at 1000. The N.W. Coast was rather sparsely represented, the residents evidently waiting for the cheap fares. At the Market Square from nine o'clock all was bustle and animation, for the general public had assembled in large numbers to watch the various participants in the coming procession arrive and depart. Captain T. H. Gould, of the Launceston Rifle Regiment, occupied the position of marshal, and mounted on a white charger, he rode from point to point seeing things moving. The centre of the roadway in such portions of St. John, Cimitiere, and William streets as are in proximity to the Market Square was kept clear of the crowd, and along the reserved space the various vehicles engaged were allotted their respective positions. The members of the societies taking part in the proceedings took up

c 2

their positions in different portions of the square. The public in great numbers lined the footpaths in the adjoining streets, the sight-seers also being spread over a considerable area of the green. Superintendent Coulter, of the Launceston police, had under his charge an efficient contingent of the city force, while a mounted detachment of the territorial constabulary did effective work in keeping the surging crowd within bounds. The idea of bringing into requisition horsed policemen on occasions when crowds are likely to assemble is one somewhat new to Launcestonians, and without doubt the orders of an officer, when given with the aid of a powerful charger to assist in enforcing compliance in case of a demur, have a wonderful effect in keeping a crowd within limits. Local and Australian detectives kept moving among the assemblage with a view of frustrating as far as possible the designs of the contingent of light-fingered gentry who honoured us with their presence for the opening of the Exhibition. By 9.45 a.m. most of the participants in the procession had reached the starting point, and affairs generally began to assume a very animated appearance. The Orange representatives were early in the field, a murmur of dissent running through many portions of the crowd as this part of the procession made its appearance, for the majority of onlookers evidently thought the occasion seized to flout emblems of religious prejudice in the eyes of a multitude was exceedingly ill-timed. The Rechabites followed, and from that period a procession of men and vehicles poured on to the scene from all directions. The roadway in St. John street to William street, in Cimitiere street from St. John to Charles street, and in William street from St. John to near George street, was filled with floats, drays, and various other descriptions of vehicles used for the displays emblematical of the various trades to be represented in the procession. Many of these called forth exclamations of approval from the crowd as they passed on to the places allotted them, and certainly the taste with which the exhibition generally speaking was arranged was exceedingly good. The butchers' brigade cut an exceedingly dashing appearance, the "boys in blue" being all well mounted. The venerable-looking Druids came in for a considerable share of attention, more especially from the country folks, many of whom saw these representatives of Britain's ancient priesthood for the first occasion. Up to 9.30 o'clock the crowd kept on increasing, until finally a waving sea of heads met the view upon all sides. The utmost good humour prevailed, and the usual amount of friendly badinage was indulged in whenever opportunity offered. Shortly before ten o'clock the work of getting the procession started upon its journey throughout the main streets of the city was commenced, and, headed by the Hobart City Band, under Conductor Hopkins, a move was made along St. John street towards the heart of the city. The incidental arrangements worked with a smoothness that was surprising considering the circumstances, for the whole proceedings must necessarily be regarded in the light of an unrehearsed effect. The order of march was given out by the marshal, and followed, with very few exceptions, with promptness and praiseworthy regularity. The various bands struck up their music as they marched at intervals from the square, and the scene became a decidedly imposing one, the onlookers signifying their approval by repeated cheering. The exhibitions of various well-known business firms were loudly cheered as they passed, each in its turn, the main body of spectators, while the appearance of some of the less pretentious shows was made the occasion for laughter and good-natured banter. The majority of our local industries were represented, and the sight presented, as the gigantic procession slowly wound along, was both attractive and instructing. At one moment the eye would be caught by an exhibition of specimens of that necessity of our earliest infancy, the cradle, and anon a contingent of those whose work it is to build for us another and final necessity sweeps by, while in between might be seen the various means by which our many wants are duly mininistered to during that brief span which intervenes between the cradle and the grave. Without doubt the many eulogisms passed upon the procession were thoroughly well deserved, and the citizens of Launceston have every reason to be proud of the show that was made. In several instances the representatives of the different trades were to be seen diligently plying their respective avocations, and this of course made the proceedings doubly interesting. By 10 minutes past 10 o'clock the whole of the procession had been got under way, the rear being brought up by a powerful Hornsby road locomotive with steam full up, which puffed and fretted its way up the incline which occurs in St. John street after the Market Square is left behind. The crowd followed, its proportions increasing as the more central parts of the city were reached, while every point of vantage along the line of route was crowded with eager spectators, windows, balconies, and housetops being in great request. The chief thoroughfares of the city were gone through, and frequent cheering was to be heard as the proportions of the procession became from time to time apparent. The only objectionable feature in the proceedings, and a most objectionable one it was too, was the throwing of bags of flour from several of the bakers' carts into crowds of expensively dressed ladies and children. The perpetrators of this outrage should have been summarily dealt with, and the vehicles they were connected with ordered at once to fall out of the procession. Several policemen were to be seen riding alongside in the immediate vicinity of the culprits, yet nothing was done to put a stop to their inexcusable conduct. At 11·30 the procession broke up in proximity to the Exhibition Building, and the crowd then concentrated its attention upon the ceremonials which were to follow.

The scene in front of the Exhibition Building in Tamar street was, from 11 a.m. until after noonday, one of great animation. The very large crowd assembled lined the footpaths on both sides of the roadway, a passage being kept clear in the centre for those taking a prominent part in the opening ceremonies. The best of order was maintained throughout, rowdyism being, happily, conspicuous by its absence.

At 10 o'clock four gun detachments of the Launceston Volunteer Artillery paraded at the drill yard, St. John street, and at 11 a.m., under command of Captain Harrap, marched, with their guns horsed and mounted, to the saluting base, on the Windmill Hill. As their Excellencies Sir Robert Hamilton and Lord Hopetoun left Struan House for the Exhibition Building, the signal was given, and a salute of 17 guns fired from the hill.

Shortly after the procession passed down Tamar street, the bluejackets marched up, headed by their fife and drum band, and were marshalled along the main entrance leading to the Albert Hall, forming a passage. The guard of honour, comprising 50 men under Captain R. J. Sadler

(Lieuts. Cragg and Chapman also being present), headed by the band of the Rifle Regiment, marched up from the drill-yard at about 11·45 p.m., and were arranged along Tamar street in front of the building, and waited for the arrival of the Governors. Their Excellencies Sir R. G. C. Hamilton and Lord Hopetoun were driven to the Albert Hall shortly before noon, and were received with the royal salute. After the reception of the Governors the guard of honour marched down Tamar street, where they were also dismissed. The bluejackets were then called out, and also dispersed until shortly after four o'clock, when they were mustered again and marched back to their boats.

THE PROCESSION.

It was conceded upon all sides that if the opening day of the Exhibition was to be an unqualified success, the procession should form a pageant such as would be a credit to all concerned. The local industries must of necessity be a leading feature in such a proceeding, while the benefit and friendly societies should, of course, be well represented. To ultimately bring about such a state of things it was considered the united wisdom of delegates from the various societies and trades should be brought to bear upon the question, and it was finally decided to form a procession committee. At first difficulties arose, but with judicious and careful management, combined with the reason that comes of concerted thought, the threatened "rifts in the lute" were avoided, and the members of the committee eventually found themselves in a fair way to make a creditable display. To attend to minor details a sub-procession committee was appointed, and from its inception it was found to work with advantage. Mr. E. B. Hornsby was the secretary of both committees, and for real hard work, combined with rare tact and judgment, it would have been difficult to have equalled him. The societies and business firms responded well to the call made upon them for co-operation and support, and the trades were not behindhand in entering with vigour into the matter, with the satisfactory result noticeable, in the undoubtedly fine display. In past years Launceston has had some presentable processions, but on no previous occasion has such a systematic and yet artistic show been seen wending its way along the streets. The nearest approach to it is the great Eight Hours Day procession held annually in Melbourne, and in proportion to population the comparison is favourable to the local march out, for in the former city the Trades and Labour Council, with its many subordinate branches, carries in its wake a large number of supporters, while in Launceston there is really no great organisation apparent in what pertains to trades-unionism. That being the case the manner in which the various industries were represented on the opening day was a clear example that both employers and employed had the welfare of the city at heart, and recognised that each contributes to the other's advantage. As a proof of the excellent arrangements that had been made, the members who intended taking part in the procession assembled punctually on the Market Green at 9·30 a.m. No confusion was experienced, and so well planned was the whole affair that each body of men knew exactly where their forces were to fall in. Captain T. H. Gould was an efficient

TASMANIAN EXHIBITION, 1891-92. 23

marshal, and to him is due much of the order and decorum which prevailed. Although it seemed only natural that some loss of time would take place in arranging the long army of men and vehicles into something like good marching order, nothing of the kind occurred. On the contrary, at 9˙45 a.m. the Hobart City Band, who were occupying the front position, struck up a martial air, and with military precision the march commenced in due order as follows :—Ancient Order of Odd Fellows; Messrs J. and T. Gunn's employés; Protestant Alliance; Mr. J. T. Farmilo's employés; Adams, Griffiths, and Dudley, timber merchants; printers; Federal Band; Loyal Orange Institution; F. Paine, coach-builder; J. Lyall, shoeing smith; J. Denton, coach-builder; J. Nichols and Son, hay and corn merchants; Nevin, Green, and Howard, coach-builders; H. Crocker and Son, coach-builders; J. Campbell, potteries; J. Boag and Son, brewers; A. G. Robins, cooper; West Devonport Band; Independent Order of Odd Fellows; M. E. Abbott, cordial manufacturer; H. Smith, cooper; W. I. Thrower, cordial factor; A. V. Cowap, cordial factor; D. Storrer, cabinetmaker; Mills Bros., cabinetmakers; F. Walker, florist; E. Jack, boat-builder; J. M'Lennan, florist; J. Moore, boat-builder; R. Newey and Son, seedsmen; E. Darcey, boat-builder; Campbell Town Band; Ancient Order of Druids; bakers; Beaumont Bros., confectioners; G. Lewis, boot factory; J. Dunning, tailor; Perth Band; I.O. Rechabites; F. Hart and Son, tinsmiths; Dunn and Williams, stonemasons; Corporation quarrymen; J. Hemp, umbrella maker; R. Gardner, tanner; South Esk Band; Fire Brigade; J. Rawson, chimney sweep; butchers; J. Ballard, jun., basketmaker; Upton and Co., soapmakers; G. Shields, wood and coal merchant; Ainley, wire mattress maker; Bond and Carr, brass founders; Peter and Son, iron founders; W. H. Knight, engineer; Salisbury, Scott, and Co., engineers.

There were 57 various societies and industrial establishments represented in the foregoing manner, and it is estimated that 2850 persons took part in the march. Having a fair start the procession was a most imposing spectacle, having all the charm of military discipline combined with variety of uniform or attire. The line of march was along St. John street to Patterson street, thence from Patterson street into Wellington street as far as Frankland street, returning by way of Charles street through Cameron street to the City Park. The marshal, mounted on a charger, preceded the rank and file, and at various distances, to preserve order, mounted constables rode on either side of the main body. The great attraction of the procession was naturally the examples of the methods employed in the various industrial or manufacturing houses of this city, and right well those engaged in playing at their daily avocations fulfilled their important parts. The building trade was exceptionally well represented by Messrs. J. and T. Gunn and J. T. Farmilo, and on the various lorries lath-splitters, stonemasons, slaters, plasterers, joiners, fitters, and blacksmiths plied vigorously with their keen or blunt-edged tools. Then, coach-building was in full swing as performed in the various well-known establishments, and those working at the fires with great gusto literally wiped the " honest sweat" of toil from off their heat-moistened brows. Cabinetmaking, with its sister trade, upholstering, had no lack of workmen, and the substantial-looking unfinished frames contrasted well with the nearly completed and elegantly finished suites of drawing-room furniture, all being apparently prepared on the somewhat prescribed limits of moving vehicles. As the various brewers' and cordial manufacturers' large and well-appointed drays and lorries passed along, heavily laden with the many cooling beverages, the parched lips of the thousands who lined the footpaths and roads bore testimony of what a quantity they could dispose of if they only had a chance to imbibe the sparkling liquids. Foremost in the ranks of this business was observable the brightly painted carts, the splendid specimens of horses, each in the pink of condition, and the highly burnished harness and trappings belonging to the Phœnix Brewery and also the Phœnix Cordial Factory, the proprietor and proprietress (Mr. W. H. Abbott and Mrs. M. E. Abbott) of which may justly feel proud of their display. J. Boag and Son also mustered their vehicles, horses, and wares in strong force and with due effect, as did Mr. W. I. Thrower and Mr. A. V. Cowap, each showing to the best advantage the extent of their cordial businesses. The Sandhill Potteries display, by Mr. J. Campbell's employés, was also a feature in the pageant. The Phœnix Foundry, with the heavy machinery, the light steel and iron work, and the many other representations of an important and growing industry, attracted the admiration of the concourse of people, all seemingly working so easily and well. One of the most taking sights was the lorry on which Messrs. Dunn and Williams, monumental masons, displayed the artistic work carved and hewn from the rough material. The cart was tastefully arranged, and the evergreens shading the workmen had a refreshing effect. Practical and eloquent was the appearance presented by the tinsmith's shop in full work by the workmen of Mr. F. Hart. The light metallic tap of the hammers had a harmonising sound mingled with the motley and many noises which filled the air; pleasant and melodious sounded popular songs as sung by Mr. J. Dunning's ubiquitous and industrious-looking staff of tailors. The butchers also made no inconsiderable show, and their appointments were all in keeping with the whole well-arranged details of the procession. In the bakers' section there was a good representation of the trade. Messrs. W. G. Porter, H. Webb, and S. Edwards were engaged at work on the lorries, and the following sent carts and lorries, viz.—Messrs. F. W. Hall, F. Crosby, G. B. Dean, W. D. Munro, P. James, J. Lane, T. B. Dean, A. Rankin, J. B. Knaggs, and Beaumont Bros. The effect of their carts being prettily decorated with flowers. entwined in evergreens, was much commented upon. The procession extended about three-quarters of a mile, and the exhibitions of industry, intermingled with the strong body of friendly societies, exemplifying thrift and forethought, conveyed to many a wholesome and retentive lesson. A Hornsby road locomotive, drawing a multitubular locomotive boiler just finished to the order of the Tasmanian Government, steamed in the rear of the line of march, and although snorting with the impatience of an iron horse, the exhibitors, Messrs. Salisbury, Scott, and Co., may congratulate themselves that it came in for a full share of general admiration. The members of the various lodges and orders indicated the strong position they hold with regard to members, but no society had more cause to take heart of grace at their display than the Ancient Order of Druids. The Druidical car with stones representing Stonehenge, the outriders in quaint blue and white robes, and the wives and daughters in the car, attractively costumed, with the long-flowing robes of the Druids on foot, gave a patriarchal and strangely varied appearance to an uncommon and unique display. The members of this society gave hearty cheers as they passed the vice-regal residence.

Upon arrival in Tamar street the procession halted outside the Albert Hall, and the members which formed it were drawn up in line on either side of the crowd to await the arrival of his Excellency the Governor and party, when the president and standard-bearers of every society entered the Albert Hall, and the procession ended.

WITHIN THE ALBERT HALL.

The arrangements at the Albert Hall for reception of the invited guests were very satisfactory. The hall had been divided into sections, each marked by a pole and banner of a particular colour, and bearing a letter. The tickets were issued in batches coloured and lettered to correspond with the sections, and as a number of members of the Exhibition Committee were on duty to receive the guests, all were marshalled to their seats without confusion. The hall was decorated with flags of all nations, and under the gallery on the eastern side a dais had been erected, carpeted, and fitted with chairs, and covered by a canopy of striped material, the effect being neat and in harmony with the surroundings. Both design and execution of this dais reflect credit on Messrs. Dempsters, to whom the work was entrusted. As the members of the Ministry and other distinguished visitors arrived they took their seats on the dais. At 11 a.m. a detachment of 86 bluejackets from H.M.S. *Katoomba* arrived, under command of Lieut. A. Gillespie and accompanied by Gunner Garland, and opening out lined the avenue from the main entrance door, in Tamar street, to the foot of the dais. Shortly afterwards Paymaster Truscott, Surgeon Jackson, and Engineers Sennett and Wall, of the *Katoomba*, arrived. By 11·30 p.m. the hall presented a very striking appearance. The galleries were filled by season ticket holders, and the spacious hall filled by a gay assemblage, the relief of colour afforded by the varied dresses of the ladies being heightened by the uniforms of military officers on the retired list and the university robes of many clergymen. The stage, which was occupied by the Exhibition choir, was arranged with taste and striking effect. The lady vocalists appeared in white dresses, the soprani and alti in separate groups in the front, distinguished by crimson and blue sashes respectively, the tenors and basses in the back, and the eye travelled over tier above tier of the singers to the orchestra, the gaily painted pipes of the large organ forming an appropriate background.

Punctually at 11·45 a.m. the boom of the howitzers of the Launceston Artillery Corps firing a salute announced that their Excellencies Sir Robert Hamilton and Lord Hopetoun and suite had left Struan House for the Exhibition, and a few minutes later the larger assemblage in the hall rose to its feet as the command "Arms" brought the double line of bluejackets to attention. A pause ensued while the Executive Commissioners were receiving their Excellencies at the entrance, and then "Shoulder" was heard, followed by "Royal Salute;" the choir rose, and as the vice-regal party entered the hall the strains of the National

Anthem broke forth from the orchestra, and preceded by Mr. Joubert, the general manager, Sir Robert and Lady Hamilton ascended the dais, followed by Lord Hopetoun and members of the vice-regal party, the President and Executive Commissioner, and a number of officers of the Launceston and Hobart Rifle Corps, who found seats near the dais.

The dais was occupied by his Excellency Sir Robert and Lady Hamilton, his Excellency Lord Hopetoun, Governor of Victoria; Captain Bickford, of H.M.S. *Katoomba*; Colonel W. V. Legge, Acting Aide-de-Camp to Sir Robert Hamilton; Captain Willoughby, Aide-de-Camp to Lord Hopetoun; Lieut.-Colonel A. H. Warner, Commandant Tasmanian Defence Force, and Staff-Adjutant Major Wallack; Surgeon H. S. Jackson, and Paymaster E. H. Truscott, H.M.S. *Katoomba*; the hon. the Premier and Mrs. Fysh; the hon. the Treasurer and Mrs. Bird; the hon. Minister of Lands and Works and Mrs. Pillinger; the hon. W. Moore, President of the Legislative Council; the Right Rev. Dr. Montgomery, Bishop of Tasmania; his Worship the Mayor of Hobart and Mrs. G. Hiddlestone; the hon. Wm. Hart, M.L.C., President Tasmanian Exhibition Committee, and Mrs. Hart; and his Worship the Mayor of Launceston, Mr. S. J. Sutton, M.H.A., Executive Commissioner, and Mrs. Sutton.

Upon ascending the dais Mr. Joubert presented Lady Hamilton with a tastefully arranged bouquet of waratah and mountain berries, which was graciously accepted.

At the side of the dais, on the floor, seats had been reserved for the executive commissioners and official agents of various countries and colonies. The principal officers of the Tasmanian Defence Force present, in addition to those already mentioned, were Major W. Martin, Captain R. J. Sadler, and Captain F. J. Read, Launceston Rifles; Major A. Reid, Captain G. Richardson, and Adjutant C. L. Cutmear, Tasmanian Rifle Regiment; Captain R. Henry and Lieutenant H. E. Packer, Torpedo Corps; Colonel R. C. D. Home, Lieutenant-Colonel A. Harrap, and Major J. H. Room, unattached. Colonel Crawford, late Madras Staff Corps, was also present.

The National Anthem was then sung by the choir with good effect and precision, the solo parts being taken by Miss Plaice and Miss Cox.

The Executive Commissioner (S. J. Sutton, Esq., M.H.A.) then read the following prayer :—

"Almighty God, accept, we beseech Thee, this our offering of praise and thanksgiving, especially now at this time, when we are about to display the fruits of our handiwork, here brought together; subdue in us all unworthy pride and self-seeking, and teach us to labour and use all that comes to our hand, that we may ever be found working out the purposes of Thy Holy Will, to the fuller manifestation of Thy glory and the great happiness of mankind. O Heavenly Father, who hast knit together all Thy creation in a wonderful order, and hast made all mankind of one blood to dwell together in unity, replenishing the earth and subduing it, pour down upon us of Thy mercy such grace as may draw us to Thyself, and in Thee to each other in the bonds of love and peace. With these our praises and prayer we offer and present to Thee the fruits of our labours, beseeching Thee to accept them, and bless them to the use of mankind, through Jesus Christ our Lord, who with Thee and the Holy Spirit liveth and reigneth ever one God, world without end. Amen."

The "Old Hundredth" was then sung by the choir, the general public not taking advantage of the announcement in the published programme that they were expected to join in.

The Executive Commissioner read and presented the following address, which had been illuminated by Mr. Long, and suitably framed, to his Excellency the Governor:—

To Sir Robert George Crookshank Hamilton, K.C.B., Governor and Commander-in-Chief of Tasmania.

Your Excellency,

We, the Commissioners for the Tasmanian Exhibition of 1891-92, desire to accord to you our heartiest welcome, and to convey to you as the representative of her Most Gracious Majesty the Queen the expression of our devoted loyalty to her Majesty's crown and person. A few years ago some of the leading citizens of Launceston met for the purpose of devising the best means of holding in this city an Exhibition where the products of Tasmania could be brought prominently before the public; but owing to a series of unforeseen obstacles, the project lay dormant, and eventually was almost abandoned during the labour crisis which prevailed throughout this and the adjoining colonies. As soon, however, as this crisis ended, the principal movers in this Exhibition met once more, and in view of the great development of the mining industry which has of late taken place in Tasmania, it was proposed to re-organise the undertaking, and abandon the idea of making it merely a juvenile exhibition, and in the early part of the current year schedules and programmes were printed and circulated throughout the world to the effect that a Tasmanian International Exhibition would be held in the City Park, Launceston, in November, 1891. The City Corporation, with a view to help the Commissioners, caused the construction of the Albert Hall to be pushed forward vigorously, and made such amendments in the original as would prove of use to the undertaking in hand. Plans and specifications were prepared and tenders called for the erection of annexes, at the rear of the hall. In view of the national character the Exhibition assumed, the Government granted a sum of money towards the construction of these annexes, provided a sum of £1500 was granted by the citizens of Launceston. The appeal made to the self-reliance and patriotism of the people met with a spontaneous and warm response. The same feeling has prompted the exhibitors from almost every district in this island to forward specimens of their industries. But we cannot refrain from expressing our special gratitude to the exhibitors from Europe, as well as the Governments and exhibitors from the neighbouring colonies, who have so liberally and largely supported our efforts to make this Exhibition the great success it undeniably now is. The area of the City Park, upon which the Tasmanian Exhibition stands, is upwards of 12 acres, the covered space being about one-fourth of that total. The countries therein represented officially are New South Wales, Victoria, South Australia, New Zealand, and Queensland, besides which a large number of valuable exhibits have been contributed by the mother country, the United States of America, France, Germany, Italy, Belgium, and Japan. In the fine arts section England, Austria, and Italy are also large contributors, thanks principally to the indefatigable assistance rendered by the Agent-General, Sir Edward Braddon, K.C.M.G., and the influential committee appointed by him in

London. We have the honour to present with this address a copy of the official catalogue of the Exhibition for your Excellency's acceptance, and trust that the results of the undertaking will prove that the confidence reposed in us by your Excellency and your constitutional advisers, as well as by the public at large, in entrusting the credit of the colony to a body of private individuals, has not been misplaced. It now remains for me, in the name of my fellow Commissioners, to request that your Excellency will be pleased to declare the Tasmanian Exhibition of 1891-92 open in the name of her Most Gracious Majesty, Queen Victoria, whom God preserve.

His Excellency, who was received with loud and prolonged cheering, replied as follows.—Mr. President, vice-presidents, and gentlemen,—It will be my pleasing duty to convey to her Majesty the Queen through the Secretary of State the assurance of your devoted loyalty to her Majesty's crown and person. I thank you for the welcome your address accords to myself, and I assure you of the pleasure it gives me to take part as her Majesty's representative in the interesting proceedings of today. You refer to delay which has taken place since the idea of holding an Exhibition in Launceston was first entertained, but I do not think that this delay is to be regretted, inasmuch as the Exhibition now is on a much more extended scale than would have been the case had the original design been carried out. In fact it is now a national Exhibition, largely subsidised by the Government of the country instead of being merely a local Exhibition, as was first intended. (Applause). You are to be congratulated on the assistance rendered by the City Corporation in pressing forward the completion of this great hall and in amending its original design to meet your requirements. The citizens of Launceston appear to have worked like one man in this undertaking, and have evinced much self-reliance and patriotism, and it must be particularly satisfactory to you, who represent them in this matter, that you have been able to get together so large and valuable a collection of exhibits, not only from Tasmania itself, not only from the other Australian colonies, but also from the mother countries as well. It is not necessary that I should enlarge upon the advantages attending exhibitions of this sort, for it is now universally admitted that their tendency is to advance culture and to improve industrial appliances, while, by increasing and disseminating a knowledge of the resources and productions of different countries, the interchange between them of such productions is undoubtedly promoted and stimulated. (Applause). I now declare open the Tasmanian Exhibition, 1891-92. (Loud and prolonged cheers.)

"Rule Britannia" was played as an air by the orchestra, and was then sung by the choir, Mrs. and Mr. Upton and Miss Cox taking the verse.

Mr. A. Day, official agent for Great Britain, was presented to his Excellency Sir Robert Hamilton by the Executive Commissioner.

M. Victor Laurelle, official agent for France, was presented in a similar manner, the orchestra playing the "Marseillaise."

MM. A. Bossomaier and O. Moser, official agents for Austria and Germany, were presented, the orchestra playing the "Austrian Hymn."

The following colonial representatives were then presented in the order named:—W. H. Vivian, Esq., Executive Commissioner for New South Wales; Mr. D. Fergus Scott, official agent for Victoria; Mr. H. J. Scott, official agent for South Australia and

Western Australia ; Mr. F. N. Meadows, official agent for New Zealand ; and Mr. A. Morton, secretary to the Hobart committee, who has worked zealously for the success of the Exhibition, and whose appearance on the dais was greeted with a spontaneous burst of applause.

The " Hallelujah Chorus " was then rendered by the choir in a manner that reflected credit upon the members and their conductor, Mr. Alex. Wallace, as well as the musical director, Mr. E. H. Sutton, jun.

His Worship the Mayor called for three cheers for the Queen, which were heartily given, and a similar request by Mr. Joubert for the Governor of Tasmania was warmly responded to.

Mr. Joubert then said : Ladies and gentlemen,—As you are aware, we have the honour on this occasion of entertaining his Excellency the Governor of Victoria, and I am sure I need not call on you to give him three hearty cheers.

The warmth of the response to this hint showed that the citizens of Launceston feel grateful and flattered at the presence of Lord Hopetoun upon such an occasion.

The vice-regal party then left the dais and proceeding into the front wing were subsequently escorted round the exhibition, spending the best part of an hour in inspecting the various courts, the fernery coming in for special commendation, and its designer, Mr. W. M'Gowan, must feel gratified at the praise it received from all visitors.

THE LUNCHEON.

At the invitation of his Worship the Mayor (Mr. S. J. Sutton, M.H.A.), about 240 gentlemen assembled in the Mechanics' Institute at the conclusion of the opening ceremony. The large hall had been decorated very tastefully for the occasion, a festoon of leaves having been hung across the platform, between which and the floor of the hall was a mass of ferns and pot plants, which produced a very pretty effect. On the platform were the Executive Commissioner, Mayor S. J. Sutton (in the chair), having on his right his Excellency Sir Robert G. C. Hamilton, K.C.M.G., Governor of Tasmania ; his Lordship Bishop Montgomery; the hon. W. Moore, President of the Legislative Council ; hon. B. S. Bird, Treasurer ; Mr. Peter Barrett, M.H.A. ; Lieutenant-Colonel Warner, Commandant Tasmanian Defence Forces; Mr. H. Button, member of general committee ; Mr. W. H. Vivian, Executive Commissioner for N.S.W. ; Mr. H. W. B. Robinson, private secretary to his Excellency the Governor; Colonel Legge, Alderman George Hiddlestone (Mayor of Hobart), Mr. Alexander Webster, treasurer executive commissioners, and Alderman David Scott. The chairman was supported on his left by his Excellency the Right Honourable the Earl of Hopetoun ; the hon. P. O. Fysh, Premier ; hon. A. T. Pillinger, Minister of Lands; hon. W. Dodery, M.L.C. ; Captain Bickford, H.M.S. *Katoomba* ; Mr. Jules Joubert, general manager of the Exhibition ; Mr. M. E. Robinson, Alderman B. P. Farrelly, Captain Willoughby, Aide-de-camp of Lord Hopetoun ; Mr. Jas. Brickhill, Colonel Home, and Mr. H. Dobson, M.H.A. The hons.

Nicholas J. Brown, Speaker of the House of Assembly, and Thomas Reibey, ex-Speaker, who were expected to be present, and were announced to speak, were unable to attend, owing to indisposition. The guests having taken their seats at the tables, the National Anthem was sung, all standing, Mr. Alexander Wallace (piano) playing the accompaniments, assisted by Mr. Andrew Wallace (cornet) and Mr. Youngman (violin). Grace having been sung, the company sat down to a well-provided luncheon; after which

The Chairman—who, on rising, was received with loud and prolonged cheering—proposed the toast of her Majesty the Queen, which was enthusiastically responded to. The company sang the National Anthem.

The Chairman then gave the toast—" Their Royal Highnesses the Prince and Princess of Wales, and other members of the Royal Family," which was also loyally received.

Song—" God bless the Prince of Wales."

The Chairman, in proposing the health of the Governor, said he had no doubt that it would be received with enthusiasm. (Cheers.) They were all pleased to have the representative of her Majesty with them. He had performed the duty of opening the Exhibition, and had carried it out well. (Cheers.)

The toast was drunk with enthusiasm.

Song—" The fine Old English Gentleman."

His Excellency Sir Robert Hamilton, on rising to respond, was received with loud and continued cheering. He said: Your Excellency, Mr. Mayor, and gentlemen,—Before I respond to this toast I should just like to read you a telegram which I have received within the last few minutes. I wrote to his Excellency the Admiral of the Station, Lord Charles Scott, asking him if he could manage to be present at the opening of this Exhibition. (Cheers.) I did so because I knew his kindly genial presence is always acceptable in Australia (cheers), but, unfortunately, H.M.S. *Orlando* is laid up just now for the purpose of refitting, and he has sent me this telegram in reply :—" Regret extremely unable to attend opening ceremony. Wish every success to the Tasmanian Exhibition." (Cheers.) I thank you very much for the hearty reception which you have given to the toast of my health as her Majesty's representative in Tasmania. You, the Commissioners of this Exhibition, are to be very much congratulated on the result of your labours so far. (Cheers.) The opening ceremony went off excellently. I was delighted with the procession, which had an earnest and business looking appearance, which I have never seen anywhere surpassed. It is perfectly evident that the hearts of the people have gone out towards this Exhibition, which has been so auspiciously started, and I think we may confidently hope that it will prove a great success. I have not yet had the opportunity of doing more than very cursorily inspecting the exhibits, but they certainly appear to be very satisfactory. It is only by the co-operation of a large number of public bodies and of private individuals that an undertaking of this sort can fulfil its objects, and this co-operation has been heartily given. But there always must be some energetic and moving spirits to set this co-operation in motion. When all connected with this Exhibition have worked so well, it is difficult to single out names for special commendation, but I feel sure that I am doing no more than simple justice in calling special attention to the very active part taken by you, Mr. Mayor, in this country, and to the valuable services rendered by our Agent-General, Sir Edward Braddon, at home. (Cheers.) You are fortunate also in your officers, and particularly in having secured the services of so experienced a man as Mr. Joubert for your general manager. As I read the excellent leaders in the two Launceston papers to-day, I felt in a state of mind similar to that of the man who is reported to have said, "Confound those fellows who have written books, for they have stolen all my best ideas." (Laughter and applause.) Exhibitions have become established as important features of the age of progress in which we live, and there is not much scope for originality in describing their objects and uses. Still, the surroundings of any individual exhibition are more or less special to itself, and I should like to say a few words as regards the benefits which we hope will accrue to Tasmania from this Exhibition. In the first place, we hope that we shall profit by the greater knowledge of the arts, the industrial appliances, and the products of other countries, which a careful inspection and study of their exhibits will afford. But we want also to make our own resources known. Tasmania does not advertise herself enough. (Hear, hear.) This Exhibition will do much in this direction. It will attract a large number of visitors to our shores, who will see with their own eyes what a favoured land ours is. They will see that our climate and scenery are unsurpassed in the Southern Hemisphere, and that our resources, particularly our mineral resources, are of boundless extent. They will see that our fruit industry, which is only at the beginning of its development, has infinite possibilities, and they have only to examine the handsome timber trophy exhibited by the trustees of the Tasmanian Museum, and the six pianos made of Tasmanian wood exhibited by the well-known firm of Collard and Collard, to satisfy themselves that we have some of the finest timber in the world, suitable for every kind of object. (Cheers.) We should take a leaf out of the book of New South Wales, which always, as she has done on this occasion, makes a great display at all exhibitions of her mineral and other staple products, and out of that of New Zealand, which advertises her picturesque and beautiful scenery all over the world. I hope that we shall not rest content with what we are doing now, but that Tasmania will also be worthily represented at the great World's Fair to be held next year in Chicago. Depend upon it the possibilities of exchange of commodities between Australia and America are very great indeed. (Cheers.) I have referred to our mineral resources, and having regard to the great interest that is being taken in these all throughout Australia, I cannot help thinking that there should have been a greater display in this Exhibition of our minerals. It is important that quantity as well as quality should be shown. We are a mining people, and it might have been expected that a very large number of specimens would have been exhibited to show the resources of the country in this direction. (Hear, hear.) In the matter of exhibits of agricultural machinery we evidently have a very fine show, and I need not point out to you how important it is that we should use the best appliances that skill can contrive in all industrial operations, in these days when science goes hand in hand with practice in the pursuit of industrial wealth. We are living in an age when to stand still is relatively to recede. It becomes therefore of the utmost importance that the young and rising generation should be instructed in those sciences and arts which lie at the basis of all industries; and it is encouraging to see that the work done by our Technical Schools, which is exhibited side by side with work sent out by the South Kensington authorities, makes a fair show. A new country like ours cannot expect to take a prominent place in matters of art, but we are favoured by having among our exhibits some fine pictures by the Tasmanian artist, Mr. W. C. Piguenit, who is acknowledged to be one of the leading, if not *the* leading, Australian landscape painter. In replying to the address presented to me to-day I referred to the three great objects sought to be attained by exhibitions of this sort, viz., an increase of culture, an improvement in the industrial appliances used, and an increase in the interchange of commodities. These are the main results to be hoped for, and surely they are in themselves most desirable. But at a social gathering of this sort I may refer to another benefit which is sure to arise from the congregating together of large numbers of people from all parts of the world interested in such matters. Old friendships are renewed and cemented, new friendships are formed, and social intercourse is promoted. (Cheers.) When we think of the extent to which social intercourse contributes to our happiness, and how large a part it really plays in our lives, I think you will agree with me that, especially on the present occasion when we are enjoying the hospitality so kindly afforded by Mr. Sutton, I am not doing wrong in assigning to the promotion of social intercourse a prominent place among the advantages to be hoped for from this Exhibition. I will not detain you longer. It gives Lady Hamilton and myself great pleasure to be living among you at this interesting time. We heartily appreciate your kindness in placing the excellent house at our disposal in Launceston which we are now occupying, and I can assure you that it gives us much pleasure to have this opportunity afforded to us of improving our acquaintance with the residents here, and with this beautiful and interesting part of the country. I am not going to anticipate what may be said in connection with the next toast, but before I sit down I must express, on my own part, the extreme satisfaction I feel in the presence here to-day of his Excellency Lord Hopetoun, who, as the representative of her Majesty in the great colony of Victoria, has done us the honour of being present on the occasion of the opening of this Exhibition. (Cheers.)

Hon. H. I. Rooke, M.L.C., in proposing the toast of his Excellency the Governor of Victoria, said he could assure them that he esteemed it a great privilege to have the honour of proposing one of the most popular toasts on the list. He felt confident that he was expressing the feelings of the people of Tasmania when he said that they greatly appreciated the presence of Lord Hopetoun. All the other colonies had responded nobly in the matter of sending exhibits, but the people of Tasmania could not forget that the colony of Victoria was their nearest neighbour (cheers); and though slight difficulties had occurred between the two colonies, and Australian federation might not be accomplished for a year or two, the presence of Lord Hopetoun might certainly have the effect of establishing closer relations between Victoria and Tasmania. They were all aware that his Lordship was one of the most popular Governors they had ever had in Victoria, and though the people of Tasmania were perfectly satisfied with the governorship of Tasmania, and would not care for a change, it was to be hoped, now that Lord Hopetoun had found his way to Tasmania, it would not be the last occasion on which he would visit the colony, and that his visit would have the effect of bringing about a feeling of genuine friendliness and sympathy between the two colonies. (Cheers.)

The toast was drunk with much cordiality.

Lord Hopetoun, on rising to respond, was received with a perfect ovation. He said: Your Excellency, Mr. Mayor, and gentlemen,—I rise to offer my very sincere thanks to the honourable Mr. Rooke for the exceedingly kind manner in which he has proposed the toast of my health, and I thank you, gentlemen, very heartily for the cordial way in which you have received that toast. I have been sufficiently long in these colonies to know that Australian hospitality is not confined to any geographical limits, and I am aware, gentlemen, that any individual representative of her Most Gracious Majesty the Queen is always assured of a warm reception wherever he goes, be it in his own colony or one of the neighbouring ones. (Cheers.) I feel that I have been very remiss during the last two years in not having visited Tasmania. I would like to explain to you how that is, and I tell you this in the strictest confidence: the colony of Victoria takes a great deal of governing (laughter, and cheers), and it is very often exceedingly difficult for me to get away. I should like to explain to you how it is that I have been able to snatch a few days to come over to see you on this auspicious occasion. I received an exceedingly kind and pressing invitation to come over from his Excellency Sir Robert Hamilton. The private individual within me rejoined and said, "Here's a chance for a nice little holiday," but the stern unbending official conscience said, "How can you go when you have so many engagements to meet in Victoria?" (Laughter and cheers.) I was torn between pleasure and duty, and in my perplexity I thought perhaps that the Premier of Victoria, Mr. Munro, might help me. So I went to him with Sir Robert Hamilton's letter in my hand and showed it to him, and asked, "What shall I do?" He replied, "This is capital: neither I nor my colleagues can get away just now." I must tell you by the way there was a crisis on just then. (Laughter and cheers.) It is all right now, gentlemen, for they have promised me that they will behave very well while I am away. "Neither I nor my colleagues," said Mr. Munro, "can go over, and you are the very man to go over and represent the colony of Victoria officially; you must go." Being backed up by my chief adviser, I need hardly say that my conscience—my official conscience—was satisfied. Here I am, gentlemen, the sole representative of the great colony of Victoria, and specially charged by my advisers to convey to you a hearty greeting, and charged by the people of Victoria to convey to you their sincere good wishes for the success of your Exhibition. Allow me to add my own warm congratulations and best wishes upon this most important occasion. Two years ago, when Lady Hopetoun had the pleasure of visiting Tasmania, she came back full of the beauties of the colony, and much impressed with the hospitality and kindness of the Tasmanian people. Now, I do not propose to restrict my few days' visit merely to Launceston. (Cheers.) I long to see a great deal more of your beautiful colony, and I hope to become better acquainted with its warmhearted people, and by the kindness of Sir Robert Hamilton, I shall have every opportunity of doing so during the next few days, and I can safely prophesy that the memory of my stay here will be among the pleasantest recollections of my life. (Cheers.) I am told by Sir Robert Hamilton that long speeches are not the fashion in Tasmania, and really I am delighted to hear this, because it is one of the "crumplings in the rose leaf" of my life in Victoria that I am always expected to turn on the tap on every possible occasion. (Laughter and cheers.) But "When you are in Rome you must do as Rome does," and being in Tasmania I will conclude my speech by thanking you on my own behalf for the kindness which you have shown towards me to-day as an individual, and on behalf of the people of Victoria for the good feeling you have exhibited and the enthusiastic reception you have accorded to their Governor. (Loud cheers; the company rising to their feet and singing "For he's a jolly good fellow.")

Mr. H. Dobson, M.H.A., in proposing the toast of "The Army, Navy, and Volunteers," said it was one which was always received with acclamation wherever Englishmen were assembled together. It must be a source of satisfaction that they were welcoming amongst them to-day the officers of a branch of her Majesty's navy, and they should feel grateful to the mother country that the shores of Australia were so efficiently defended. But they should remember that it was not Englishmen alone who could stand fire. Carlyle when he borrowed from a library a copy of an old work containing an old version of "Rule Britannia" had the impertinence to write under that song "Cock-a-doodle-doo!" Carlyle had one of the characteristics of politicans in using strong language, and his comment was a little unjust and unfair. But there were victories which our army and navy had gained, of which they had good reason to be proud—such as the defence of Rorke's Drift, the Charge of Balaclava, and the repair of the steamer within 500 yards of Khartoum under a heavy fire from the enemy's guns. The men who performed those heroic deeds were those of whom the volunteer forces had reason to feel proud. It might sound incongruous to talk of war on a peaceful occasion such as the present, but he believed he expressed the wishes of the people of Tasmania when he hoped that the colony would be represented at the Great World's Fair in Chicago, of which Colonel Campbell was the accredited agent. But if Tasmania desired to possess efficient defences, the Government should see that the guns were all of one pattern—that there should be a dock and coaling station at Hobart, and coaling stations on the south and western shores of Australia. If any attempt were made to introduce socialism into Tasmania, or to separate Australia from the mother land, the duty of every loyal colonist would be to support the maintenance of the Imperial connection. In conclusion, the speaker expressed a hope that the federation of the Australasian colonies would shortly be an accomplished fact.

Captain Bickford said, in returning thanks on behalf of the senior branch of the service which he had the honour of representing—H.M.'s navy—he regretted in the first place that more of her Majesty's ships were not present, so that many more representatives might have taken part in the very interesting event of the day, the more so as their Admiral—whose telegram had just been read, and under whom he had the very great honour and privilege (at the same time, he might add, the very great pleasure) to serve—was not there. They had received the toast of her Majesty's navy in the way he expected they would receive it, and, if he might be allowed to say so, it would be an evil time for England when her sons would not receive it in the same way. (Cheers.) On that navy, as they knew, the safety, honour, and welfare of the nation depended. Take away her navy and what would become of England? From her proud position of mistress of the seas she would sink into the position of a third or fourth class power. Therefore, he said it was the duty of every true Englishman to not only receive the toast as they had received it on that day, but also to do all they could to make their safeguard as efficient as possible. (Cheers.) He referred to the improvements that were being effected in the navy, and said that at the end of another twelve months further progress would be made, and a few years hence there would be a powerful addition, very much more so than had taken place during the last thirty years. (Cheers.) They would then have a powerful fleet, and no other nation in the world would be able to compare with the English nation. (Cheers). They would also have a very large number of cruisers, which were for the protection of their commerce and to act as scouts for the protection of the nation. He thought that they might regard it as a certainty that in 1892 the navy of England, in respect to material, would leave very little, if anything, to be desired. (Cheers.) As regarded personal element, of course it was difficult for him to speak. Neither in officers nor men was H.M.'s navy sufficiently strong. He would not, however, enter into a disquisition on the state of the navy, but he thought it was the duty of every naval officer, when addressing a number of intelligent Englishmen, such as he had the pleasure to address on that occasion, to point out the weak spots in their navy. He would take their personality as they had it, then, and speak of the rank and file. He would not speak of the officers; he was going to say he would leave them to speak for themselves, but as a rule an officer would not get up and talk about what he would do. He held that they should be judged, as their forefathers were judged, by their deeds. But as regards the British blue-jackets, he could speak from an experience as an officer of thirty-three years, and was entitled to express an opinion. They had seen a detatchment from H.M.S. *Katoomba* that day, and they could judge of their physique and general appearance. He could assure them that it was his honest opinion that these men, as regarded their morality, education, and conduct, were far superior to those whom they had in the service before. (Cheers.) As for that important factor, British pluck, they had not had many opportunities in the immediate past for displaying their courage, but when the opportunities had taken place they certainly had not been backward in coming forward, and had shown themselves to be worthy descendants of their heroic forefathers. He could only hope that that state of things would continue in the future, and that the traditions of that glorious service to which he had the honour and privilege to belong would be maintained without tarnish, and that when the future history of the navy came to be written the British sailor of the present would be found to have done his duty. (Cheers.)

Lieutenant-Colonel Warner, in responding on behalf of the army and the volunteers, said, as regarded the former, its deeds were so well known that it was only necessary to refer to the volunteers, and more especially to the Defence Force of Tasmania. Mr. Dobson had referred to the various types of guns now in use in the colony, but Tasmania was not a rich country, and was therefore obliged to procure guns as they came out, and was unable to obtain enough to entirely replace the old ones. That was the reason that the colony now possessed so many old types of artillery. If the colony of Tasmania could afford to arm her forces with new guns, he (Colonel Warner) would for one be very glad; but there was one matter of greater importance, and that was to get a sufficient number of men to man the guns. At present the defence forces of Tasmania were not as liberally supported as the forces in the neighbouring colonies, and the men did not get enough of daylight training, except at the camps. They were expected to learn everything at night drills, and only received pay for four days in the year. In New South Wales, Victoria, and South Australia the forces were paid for a large number of daylight drills. There was ample material of excellent physique in this colony, particularly in the country districts, where there were 1500 men all well equipped and armed, and he felt confident that if occasion arose, and they were put to the test, they would equal the deeds of armies in other parts of the world. (Cheers.)

Mr. Henry Button proposed the toast—"The Government and Parliament of Tasmania." He said he was placed in a very awkward position after the remarks which had fallen from Lieutenant-Colonel Warner regarding the inadequate support which the Government had given to the Tasmanian defences. He was confident, however, that if Parliament provided the means the volunteers would be a credit to the colony, though there would be many demands on the finances when Parliament again met. The representative system of government had been in force for many years in Tasmania, but, on the whole, Tasmania had reason to be proud of her Parliament, which, after all, was what the people made it. The present Government had taken office at a time of financial embarrassment, but they had applied themselves to bringing about an improvement, and it was for the electors to say whether they had succeeded. He thought that on the whole they must give the Government credit for disinterestedness, and a desire to advance the welfare of the colony. They must remember that Parliament was what the people made it, and that as the Ministry was formed from the ranks of members of Parliament, if they traced back to the origin of things, they must admit that the Government was also what the people made it. Tasmania was now in the best position of any of the colonies, but he deprecated the practice of attributing improper motives whenever any hitch occurred in public affairs.

The Premier, in responding on behalf of the Government, alluded to the true ring of honest hearty loyalty which he thought existed in the hearts of Tasmanians, spite of what was said by those who came amongst them and wrote books; and to the great privileges and blessings which they enjoyed, and which they could hand down to posterity.

The hon. W. Moore, President of the Legislative Council, expressed pleasure at the manner in which the Exhibition had been carried out.

The hon. A. T. Pillinger, Minister of Lands, also responded, and apologised for the unavoidable absence of the hon. N. J. Brown, Speaker of the House of Assembly, through illness. He (Mr. Pillinger) had been struck with the progress made by the colony during the past two years.

Mr. P. Barrett, M.H.A., proposed the toast of "The British and Foreign Representatives," and referred to the liberal manner in which

Great Britain, the neighbouring colonies, and foreign countries, had supported the Exhibition. He also eulogised the energy displayed by Sir E. Braddon.

Mr. Arthur Day, in responding to the toast, referred to the kindness and courtesy which he had received as the representative of the mother country, which he thought should have precedence. He also spoke in high terms of the exertions of the Mayor, and predicted a brilliant success for the Exhibition.

Mr. W. Hussey Vivian also responded on behalf of New South Wales, and said he felt in the position of a parent celebrating the coming of age of her youngest son. He referred to the opening of the Exhibition as a marvellous and magnificent spectacle, and eulogised the enthusiastic loyalty which had characterised the proceedings. He might mention, as showing the deep interest New South Wales felt in the Exhibition, that he was the only representative present besides the Mayor of Launceston who held the position of executive commissioner under the great seal of the colony. In a few minutes after the close of the proceedings he would telegraph to his Government, intimating that the Exhibition had been a splendid success.

Mr. D. F. Scott (official agent for Victoria) spoke of Tasmania as the worthy old mother of Victoria, who had colonised it.

Mr. H. J. Scott acknowledged the toast on behalf of South Australia.

Mr. M. E. Robinson gave "Our Visitors," which was responded to by Mr. Campbell.

The hon. B. S. Bird proposed "The Mayor and Aldermen of Launceston," and in a felicitous speech expressed the opinion that they should be regarded as a model Corporation; speaking in eulogistic terms of the way in which they conducted business and the improvements effected under their administration.

The Mayor returned thanks on behalf of the Council, and alluded to the past history of the Exhibition, expressing the gratification which he in common with his fellow commissioners experienced at the success which he felt sure would accrue from their endeavours.

The following were the remaining toasts: "The Ladies," by Alderman B. P. Farrelly, responded to by the City Clerk, Mr. C. W. Rocher; "The Press," proposed by the hon. A. T. Pillinger, responded to by Mr. Jas. Brickhill; "Success to the Tasmanian Exhibition," proposed by hon. P. O. Fysh, responded to by the Executive Commissioner (Mayor Sutton) and the general manager, Mr. Jules Joubert.

The company sang "Auld Lang Syne," after which the proceedings terminated.

THE EVENING'S PROCEEDINGS.

In the evening the interior of the Exhibition Buildings was seen to marked advantage, the display by gas and electric light being brilliant. The attendance was very large, an almost constant flow of visitors passing the turnstiles from the opening hour until nine o'clock. The fernery, into which portion of the building the visitor first enters, constitutes a most charming feature of the Exhibition, the atmosphere inside proving delightfully cool, while the giant ferns lend their aid in imparting a thoroughly sylvan air to the whole surroundings. Upon entering the portion of the building devoted to the many and various exhibits, the scene was striking in the extreme, the contents, generally speaking, showing to advantage. The passages were crowded by admiring throngs of sightseers, and loud praises of the Exhibition were to be heard upon all sides.

INAUGURAL CANTATA.

The Inaugural Cantata for the Tasmanian International Exhibition, composed by Mr. John Plummer, of Sydney, is as follows:—

OPENING CHORUS.

Of Tasman's Isle the children, we
   Step forth this day to take our stand
With those—earth's truly great and free—
   Who seek to crown each smiling land
With laurels gained in braver strife
   Than that in which the sword hath part;
The fruitage of a people's life,
   Of willing hand and earnest heart,
Of patient skill, heroic deed,
   Of thought unbound by error's thrall,
Of quenchless faith in Nature's creed—
   "'T is toil that e'er ennobleth all."

RECITATIVE.

But yesterday we had no place
   On history's board and varied page;
But yesterday a savage race
   Dominion owned where now we wage
The arts that from a grateful soil
   Abundance bring, or proudly rear
The shrines wherein the priests of toil
   Hold worship through the changing year;
The arts unknown to people rude
   Yet can the poorest nation bless,
And make the wildest solitude
   A world of light and loveliness.
Three hundred years! how short the span!
   A drop in time's eternal sea!
Yet scarce three hundred years have ran
   Their silent course, no more to be,
Since he, the bold explorer, came—
   The future's sturdy pioneer—
A new Columbus, borne to fame,
   To bring two worlds to each more near,
Like wandering knight, in fable old,
   Impelled by love's consuming drouth,
He found, enrobed in green and gold,
   The sleeping beauty of the south.

Quartet or Trio.

A land of sunny warmths and flowers
    Than poet's dream more fair and bright,
Where gaily dance the laughing hours,
    Enwreathed with garlands of delight;
Where stately hills and spangled plains
    Are kissed by soft and cooling breeze,
And silvery streams breathe glad refrains,
    Beneath the broad o'er-reaching trees;
A land encircled by a zone
    Of purple seas and golden skies,
Where freedom finds a stainless throne
    And freedom's sons a paradise.

Solo (Soprano).

But oft the brightest eyes are those
    That weep the saddest tears of pain;
And oft the heart that warmest glows
    Is chilled by sorrow's icy rain.
And so with us: not always bright
    Hath been our ceaseless onward way,
But hope hath borne us through the night,
    Into the realms of cheery day,
Till with the cross we gained the crown
    That none but freedom's sons may wear,
And sternly cast our burden down—
    In God our trust, to God our prayer.

Quartet and Chorus.

Then stouter grew the arms that bore,
    With brawny strength, the axe and spade
Through regions strange, where mountains hoar
    Rose high o'er wood and ferny glade.
To where the pastures, spreading wide,
    In silence yearned for sheep and kine;
To where the upland's sloping side
    Concealed the wealth-producing mine;
And soon was heard the stockman's cheer,
    The shearer's song, the anvil's clang,
Where oft was hurled the cruel spear,
    Or snake-like hissed the boomerang.

Solo (Tenor or Bass).

As tender shoot from acorn small
    In time becomes the lordly tree,
Whose leafy branches shelter all,
    So have we grown, a nation free;
A people strong in loving faith,
    Which of the future hath no fear,
And to its distant kinsman saith—

"Come, come, for ye are welcome here;
  No longer sad and weary pine,
  No longer fate and hungered moil,
But come where hearts with gladness shine,
  And roses strew the paths of toil."

Quartet.

Oh, sturdy toil! Thy aid divine
  Hath blessed the field, the farm, the fold;
Bade fruit the orchards rich entwine,
  And brought us store of wool and gold.
To thee we owe the storeyed mill,
  The dainty wonders of the loom,
The workshop where the sculptor's skill
  Bids shapeless blocks with beauty bloom;
The shelving mine, the iron way
  O'er which the harnessed engine roars,
The busy mart, the crowded bay
  Where float the flags of distant shores.

Chorus.

No ingrates we. Behold this fane
  To which we votive offerings bring,
And aid to swell the glory strain
  That heralds toil as lord and king.
Around are ranged the trophies vast
  Of art and science, brain and hand—
The present, learning from the past,
  Calm building up a future grand;
A time when hate and strife shall cease
  To mar the beautiful and good,
When all mankind shall dwell in peace
  In close unbroken brotherhood.

Grand Finale.

So shall it be. Though some may sneer
  At truths they cannot comprehend,
Still onward will we persevere—
  Still angel-heights our hearts ascend;
Still undeterred by scoff or scorn,
  Prepared to battle for the right,
We'll fearless wait the promised dawn,
  Through trouble's dark and gloomy night,
Till all the world be filled with love,
  By war unstained the grassy sod,
The ancient curse a blessing prove,
  And man be reconciled to God.

A BIRD'S-EYE VIEW OF THE INTERIOR.

The public entrance was through the fernery, which, under the unremitting supervision and artistic skill of Mr. M'Gowan and his assistants, was a veritable fairy scene, the beautiful specimens of the *Dicksonia, Alsophilus, Australis, Tomarias,* and other specimens from Denison Gorge, the staghorns and elkhorns from Queensland, birds' nest ferns from Sydney, *Australia Todea* from the Forth, and *Cyathea Medularis* from Stanley, are specially conspicuous. Right in the centre, and in the best position which could have been possibly selected for it, was the unmatched trophy composed of specimens of the native timbers of Tasmania, beautifully polished, and effectively arranged, and indicating the capabilities of the indigenous woods of the colony for ornamental, industrial, and commercial purposes. Emerging from the cool shades of the fernery into the annexes, the eye was charmed with a variety of brilliant colours, formed by a profusion of flags, ornamental trophies, kiosks, and pavilions, amongst which the splendid pyramid of the Mount Bischoff Tin Mining Company shone in all its silvery splendour. At the first glance the effect was somewhat confusing, the various exhibits being so closely grouped that the colours blended into each other. One of the first objects on the left of the entrance was Mr. F. Jackson's exhibits, of patent locks, and on the right the *Launceston Examiner* and *Tasmanian* section, which displayed a large variety of samples of the printing trade in all its branches. To the right the beautiful stained window representing the "Calling of St. Matthew," made by Messrs. Brooks and Robinson, Melbourne, for Christ Church, Launceston, at once attracted attention; and on the same side were the exhibits of Messrs. F. and W. Stewart, jewellers, of Charles street, who performed the work of stamping the award medals for exhibitors. Adjoining this was the section of Mr. Storrer, among whose exhibits were a beautiful sideboard, made from the wood of an English oak grown in the City Park; the first article of the kind made from that brave old tree of colonial growth. In front of these exhibits were show cases containing specimens of flowers cut with the scissors from rice paper, dahlias made from coloured paper, and waxen paper flowers, shown by Mrs. D. Room, of Mayfield, and so closely resembling nature's handiwork as to—at the first glance—be mistaken for real flowers. Next these were some neat exhibits from the Kindergarten School, held by Miss Fletcher, all the work of children ranging from four to six years of age. Immediately on the left of the Avenue of All Nations were to be found the pretty models and photographs of the crack steamers of Messrs. Huddart and Parker's fleet, and on the right the collection of pianos and organs shown by Messrs. Walch Bros. and Birchall. Further on the left the fine exhibits of pottery, pipes, and tiles from Mr. Campbell's works, the trophies from the Cornwall and the Esk Breweries, pyramids of bottles of tomato sauce, Peacock's jams, an artistic arrangement of the manufactures of the Tasmanian Soap and Candle Factory, and the important section of the Launceston Gas Company, with a varied collection of gas stoves, lamps, globes, and lighting appliances, commanded attention. Mr. Russen's confectionery works, situated in the model bakery close by, were contiguous, exhibiting all the latest appliances for producing the delicacies of the trade. Behind these, on the right of the entrance to the Albert Hall, the model dairy was at work, under Mr. Bartlett, the appliances of which were run by a Victory gas machine, which was started by his Excellency the Governor. The trophy shown by Messrs. Monds and Son, Carrick Roller Mills, also attracted favourable notice.

In the Tasmanian Court the most conspicuous features were some fine specimens of tweeds, etc., from the Waverley Mills, Cornish American organs shown by Newton and Son, a case of medicines from the establishment of Mr. J. D. Johnston, and a very fine exhibit of electroplate ware exhibited by Messrs. Hart and Sons. The mining exhibits next deserve a passing notice. Among these the Balstrup's mine showed specimens of ore, and the Sylvester S.M. Company, Mount Zeehan, some rich samples. Mr. J. T. Blackman, Invermay, had a very interesting and well-arranged show of paints and pigments manufactured from Tasmanian products. A pyramid from the Cornwall Coal Mine led the way to the magnificent locally built boarding boat of the Marine Board, showing to advantage the capabilities of our Tasmanian woods. Near this were appropriately placed some specimens of skilfully-made mats, and further on mineral exhibits from the Comet (Dundas), Whyte River S.M. Company, and Great Republic T.M. Company. Mr. J. Barclay exhibited a collection of safes, cooking ranges, baths, etc., and further on in the same avenue of the Tasmanian Court were specimens shown by the Western S.M. Company, Mount Zeehan Silver-Lead Mining Company, Fahl-Ore Company, Heazlewood S.M. Company Limited, and rocks and minerals from Mount Claud exhibited by Mr. C. W. J. Mansfield. Messrs. Bernacchi and Co., of Maria Island, had a number of fine exhibits of patent natural cement, white freestone, specimens of silver and gold, kaolin clay, and other products; and adjacent was the fine trophy of the Mount Bischoff Tin Mining Company. Quibell's pagoda, with its rich scarlet curtains and gilt poles, was also a prominent feature of this part of the annexes. The New South Wales Court made a splendid show, being artistically arranged and varied. The mineral resources of Broken Hill and other mining districts of the parent colony, including some splendid specimens of coal from the mines of the Wickham and Bullock Coal Company Limited, formed, of course, a prominent feature in this court, and were aptly illustrated by photographs. The cycloramaic view of Broken Hill, with a most realistic foreground, was one of the *pieces de resistance*, and attracted a large number of visiters. The aviary, filled with birds indigenous to New South Wales, the Fallon (Albury) wine exhibits, specimens of printing, bookbinding, and endless rolls of paper, from the *Sydney Morning Herald* office, funny sketches from the *Bulletin*, and an innumerable variety of other exhibits, combined to render this court one of the best in the building.   Messrs. J. C. Ludovici and Sons' exhibits of leather belting, oak tanned belting, and other goods of the same kind for engineering purposes, were one of the features of this court. A pretty entrance from the Avenue of All Nations, an effective arrangement of ferns, a ceiling in harmony with the general colour, a profusion of shields, banners, and flaglets, and a general study of completeness and method, showed that the staff under the Executive Commissioner, Mr. Vivian, worked with energy and enthusiasm to maintain the credit of the pioneer colony.   In the next bay the Union Steamship Company of New Zealand displayed some fine models of their steamboats, together with photographs and water-colour pictures of the places included in the extensive routes served by this enterprising company.   One of the most interesting features of this section was a chart table depicting the routes from New Zealand to Australia, Tasmania, Fiji, and other parts of the Southern Hemisphere served by this company's magnificent fleet of fifty-three steamers, all represented in the exact positions they occupy every morning, and giving at a glance a bird's-eye view of the regularity and extent of the service.   The larger models of the Company's steamers included the *Mararoa, Waikatipu*, and *Rotomahana*.   Continuing progress along the Avenue of Nations, were found the Fine Art Galleries, in which the British, Australasian, and Tasmanian Courts had many admirable exhibits.   Outside, the Technical Schools of Hobart and Launceston made a fine display of samples of really meritorious work, having regard to the short period that they have been established.   On the left were the South Australian wine rooms, with a very handsomely furnished sitting-room, and an assortment of the best viticultural products of that colony.   Coming to the Victorian Court, which shows well, thanks to private enterprise and the admirable arrangements of Mr. D. Fergus Scott, the official agent, were well-made exhibits by Messrs. Danks and Son, Perry and Co., the well-known coach builders, Falshaw Bros., Dowling of South Melbourne, Tech, Morgan, M'Laren, Greer, wine merchants, Jack Frost freezing appliances, Alcock's billiard tables, V. Pride's (Geelong) saddlery, Carter and Werner's optical goods, and Braybrook Company's Phœnix Fireworks manufactures, Brache's varied and well got-up samples of wine, Mephan-Ferguson's iron water-pipes and fluming, Thompson's (Castlemaine) machinery, Pearson's Richmond Brewery stout, Farrow and Company's cocoa and whiskey (a novel combination), Sargood, Butler, and Nichol's exhibits of clothing, and the very interesting and valuable exhibits of the Australian India-rubber Company.   Messrs. Swallow and Ariel had a very cleverly arranged trophy composed of their celebrated biscuits, and there were also Morgan's tents and flags, the Australian Wine Company, A. Weigel and Co.'s champagne bar, Donaghy and Son's (Geelong) rope and twine exhibits, and Budam's Microbe Killer.   In the British Court, Mr. Arthur Day's exhibits at once commanded attention by the superior appearance of the show cases, and the effective arrangement of the section.   The models of the steamers *Ophir* and *Ormuz*, in the centre of the main avenue, were magnificent samples of marine architecture.   A noteworthy feature at this point was the fountain, which assumed quite an imposing appearance with its coating of bronze, and artistic setting off of flowers, ferns, and evergreens.   Mr. A. Munnew's pretty pavilion, and the effective display of Messrs. Collard and Collard's fine pianos and American organs, attracted much attention, and were a credit to the firm, the decorations having been most artistically done by Mr. Little, scenic artist, the pavilion being surmounted by a pretty tapestry design with the motto "Packard's Fort Wayn American Organs" suspended on gold-tipped spears. In the foreign courts, to the left, Mr. Singer's mannikins excited some amusement, and the Bohemian glassware was much admired. Mr. Nason's beautiful ware and the varied exhibits of M. Bossomaier could not be passed without appreciation of their beauty. The French Court did not make any elaborate display, though M. V. Laurelle had a fair stock of exhibits. Opposite this court, on the right of the Avenue of Nations, Mr. Saunders, the representative of a large number of leading English firms, made a creditable display in the absence of some of his principal exhibits, and Mr. Jacob Hillman had a thoroughly typical example of British industry in Messrs. Clark and Company show case of cottons from the Anchor Mills, Paisley, the reels being built up in artistic coloured designs. There were also in the same case novelties in the shape of globes, containing winds of cotton for ladies' work tables. Mr. Hillman also exhibited some very fine samples of pottery from designs by Sir Edward Elton, Bart., of the Clevedon Court Estate, Somerset. Further on in the main avenue, Messrs. James Miller and Company showed several samples of the manufactures of the Victoria Rope, Twine, and Mat manufactory, Melbourne, arranged in cases and in pillars; and Messrs. Craddock and Company, Wakefield, one of the most genuine samples of the durability and compactness of British workmanship, in the form of a trophy composed of samples of cables, wire ropes, etc. The Machinery and Implement Court made an excellent show, and though the space had been extended there was none too much room.

DEATH OF THE DUKE OF CLARENCE.

On the 16th January news was received of the death of H.R.H. the Duke of Clarence, and the various sections of the Exhibition were draped in black, the British Court being closed until after the funeral, and some of the mourning manifestations, especially those made by Mr. Arthur Day, official agent for Great Britain, and Mr. D. Fergus Scott, official agent for Victoria, were costly and elaborate.

On the 18th of the same month, the date of the late Prince's funeral, a solemn requiem service was held in the Albert Hall. It was, as Mr. Sutton remarked, " peculiarly fitting that a requiem should be sounded within the walls of the Exhibition " for the late Duke of Clarence, and it was equally fitting that the address upon the occasion should have been delivered by the gentleman who was mainly instrumental in calling the Tasmanian International Exhibition into existence. It was a happy inspiration, then, which prompted the gathering, and the large attendance endorsed the action taken by Mr. Sutton and Mr. Joubert, and rewarded the efforts of those who planned out the requiem and brought it to a successful issue. The building was tastefully draped in black, and the ladies in the choir wore mourning sashes. The audience was an exceedingly large one, and the programme commanded respectful attention from its commencement to its close. The arrangement of the order of the ceremony was excellent, and the selection of the various items set down in the programme was in the best possible taste. Miss Frost having played an organ voluntary, " Eternal Rest," Mr. S. J. Sutton, M.H.A., delivered the following panegyric:—"The Great Angel who is ever calling over the muster roll of human names came on Wednesday last to that of Albert Victor, Duke of Clarence, second in right of succession to the Crown. The nation upon which the sun never sets is plunged in grief at the decease of one so near the throne; and we, in common with other parts of the empire, pay our tribute of respect to his memory. It seems to me that it is peculiarly fitting that a requiem should be sounded within the walls of the Tasmanian International Exhibition, because, as you will all remember, it was the late Duke's illustrious grandfather who conceived and worked out the scheme which led to the inauguration of the system of exhibitions which we are perpetuating here. Of the late Prince I need say little. His career was finished almost before it was begun. It is enough for us to remember that those who knew him best loved him best, and the British people all over the world honour the Queen, and love the stricken mother who so tenderly nursed the dying Prince. The cablegrams this morning especially draw our feelings to the young Princess who was so shortly to consummate by marriage the love of many years. That the joys of her approaching wedding should so suddenly be changed into bitter mourning over the bier of her betrothed is a circumstance of so extremely pitiful a character as to demand our heartfelt sympathy. Let us then place our mourning wreath—the waratah, the clematis, and our own sweet wild flowers of affection—upon the tomb of the Prince's memory, in the full assurance that they will be deemed worthy of a place beside those from the old historic world, and let us hope that our present sorrow will bind closer the bonds which unite the empire." The "Dead March in Saul" was then rendered by the City Band, after which the Exhibition Choir sang that sweetly pathetic hymn from the "Ancient and Modern" collection, "Now the labourer's task is o'er." Mr. O. B. Balfe followed with a reading comprising selections from Tennyson's "In Memoriam" and the concluding portion of the dedication to the Idylls, given in magnificent style, the lines breathing a prayer for comfort for the sorrowing Queen being rendered with splendidly pathetic effect. The choir followed with the hymn " God moves in a mysterious way," after which the band played the Requiem March; the service was then concluded with the National Anthem, rendered by the choir, Miss Cox singing the solo in her usual finished style. The Requiem service was a credit to the management of the Exhibition and an additional testimony of the loyalty of the people of this city.

THE MINERAL ARCH.

This handsome structure at the main entrance to the Exhibition, and composed entirely of Tasmanian material, stone, brick, terra-cotta, cement, lime, minerals, etc., was supplied gratuitously by manufacturers, quarry owners, and mining companies. As it is intended that the Arch shall be a permanent structure, more care was expended in its erection than is usual with Exhibition work of this character. Consequently, it reflects much credit upon its designer, Mr. A. E. Luttrell, architect, of Cameron street, and builder, Mr. J. T. Farmilo, of Cimitiere street.

The following is a list of the donors and materials supplied by them :—

LAUNCESTON CORPORATION.—Bluestone.

MESSRS. JORY AND CAMPBELL, LAUNCESTON.—
1. Fire-clay brick, manufactured by the firm of material lately discovered by them.
2. Machine-made plain and moulded bricks.
3. Terra-cotta.

T. B. INNOCENT, LAUNCESTON.—Hand-made and machine pressed and moulded bricks.

BERNACCHI AND COMPANY, MARIA ISLAND.—Native cement.

COSGROVE BROS., LAUNCESTON.—Hand-made bricks.

SHERIFF AND JARVIS, LATROBE.—Ditto.

J. BLENKHORN, RAILTON.—Lime.

FYSH BROS., OATLANDS.—Brown stone.

J. WALKER, ROSS.—White and light brown stone.

The mineral specimens in the panels were received from various mining companies and others, and represent but a few of the many minerals found in Tasmania, and which were seen to the best advantage in the Mineral Section of the Tasmanian Court.

THE FERNERY.

(From the "Launceston Examiner.")

"On entering the Fernery for the first time the visitor might imagine himself suddenly transported to some quiet cool sylvan glade in the depths of the forest primeval, far away from the haunts of men, so realistic is the scene presented and so complete and effective the *coup d'œil*. By an ingenious arrangement of 'wood borders' the harmony is preserved between the natural foliage and the ceiling, and a pretty piece of Tasmanian landscape at the far end of the fernery, with waterfalls and a range of mountains in the distance make a most effective background and give depth to the view. The sides of the fernery are also effectively painted in harmony with the trees, opening up vistas which seem to recede away into the distance. The artistic accessories are so blended with the real as to perfectly harmonise with the natural foliage, the waterfalls in the background descending into a rustic structure representing cliffs over which three natural cataracts tumble down through masses of creepers and rock lilies. On either side of the avenue the fernery is planted with splendid specimens of the common *Dicksonia* and *Alsophilus Australis, Lomarias* and other varieties from Denison Gorge, the beautiful staghorn and elkhorn ferns from Queensland, bird's nest ferns from Sydney, and several very fine specimens of the *Australia Todea* from the Forth. Intermingled with these are rock lilies, creepers, and dwarf ferns, which form the undergrowth to the tree ferns with their spreading fronds, and on one side is a bit of natural forest. At intervals are arranged little rivulets, water-falls, fountains and jets, which will serve to keep the air deliciously cool during the summer months. . . . . The splendid specimens of the staghorn ferns received from Sydney were very skilfully packed under the superintendence of Mr. C. Moore, director of the Botanical Gardens. All the ferns and plants wear a healthy and thriving appearance, and the whole of the work reflects much credit on the artistic taste and energy of Mr. McGowan and his assistants."

There was also to be noticed a very interesting fern (*Cyathea Medularis*) which although fairly plentiful in New Zealand and some other colonies is confined to a very limited area near Stanley, in Tasmania.

THE MODEL DAIRY.

On the visitor's left hand after passing through the Fernery was to be found the Model Dairy in full working, butter and cheese being made by machinery. It was equipped with a complete plant, such as is now in use in almost every farming district in Victoria. The full working capacity of the Dairy was 960 lbs. of butter per week, the advantages of machinery over the old style being apparent. The Alexandra Separator at a speed of 6000 revolutions per minute will separate 100 gallons of milk per hour; the cream can be made either thick or thin, and the separated milk being sweet is far superior for most purposes than the majority of that skimmed by hand. The churn employed was what is known as a concussion churn, the interior being devoid of beaters and agitators. Finer grained, better flavoured, and better keeping butter results from this method. The next utensil, the butter worker, is the most important in a dairy. Good butter may be made in almost any churn, but its keeping depends entirely on the thoroughness of the working and washing, which operations are admirably performed by the use of the butter worker. A butter press and printer was to be found in close proximity to the foregoing. The advantages obtained by the use of this machine are considerable. By extreme pressure of the screw a large percentage of the remaining moisture runs out, and the butter on being forced through the opening is stamped and formed into long cubes uniform in shape and size. The cutting frame is then brought into action, and the cube by one operation divided into pounds or half-pounds as desired. Hot water, so indispensable in a dairy, is obtained by the employment of a patent steam generator, which with other plant was supplied by Messrs. A. G. Webster and Son, of Hobart. By the use of this patent 250 gallons of water can be raised to boiling point in 25 minutes. The Cheese-making Plant in the Model Dairy was complete in every detail, manufactured by Messrs. Lister and Co., of England. The motive power was furnished by means of a "Victory" gas engine of four-horse power. This engine is an improvement on the well known "Otto," and is manufactured in Melbourne by Messrs. J. A. Brierly and Co. In addition to demonstrating the science and practice of butter and cheese making, the Manager, Mr. A. P. Bartlett, delivered a course of Lectures, illustrated by means of diagrams and the use of the various appliances, on subjects of interest to dairy farmers.

LIST OF JURORS.

Group A.—Works of Art.

Class 1. Oil paintings on canvas, panel, or other grounds.
Class 2. Miniatures, water-colour paintings, pastels, and drawings of every kind.
Class 3. Sculpture and die sinking, medals, cameos, engravings, etc.
Class 4. Architectural drawings and models, elevation and plans of buildings.
Class 5. Engraving and lithographing, chromo-lithographs, etc.
    Messrs. GEORGE COLLINS,
          HENRY EDGELL,
          JULES JOUBERT, Chairman.

Group B.—Education and Instruction; Processes of the Liberal Arts.

Class 6. Plans and models of schools, asylums, furniture for same; ditto for blind, and deaf mutes; work of pupils of both sexes.
Class 7. Stationery, bookbinding, painting and drawing materials.
    Messrs. S. HOPWOOD,
          J. N. CLEMONS,
          E. H. SUTTON, JUN., Chairman.

Class 8. Photographs on paper, glass, wood, and enamel; heliographic engravings, photo-lithographic specimens, enlargements, coloured photographs, instruments, apparatus, chemicals, and all materials used in photography.
    Messrs. J. G. S. FAWNS,
          A. J. ALLOM,
          JULES JOUBERT, Chairman.

Class 9. Musical Instruments.
    Messrs. ALEX. WALLACE,
          T. H. Bosworth,
          JULES JOUBERT, Chairman.

Class 10. Medicine, hygiene, and public relief.
    Dr. L. G. THOMPSON,
    Mr. JULES JOUBERT, Chairman.

Class 11. Mathematical and philosophical instruments.
Class 12. Maps, geographical and cosmographical apparatus.
>   Messrs. S. HOPWOOD,
>   J. N. CLEMONS,
>   E. H. SUTTON, JUN., Chairman.

Group C.—Furniture and Accessories.

Class 13. Cheap and fancy furniture.
Class 14. Upholsterers' and decorators' work.
>   Messrs. C. W. JOSCELYNE,
>   W. COOGAN,
>   JULES JOUBERT, Chairman.

Class 15. Crystal glass, and stained glass.
>   Messrs. W. R. MARSH,
>   HERBERT SAUNDERS,
>   JULES JOUBERT, Chairman.

Class 16. Pottery, including bricks, tiles, drain and other pipes, etc.
>   Messrs. A. E. LUTTRELL,
>   J. T. FARMILO,
>   JULES JOUBERT, Chairman.

Class 17. Carpets, tapestry, and other stuffs for furniture.
>   Messrs. C. W. JOSCELYNE,
>   W. COOGAN,
>   JULES JOUBERT, Chairman.

Class 18. Paper-hangings.
Class 19. Cutlery.
>   Messrs. ALEX. WEBSTER,
>   J. R. MASON,
>   JULES JOUBERT, Chairman.

Class 20. Gold and silver smith's work.
Class 21. Bronzes, art castings, and repoussé work.
Class 22. Clocks and watches.
>   Messrs. J. G. PIPER,
>   J. M. PROCTER,
>   JULES JOUBERT, Chairman.

Class 23. Apparatus and process for heating and lighting, matches, etc.
>   Messrs. A. E. LUTTRELL,
>   J. T. FARMILO,
>   JULES JOUBERT, Chairman.

Class 24. Perfumery, toilet, and other soaps.
>   Messrs. F. K. FAIRTHORNE,
>   C. RAWSON,
>   JULES JOUBERT, Chairman.

Class 25. Leather and basket work and fancy articles, including pipes, ivory, and tortoiseshell, bone, and wood work.

  Miss Kate Farrell,
  Mrs. Moser,
  Mr. Jules Joubert, Chairman.

Group D.—Textile Fabrics, Clothing, Etc.

Class 26. Cotton, cotton fabrics (pure and mixed).
Class 27. Flax, hemp, and linen fabrics
Class 28. Wool and all woollen fabrics, flannels, blankets, tweeds, etc.

  Messrs. J. W. Pepper,
    A. Bossomaier,
    Jules Joubert, Chairman.

Special Jury for Wool.

  Messrs. J. B Curran,
    E. Whitfeld,
    G. P. Hudson,
    W. R. Marsh,
    Jules Joubert, Chairman.

Class 29. Silk and all silk fabrics.
Class 30. Hosiery and underclothing.

  Messrs. J. W. Pepper,
    A. Bossomaier,
    Jules Joubert, Chairman.

Class 31. Clothing for both sexes, boots and shoes, artificial flowers, hair, wigs, etc.

  Messrs. W. F. Petterd,
    J. H. Room,
    Jules Joubert, Chairman.

Class 32. Jewellery (other than gold and silver); plated ware; jet, amber, coral, mother-of-pearl, steel; precious stones, real and imitation.

  Messrs. N. Aronson,
    O. Moser,
    Jules Joubert, Chairman.

Class 33. Portable weapons — guns, pistols, side-arms; hunting and sporting equipments.

  Messrs. T. S. Cleminshaw,
    Louis Saber,
    Jules Joubert, Chairman.

Class 34. Travelling and camp equipage—tents, tent furniture, hammocks, beds, camp stools, trunks, valises, bags, rugs, cushions, equipments, and all implements for geologists, mineralogists, naturalists, etc.

  Messrs. M. Singer,
    L. R. Castray,
    Jules Joubert, Chairman.

Class 35. Toys, dolls, and playthings; games for adults and children.
> Messrs. CHAS. DAY,
> HERBERT SAUNDERS,
> JULES JOUBERT, Chairman.

Group E.—Mining; Mining Industry; Raw and Manufactured Products.

Class 36. Collections of rocks, mineral ores, stones, refractory substances, earths and clays, rock salt, mineral fuels, asphalt, bitumen, mineral tar, petroleum, etc.; process of washing and extracting precious metals; metals in crude as well as manufactured; tools, and all kinds of hardware.
> Messrs. Alex. MONTGOMERY, M.A.,
> W. F. PETTERD,
> JULES JOUBERT, Chairman.

Class 37. Products of forestry: specimens of timber; wood for cabinet work, for building and other purposes; barks for tanning or textile purposes; colouring and resinous substances; charcoal, dried wood, potash; turnery; straw work, etc.
> Messrs. D. SCOTT,
> J. T. FARMILO,
> JULES JOUBERT, Chairman.

Class 38. Products of hunting, fishing, etc.: collections or drawings of terrestrial and amphibious animals; birds' eggs, fishes, mollusca, and crustacea; furs and skins; undressed feathers; horn, teeth, ivory; tortoiseshell; sponges; gums; traps, snares, fishing nets, lines, hooks, etc., etc.
> Messrs. HOWARD E. WRIGHT,
> W. F. PETTERD,
> JULES JOUBERT, Chairman.

Class 39. Agricultural products NOT used for food: raw cotton, flax, hemp, and other fibres

Rope.—
> Capt. BARWOOD,
> Messrs. WM. GURR,
> JULES JOUBERT.

Class 39. Wool, washed and greasy; pharmaceutical substances; tobacco, raw and manufactured; tanning and dyeing substances; preserved fodder, and substances for feeding cattle, sheep, dogs, etc.
> Messrs. GEO. E. HARRAP,
> GEO. P. HUDSON,
> W. R. MARSH,
> JULES JOUBERT, Chairman.

Class 40. Leather and skins : raw and salted hides; tanned, curried, dressed, and dyed leather; varnished or patent leather; morocco and sheepskin; skins grained, chamoyed, tanned, dressed, or dyed.
 Messrs. H. B. Hardt,
  Joseph C. Genders,
  Jules Joubert, Chairman.

Group F.—Apparatus and Processes used in Mechanical Industries.

Class 41. Mining and metallurgy : boring machines; artesian, diamond drills, etc., for cutting coal, rocks, etc.; for working mines or quarries; appliances for lowering and hoisting miners, pumping water, ventilating shafts, etc.; safety lamps; apparatus for saving life; apparatus for the mechanical dressing of ores; fuel for metal work of all kinds.
 Messrs. Jas. Scott,
  W. R. Marsh,
  Jules Joubert, Chairman.

Class 42. Agricultural implements : tools; machines used in the cultivation of fields and forests, in all branches of husbandry, sowing, planting, or harvesting, whether worked by hand, horse, or steam-power; carts and other rural means of transport; manures, organic or mineral.
 Messrs. Jas. Scott,
  Wm. Luck,
  W. R. Marsh,
  Jules Joubert, Chairman.

Class 43. Apparatus and processes used in agricultural work and used for the preparation of food, including milling flour, kneading, baking, ice-making, and refrigerating machines.
 Messrs. Jas. Scott,
  W. R. Marsh,
  Jules Joubert, Chairman.

Class 44. Machines and tools in general, not specified.

Typewriters.—
 Messrs. T. S. Cleminshaw,
  W. Paxman,
  Jules Joubert, Chairman.

Oils and Tallow.—
 Messrs. W. R. Marsh,
  Jas. Scott,
  Jules Joubert, Chairman.

Class 45. Carriages and wheelwrights' work.
Class 46. Harness and saddlery.
 Messrs. W. R. Marsh,
  J. T. Smith,
  Jules Joubert, Chairman.

Class 47. Railway apparatus: engines, carriages, etc.
  Messrs. W. R. MARSH,
    JAS. SCOTT,
    JULES JOUBERT, Chairman.

Class 48. Telegraphic appliances—electric and all appertaining to electricity.
  Messrs. E. WHITFELD,
    W. R. MARSH,
    JULES JOUBERT, Chairman.

Class 49. Building materials of all kinds; drawings, models, etc., of public buildings, mansions, cottages, lighthouses, industrial dwellings, etc.
  Messrs. A. F. LUTTRELL,
    J. T. FARMILO,
    JULES JOUBERT, Chairman.

Class 50. Navigation: drawings or models of ships, boats, steamers, floating docks; materials for rigging; apparatus for saving life at sea; diving bells; rocket apparatus; flags and signals.
  Capt. W. R. BARWOOD,
  Messrs. W. R. MARSH,
    E. WHITFELD,
    JULES JOUBERT, Chairman.

Class 51. Material and apparatus for military purposes, engineering, fortifications, artillery, guns and gun carriages, military equipment, clothing, military transport service, armaments, etc.

Group G.—Alimentary Products.

Class 52. Cerals, farinaceous products; wheat, rye, barley, rice, maize, millet, and other cereals, in grain and in flour; grain without husk, and groats; bread and pastry; biscuits, etc.

Cereals and Farinaceous Products.—
  Messrs. S. J. SUTTON,
    W. H. GIBSON,
    JULES JOUBERT, Chairman.

Bread, Pastry, and Biscuits.—
  Messrs. S. J. SUTTON,
    W. G. PORTER,
    JULES JOUBERT, Chairman.

Class 53. Fatty substances and oils good for food; milk, fresh and preserved; butter, fresh, salt, or tinned; cheese.

Class 54. Meat and fish, salt, preserved, smoked, and salted.
  Messrs. J. N. SERGEANT,
    A. MURRELL,
    JULES JOUBERT, Chairman.

Class 55. Vegetables and fruit, fresh, dried, and preserved.
Class 56. Condiments: sugar and confectionery, including jams, preserves, sauces, etc.
 Messrs. R. F. IRVINE,
  J. N. SERGEANT,
  JULES JOUBERT, Chairman.

Cocoa and Chocolate.—
 Messrs. T. H. GOULD,
  W. R. MARSH,
  JULES JOUBERT, Chairman.

Class 57. Fermented drinks: wines, still and sparkling; beer; cider, perry; brandy, whiskey, gin; liqueurs, etc., etc.

Wines, Spirits.—
 Messrs. W. R. MARSH,
  E. WHITFELD,
  JULES JOUBERT, Chairman.

Beers.—
 Messrs. W. R. MARSH,
  JOHN MORTON,
  JULES JOUBERT, Chairman.

Aerated Waters and Cordials.—
 Messrs. W. R. MARSH,
  E. WHITFELD,
  D. FERGUS SCOTT,
  JULES JOUBERT, Chairman.

Special Jury for Adjudicating upon Unclassified Exhibits.

 Messrs. W. R. MARSH,
  E. WHITFELD,
  JULES JOUBERT, Chairman.

Class 58. Horticulture; floriculture; arboriculture; flowers, etc.
 Messrs. P. LORD JOHNSTONE,
  E. WHITFELD,
  JULES JOUBERT, Chairman.

Group H.—Music and Singing.

 Mrs. A. MUNNEW,
 Messrs. W. W. THORNTHWAITE,
  JULES JOUBERT, Chairman.

AWARDS.

GROUP A.—FINE ARTS.

The Fine Art collection, though somewhat limited in the number of exhibits, was a main feature in the display. The collection occupied a capital position in spacious galleries facing the main avenue, whilst a magnificent collection of choice Italian Statuary was displayed in the Fernery, and materially added to the beauty of that picturesque section of the Exhibition. The Fine Arts Gallery proper was divided into three sections, viz.—British, Foreign, and Tasmanian. And in the first department the choice oil paintings procured by Sir Edward Braddon, including the full length portrait of Queen Victoria, lent by her Majesty, were a source of never-failing interest to the visitors; whilst the works of Tasmanian and intercolonial artists were very greatly admired, and the Austrian pictures displayed by Herr Bossomaier attracted considerable attention. It is hoped that the exhibition of such magnificent works of art will confer material benefit upon the people by increasing an appreciation of the beautiful, and making art and its softening and subduing influences part and parcel of the daily life of the community. The work of the judges was long and arduous, and the following are their awards:—

CLASS I.

Brent, Rose T., Invermay. Chess table top, two views painted in Indian ink—Second award.

Burrowes, Mrs. A. E., Launceston. Small folding screen, four panels, painted in oils on canvas, Tasmanian lake scenery, native flowers, etc. —Second award. Fire screen, transparent painting on glass in oils, fuchsias and poppies—Highly commended. Large folding screen, four panels, painted in oils on canvas; views of Hobart and Launceston, also miscellaneous subjects—Highly commended.

Browne, F. Styant, Launceston. Original oil painting, the work of exhibitor, "S.S. *Oonah* leaving the River Tamar on a misty morning"—Second award.

Bates, Edward S. Designs in oil for decorating ball room, dining room, and hall—Highly commended.

Barrett, Alfred Warshop, Trevallyn, Launceston. "Fruit"—Second award.

Dodery, Emmeline, Lauraville, Longford, "Scene on Upper Yarra—Highly commended. "Scene on Goulburn, N.S.W."—Highly commended.

Farrelly, B. P., Launceston. "Landscape"—Highly commended. "The Magdalen Reclining"—Highly commended.

Gurr, M. E., Launceston. Group of flowers painted on ground glass, in oils—Second award.

Greig, Mrs. C. G., Launceston. "Scene, River Ouse"—Highly commended. "Lake St. Clair"—Second prize.

Halligan, Mrs. G. H., Riversleigh, Hunter's Hill, Sydney. Oil painting, "Queen of White Flowers"—Second award.

Higgs, Joshua, jun., Trevallyn. "Low Head, River Tamar"—Highly commended. "Don Plains, River Mersey"—Highly commended.

Hall, Alfred J., Launceston. "Victoria River, Huon—Morning," by W. C. Piguenit—First award.

Kenworthy, Miss Rosina, Launceston. Hand-painted table top in oils; half wreaths of genuine blossoms on a black ground—Second prize. Hand-painted door in oils, Tasmanian wild flowers and berries, taken from nature—First prize.

Mace, Miss Kate Lee, Hobart. Hand-painted screen and several oil paintings—Second award.

Maxwell, Mrs. P. C., Latrobe. "A bush road near Port Sorell"—Highly commended. "Spring in the Tasmanian bush"—Third award. Miniature views of Tasmanian scenery—Highly commended. Hand-painted walnut screen of "Tasmanian river scenery" in brown and white oils, with "native flowers" on the back in colours—Second award.

Nicholas, R. J., Launceston. Oil painting on canvas of Cataract Gorge in flood—Second award. "Eventide," painted entirely with the palate knife—Second award. "Corra Linn"—Highly commended. Oil paintings from life—No. 1, His Worship the Mayor of Launceston, S. J. Sutton, Esq.; No. 2, Mrs. S. J. Sutton; No. 3, J. Joubert, Esq.; No. 4, G. Horne, Esq. Oil painting on canvas *from* photograph (not *on* photograph), Mrs. Nicholas, sen. (collective exhibit)—First award.

Purdue, Ralph, Launceston. Oil paintings (40) of prominent Launcestonians, including previous mayors and present aldermen—Second award.

Pousty, William, Launceston. "Corra Linn"—Highly commended. "Glen Fallon, etc., Scotland"—Second award.

Scott, Mary Teresa, Launceston. "Entrance to the Huon"—Highly commended. "Freycinet Peninsula"—Highly commended.

Smith, Henry E., Hobart. Oil painting, "The Sly Glass"—Highly commended.

Walker, Mary, Longford. Copy of painting, racehorse "Camel"—Highly commended.

Williams, Maud Marion, Hobart. Black octagon table top, in oils; Tasmanian native flowers and berries—First award.

Weetman, Mabel L., Launceston. Collection of oil paintings—Highly commended as a collection.

Colonial Architects' Department, Sydney. Oil paintings of old N.S.W. identities—Second award.

New South Wales Fisheries Department. Paintings of edible fish—First award as a collection.

Piguenit, William C., Hunter's Hill, Sydney. Oil painting, "Out West, during the flood, 1890" (the Gundabooka Range, N.S.W.)—Special first award.

Anscombe, Eliza, Dunedin, N.Z. Oil painting, "Lawyer's Head above St. Clair, Dunedin"—H.C. "Holly Branch" on wooden panel—Second award.

Gibb, J., Christchurch, N.Z. Wellington Harbour—First prize. "A bush saw pit—Second award.

Murray, Geo. Read, Port Chalmers, N.Z. "Mount Cook, Middle Island, N.Z.—Second award. "Dusky Coast, West Coast"—Second award.

Binney, Florence Walker, Moonee Ponds, Victoria. "Through Morley's Track, Fernshaw, Victoria"—Second award.

Binney, Catherine, Footscray, Victoria. Hand-painted dessert service; waterpot, portrait, etc.—Very highly commended.

Coulson, G. J. R., Mercer road, Melbourne, Victoria. "Sunset at Lorne, Victoria"—Second award.

Creed, Lila, Victoria. Oil paintings, "Single white roses"—First award. "Rhododendrons"—Second award. "Study of foliage"—Second award. "Waratah"—Second award.

Irvine, John L., St. Kilda. Rolando's oil painting "Sunset on the Buffalo Ranges"—First award. Rolando's oil painting "Mount Feathertop"—First award.

Lyall, Alex. S., St. Kilda, Victoria. Picture of New Zealand—Second award.

Maffey, Mabel, Melbourne. "Moonlight"—Highly commended. "Dog's Head"—Highly commended. "Eucalyptus" on glass in plush frame—Highly commended.

Sinclair, Catherine S., Kew. Oil painting "French poppies"—Highly commended.

Weir, Elizabeth P., Prahran, Victoria. "Sunshade and shower," Whittlesea, Victoria—Highly commended. "Sunset near Yan Yean," Whittlesea, Victoria—Highly commended.

Guban and Follerman, Vienna. Oil paintings—Second and third awards.

Robitsek, H., and Co., Vienna. Collection of oil paintings—Very highly commended.

CLASS II.—Miniatures, Water-colour Paintings, Pastels, and Drawings of every kind.

Allom, Albert J., Launceston. View on River Esk, South Wales—Second award.

Archibald, Carl, Warrnambool, Victoria. Frame containing series of illustrations of Eureka Stockade riot; series original drawings of Australian explorations, illustrating incidents in Australian history—First award.

Archibald, Lucy, Warrnambool, Victoria. Water-colour sketches from life (collective exhibit)—Highly commended.

Barrett, Walter, Launceston. Water-colour, "On the Tamar," Tasmania—Highly commended.

Boyd, Allan, West Melbourne. Design for certificate—Highly commended.

Bates, S. E., Launceston. Designs for decorations of ball-room, dining-room, and hall—Second award.

Bell, Lionel E., Ross. Three crayon drawings of animals—Highly commended.

Cathcart, May, Invermay. Two pen and ink sketches—Two first awards.

Entwistle, Arthur, Hobart. Pen and ink drawings from a copy titled "Surrender"—Highly commended.

Charlton, Arthur Esam, St. Kilda. Collection of water-colour paintings—Highly commended.

Ford, William, Bracknell. Lightning flourished bird sketch and cards—Highly commended.

Ferguson, Ethel May, Launceston. Three crayon drawings—Second award.

Gravatt, Emma Jane, East Devonport. Two water-colour paintings—Highly commended.

Gurr, L. R. and E. E., Launceston. Crayon drawings (2), "Moonlight on the Alps"—Second award.

Godfrey, Charles D., South Melbourne. "Ill-fated Steamships"—First award.

Home, Nellie C., Quamby, Hagley, Tasmania. Hand-painted screen from nature, centre "Arum lilies," side panels "Poppies and chrysanthemums"—Second award. Hand-painted fire screen, "Tasmanian flowers and berries," from nature—Highly commended. Group of lemons painted from nature on wood panel—First award.

Hudson, Kate, Launceston. Four hand-painted vases—Second award.

Hopkins, Maggie, Launceston. Crayon drawing enlarged from a painting of Mary Anderson as "Parthenia," from "Ingomar," a drama by Mrs. Lovell—Highly commended. Crayon drawing enlarged from a photo of Mr. Hopkins's dog "Laddie"—Highly commended.

Hall, Alfred J., St. John street, Launceston. "Three scenes on the Upper Yarra, near Kew, Victoria," by the late T. S. Hall—One first and two second awards.

Halligan, Mrs. G. H., Hunter's Hill, Sydney. "Spring flowers" (in white and black), "Tasmanian waratah and arbutus" (in white and black), "Tasmanian gorse tree"—Two first awards and one second.

Huddart, Parker, and Company, Melbourne. Pictures of steamers—Second award.

Kent, David, St. Kilda. Pen and ink drawing, "Lioness and cubs"—First award. Design for a certificate of merit—Second award.

Kildea, Francis T., New Town. Crayon, "Modern Heroes"—Second award.

Lawrence, Edgar, Launceston. Water-colour, "Lake Arthur," Tasmania—Highly commended.

Lloyd, H. G., Dunedin, N.Z. Collection of water-colours—Highly commended.

Long, C. Edward, Launceston. Illuminated address to the Governor—Second award.

Mansell, Hunt, Catty, and Company, London. Collection of etchings—Special first award.

Marchant, Annie Ellen, Mole Creek. Poonah painting of a group of roses (on silk); also, wreath or spray of roses (painted on velvet)—Highly commended as collective exhibit.

Sinclair, Catherine P., Kew. Chalk drawing, " Letter from Home "—Highly commended.

Shearn, Percy C., Launceston. Chrystoleum, subject, " Basket of flowers "—Highly commended. " Likeness of Mrs. Langtry "—Highly commended. " Scene on the Scottsdale road "—Highly commended.

Union Steam-Ship Company of New Zealand. Two water-colour paintings—First award.

Vellacott, John W. Water-colour paintings on opal (2), " Clipper ship *Sobraon*," " R.M.S. *Victoria* "—Two second awards.

Waldron, Mabel Ethel, Launceston. " Lilies and dielytra "—Second award. " White violets, primrose, and ivy "—First award.

Weetman, Mabel L., Launceston. Collection of water-colour pictures —Highly commended.

Weetman, H. J., Launceston. Patch-board, consisting of pen and ink sketches, with tiled background—First award.

Willis, Helen. Study of nasturtiums—Second award. " Study of actimostus " (flannel flower of N. S. Wales)—First award.

Wilson, Mrs. L. S., Port Sorell. Portfolio of water-colour paintings Tasmanian wild flowers—First award.

CLASS III. — Sculpture and Die Sinking, Medals, Cameos, Engraving, etc.

Cecchini, G., Pisa, Florence, Italy. Carrara marble statuary (collective exhibit)—First award.

Entwistle, Arthur, Hobart. General engraving on gold, silver, ivory, brass, steel, and wood: coats of arms, crests, monograms, cyphers, brass name and memorial plates, etc.—First award.

Fontana, Signor, Chelsea, England. Sculpture—Special first award.

Killalea, Henry, E., Launceston. Marble statue of the Lady of Lourdes, and marble cross and figure of the Crucifixion (collective exhibit)—Third award.

Warrington, S. A. and E., Launceston. Stone altar, stone bridge, stone lighthouse—Third award.

Watson, Charles C., Hobart. Carving in stone representing tree, ivy, and birds—Second award.

Doulton and Co., London. Terra-cotta sculpture, by George Tinworth—Special first award. Sculpture in Doulton ware, by George Tinworth—First award.

Moran, A. W., Melbourne. Medal making and die sinking—First award.

CLASS IV. — Architectural Drawings and Models, Elevation and Plans of Buildings.

Science and Art Department, South Kensington, series of 37 drawings (collective exhibit)—Special first award.

Scholars' Science and Art Department, South Kensington. Isabella L. Bebb—First award. E. Piper—Special first award. D. S. Grubb—Special first award. T. W. Cole—Special first award. J. M. Dunlop—

TASMANIAN EXHIBITION, 1891-92.   63

First award. C. D. Hodder—First award. Isabella L. Bebb—Special first award. A. G. Scrange—Special first award. Frank W. Wood—Hon. mention. T. W. Cole—First award. W. J. Merriot—First award. W. M. Grubb—First award. J. T. Cook—Special first award. C. Cortinoss—First award. Alfred Lewis—Hon. mention. M. A. Heath—First award. F. Brown—First award. M. A. Heath—First award. Agnes G. Farmer—First award. John Lee—First award. J. T. Cook—Special first award. W. M. Grubb—Special first award. Rider Haywood—Special first award. Arthur Legge—Hon. mention. C. S. Perkin—First award. C. S. Millard—Hon. mention. A. C. C. John—Special first award. G. W. Harley—Special first award. A. C. C. John—Special first award. W. M. Grubb—First award. Arthur Whitehead—Special first award.

Launceston Technical School. Sheets of workings in solid geometry and projection, 14 original designs modelled in clay and re-produced in plaster and terra cotta; or carvings in wood, original designs; five models, door, photo frame, mantelpiece, gate, circular staircase (collective exhibit)—Special first award.

Scholars of the Launceston Technical School. A. E. Morgan, original designs modelled in clay and re-produced in plaster—Hon. mention. S. Morgan, frieze and scrolls modelled in clay and re-produced in plaster—Hon. mention. C. Tyson, original designs modelled in clay and re-produced in plaster — First award. R. Gow, mantelpiece, original design, modelled in clay and re-produced in plaster—Special first award. C. Beaufoy, carved front of chiffonnier, original design (blackwood and Huon pine)—First award. A. E. Evershed, carved coat of arms in Huon pine—Special first award. C. Sargeant, blackwood mantelpiece—Hon. mention. T. Earley, model of circular-staircase—Special first award.

Machine Construction Class, Launceston Technical School. 18 drawings to scale from fully dimensioned sketches supplied, five drawings being designs of details of machinery from data supplied; 11 drawings, full size, and to scale from data supplied by student himself; 12 drawings, shaded and coloured from copy (collective exhibit)—Special first award.

Scholars' Machine Construction Class, Launceston Technical School. John Clark, drawings to scale from fully dimensioned sketches supplied, being Tasmania Gold Mine pumping engine and marine engine—First award. Thomas Turner, drawings to scale from fully dimensioned sketches supplied, being marine engine and cylinder marine engine—Special first award. John Wilson, drawing to scale from fully dimensioned sketches supplied, being safety valve for marine boiler—Hon. mention. John Batchelor, drawings full size and to scale, details of machinery from data supplied by the student himself, being locomotive connecting rod and locomotive cross-head—First award. James B. Massey, drawing full size and to scale from data supplied by the student himself, being marine boiler—Hon. mention. H. R. Evershed, detail drawings, shaded and coloured, from copy, being plummer block, bevel wheel gearing, connecting rod, crane hook—Special first award.

Allen, Albert G. H., Invermay. Collection of architectural designs and sketches—Second award.

Hardt, H. B. Designs of the arches, all decorations, and allotments of space in N.S.W. Court of the Exhibition—First award. [The jurors consider that the design and especial care shown in the setting out of the N.S.W. Court entitle it to special notice by the commissioners, and therefore suggest a first award be granted.]

Luttrell, Alfred E., Cameron street, Launceston. Perspective drawing, Marine Hotel, pen and ink isometrical perspective drawing of Tasmanian Exhibition and surroundings—Second award. Pen and ink drawing (first prize Exhibition certificate competition)—First award.

Maurice, F., Melbourne, Victoria. Plan (in relief) of Tasmania, showing by scale (horizontally and vertically) rivers, mountains, roads, railway lines, towns, townships, divisions, etc.—Second award.

M'Kinnon, Gordon, Parramatta, N.S.W. Front elevation design of the Albert Hall, Launceston—First award.

Fagg, Mr., Hobart. Two architectural drawings—Second award.

Warry, D. R., Greenwich, London. Architectural design for cathedral—Special first award.

CLASS V. — Engraving and Lithographing, Chromo-Lithographs, etc.

Bulletin Newspaper Company, Sydney. Original "Bulletin" drawings by Livingstone, Hopkins, and Phil May; 38 engravings, zincography, photo-negative drawing, print on negative on silver zinc ready for engraving, zinc block engraved ready for printing—First award.

Dunlop and Brown, Melbourne. Show case or frame of window tickets—Second award.

Milne, Angus, Footscray, Victoria. Picture, freehand—Second award.

Osborn, Alf. P., Christchurch, N.Z. General engraving on brass plates, copper, gold, silver, and wood—First award. Caligraphy—Second award.

Waterworth, John J., Hobart. Collection of engravings—Second award.

Patent Borax Company, Birmingham, England. Collection of artistic show cards—Second award.

Keen, Robinson, and Belville, London. Collection of artistic show cards—Second award.

Birmingham Vinegar Brewery Company, Birmingham, England. Collection of artistic show cards—Second award.

CLASS Va.—Amateur Photographic Exhibits.

Browne, F. Styant, Launceston. Bromide enlargement, untouched, "Study of a head"—Second award. Frame of landscapes of Tasmanian scenery and portraits—First award.

Northern Tasmanian Camera Club. Frame of platinotype prints, frame of silver prints, the work of members of the Club—First award.

Gruncell, Charles, Hobart. Tasmanian views—Second award.

Hyslop, H. F., St. Kilda, Victoria. Landscape photos of Victorian scenery—Third award.

Parker, R. L., Launceston. Collection of photos of Tasmanian scenery (platina)—First award.

Roome, Dr. H. A., Westbury. Photograph in platinotype, "Scenes in the Alps"—Second award. Ditto, "Studies on Lake Como, Italy"—First award. Ditto, "An Italian Peasant"—Special first award. Photograph in platinum, "Springtime in Surrey"—Special first award.

Colliver, N., Ballarat, Victoria. Cabinet of photographs—Fourth award.

Kermode, Robert, Mona Vale, Ross. Photographs of Tasmanian views—Second award. Photographs of Tasmania and Australia—First award.

Grange, John Stuart. Photographs of Tasmanian scenery—Second award.

New South Wales Government Railway Department. Amateur photography—Hon. mention.

CLASS VI.—Plans and Models of Schools, Asylums; Furniture for the same; ditto for Blind and Deaf Mutes; Work of Pupils of both sexes.

Easton, Thomas J., Venus School, Zeehan. Oil paintings of maps of Tasmania and Australia, poetry, pen and pencil sketches, mechanical drawings, collection of specimens, flowers, ferns, etc., mounted—Commended.

Corp, John Francis, Commercial College, Latrobe, Tasmania. Work done in school, maps of New Zealand (by pupils over 14), Australia (under 14), Tasmania (under 12), plan (under 15)—Special mention for plans and maps.

Fletcher, Mary A., Launceston. Kindergarten system, occupations done by the children—First award.

Nathan, E. A., High School, Launceston. Plain penmanship by the pupils—Highly commended. Fancy penmanship by the pupils—Commended. Mapping by the pupils—Highly commended.

Rees, John D., State School, Lilydale. Three maps of Tasmania and writing cards—Commended.

Stopford's Preparatory School, Bellerive. Copy slip and angle in use at Hobart Junior School, with samples of writing to show the improvements made in six months—Commended.

Government Technical School, Hobart. Work by students in art, modelling, and maritime construction classes—First award.

Phillips, James, Launceston. Map of New Zealand, ornamental and plain writing—Highly commended.

Launceston Technical School. Modelling, "Survival of the Fittest," from *Illustrated London News*—First award.

Scholars of Hobart Technical School. G. Howe, iron gutter—Special first award. [The jurors beg to note the excellent workmanship of the student in this exhibit.] R. Green, details of roof, two boxes, bread platter—First award. Glastonbury chair—Special first award. Model of staircase—First award. C. Green, folding shutter window—First award.

Hobart Technical School. Four paintings—First award.

F

Class VI.—Maps and Penmanship.

Lilydale State School. Work done by scholars. Coloured map of Tasmania by George Proctor, aged 12 years; ditto by Elsie Proctor, aged 12 years; specimen of writing by Robert Arnold, aged 13 years; Grace Erb, 13; Elsie Proctor, 11; Margaret Brewer, 15; Hannah Proctor, 15; Louisa Brooks, 12; Amy Christie, 12; Robert Power, 13; and Matthew Phillips, 11—Hon. mention.

Class VI.—School Exhibits.

Corp, John Francis, Latrobe. Collective school exhibit—Very highly commended.
    Ford, W. (over 16). Ornamental penmanship—Special first award.
    West, V. B. Map of New Zealand—Highly commended. Ornamental penmanship—First award.
    Addison, H. W. Map of New Zealand—First award.
    Phillips, J. Plain penmanship—First award.
    Kelly, W. Map of Australia—First award.
    Kildea, F. J. Crayon drawings—First award.
    Jones, H. Fancy penmanship—First award.
    M'Ilwaine, J. Map of Tasmania—First award.
    Sidebottom, —. Plain penmanship—First award.
    Kidd, R. A. Plain penmanship—Second award.
    Beck, Ernest. Plain penmanship—First award.
    Jackson, L. Plain penmanship—First award.
    Ferguson, J. Plain penmanship—Commended.
    Nathan, E. A. Collective school exhibit—First award.

Class VII.—Stationery, Bookbinding, Painting, and Drawing Materials.

Button, Henry, proprietor of the *Launceston Examiner* and *The Tasmanian*. Specimens of materials used in various stages of paper-making, from Messrs. J. Spicer and Sons, London, and J. Joynson and Sons, London—First award. Demy folio "Quadrat" cylinder machine (in operation)—First award. Specimens showing progressive stages in the manufacture of black lead pencils, from Mr. B. S. Cohen, London—First award. Specimens showing progressive stages in the manufacture of steel pens, from a sheet of metal to the finished pen, from Mr. William Mitchell, London—Highly commended. Specimens of paper-ruling, done by the exhibitor—Highly commended. Specimens showing progressive stages in the manufacture of steel pens, from a sheet of metal to the finished pen, from Messrs. G. Brandauer and Co., London—First award. Post octavo "Model" platen machine (in operation)—First award. Specimens of printing, letterpress, lithographic, embossing, etc. —First award. Specimens of account books made by the exhibitor—Highly commended. Specimens of photo-engraving, plates etched and mounted by the exhibitor—Highly commended. Specimens of stereotyping, moulds, plates, as cast and mounted by exhibitor—First award. Bookbinding in morocco—First award.

    Bellett, S. J., St. Kilda, Dunedin. Black, blue black, and copying ink, scarlet ink, gold paint, raven black, cold water ink—First award.

TASMANIAN EXHIBITION, 1891-92. 67

Meek, W. J., Dunedin. Blue black, copying, and coloured inks—First award.

Walch Bros., and Birchall, Launceston. Finest pencils, Johann Faber, Nuremburg, Bayern ; steel pens and method of manufacture, G. Brandauer and Co., Birmingham ; Swan Quill steel pens, A. E. Lamdin, Liverpool ; sealing wax, Bee brand, George Waterston and Sons, London ; steel pens and method of manufacture, Joseph Gillott, Birmingham ; frames steel pens, John Heath, Birmingham—First award for collection. Manufactured account books, made by J. Walch and Sons, Hobart—First award.

Reeves and Sons, London (Artistic Stationery Company, Melbourne, agents). Artists' materials, water and oil colours, brushes, etc., easels, canvases, drawing boards, studies, drawing paper, oil and water colour blocks, architects' instruments, etc.—First award.

Orient Steam Navigation Company. "The Orient Line Guide"—First award.

Hinton, T. H., Chelsea, England. "Some of the postage stamps of the British Empire"—First award.

Mines Department, Victoria. Mining reports and publications—First award.

Government Statist's Department, Victoria. Statistics, handbook, and large statistical table showing progress of the colony—Special first award.

Lands Department, Victoria. Reports and publications—First award.

"Year Book of Australia" Publishing Company, Limited, Melbourne. The "Year Book of Australia"—Special first award.

Strutt, W. T., Hobart. Specimens of bookbinding done at the Government Printing Office, Hobart—Highly commended.

Walch Bros. and Birchall, Launceston. "Walch's Red Book" (Tasmanian Almanac)—First award.

Victorian Postal and Telegraph Department. Two frames, containing —No. 1 frame, view of Melbourne General Post Office in the year 1853, and view of Melbourne General Post Office in the year 1890, handsomely illuminated and surrounded with revenue and postage stamps of Victoria of denominations up to £9, stamps entwined amidst Australian foliage ; No. 2 frame : views of the principal post and telegraph buildings in Victoria, surrounded with stamps of current issue in Victoria; both frames are in Tasmanian figured blackwood—Special first award.

CLASS VIII.—Photographs on Paper, Glass, Wood, and Enamel ; Heliographic Engravings, Photo-lithographic Specimens, Enlargements, Coloured Photos, Instruments, Apparatus, Chemicals, and all materials used in Photography.

Fairfax, John, and Sons, *Sydney Morning Herald*, Sydney. Illustrations of daily and pictorial newspaper work, stereotype and rare specimens of printing, newspaper literature, engraving, and typographical art—Special first award.

Skinner, J. H., and Co., East Derham, Norfolk. Photographic apparatus—First award. Patent photographic turntable—First award.

Nicholas, R. J., Launceston. Photographic portraits—First award. Christmas, New Year, and birthday cards—First award. Water-colour enlargements of photographs of the late Judge Giblin, and Miss Simonson and child; plain enlargements of photos of Sir R. G. Hamilton, S. J. Sutton, Esq., and Miss Tulloch—Special first award.

Doulton and Co., Lambeth, London. Series of 19 photographs of the works of George Tinworth in terra cotta—Special first award.

Wherrett Bros. and Co., Hobart. Photographic portraits in platinum and silver—First award.

New Zealand Midland Railway. Collection of photographs of New Zealand scenery—First award.

Union Steam-Ship Company of New Zealand. Collection of photographs of New Zealand scenery—First award.

Government Printer, New South Wales. Photographs of New South Wales scenery—Special first award.

Colonial Secretary, New South Wales. Photograph of delegates to the National Convention, 1891—Hon. mention.

Class IX.   Musical Instruments.

Fincham and Hobday, Richmond, Victoria. Organ—First award.

Gee, Richard, Launceston. The Bell and Company American cabinet organ—Second award.

Karrer, S., Teufeuthal, Switzerland. Musical boxes—First award.

Munnew, A., Launceston. Packard's cottage and parlour organ—First award.

Milner and Thompson, Christchurch. Thompson's patent tuning attachment—Special first award. Patent piano, with new tuning attachment—Second award.

Walch Bros. and Birchall, Launceston Set of brass band instruments —First award. Two upright grand pianos by Kanhauser—First award. Four American organs by Mason and Hamlin—First award for church organ. Kanhauser cottage pianos—First award.

Young, Alexander, Trevallyn, Launceston. 1 violincello, 1 viola, 2 violins—Special first award.

Broadwood, John, and Sons, London, England. Cottage pianoforte, with complete metal frame, patent tuning pins, full trichord stringing, and improved front, in early English design, of the choicest satinwood, with handpainted centre panel—Special first award for quality of tone and superior workmanship and material.

Class X.—Medicine, Hygiene, and Public Relief.

Bosisto and Co., Richmond, Victoria. Preparations obtained chiefly from the indigenous vegetation of Australia, consisting of essential oils, eucalyptus, alkaloids, gums, and resins—First award.

Draper and Son, Melbourne. Microbene and closet disinfectant—First award.

Burroughs, Wallcome, and Co., London. Kepler's cod-liver oil—First award. Compressed drugs, medicines, etc.—First award. Medicine chests—Special first award.

Girdwood, John, London. Patent asthma remedy—Highly commended.

Kearsley, C. and J., Westminster. Pills—Highly commended.
Hatton and Laws, Launceston. Drugs, chemicals, patent and proprietary medicines—First-class award for collection.
Chassaing and Co., Paris. Pharmaceutical and physiological produce, pepsine drug and medicine—First award.
Cornu, Ch., Paris. Medicinal capsules—First award.
Browne, F. Styant, Launceston. Pyramid of proprietary medicines manufactured by exhibitor—Highly commended.
Carter and Werner, Ballarat, Victoria. Scientific optical instruments to measure sight, etc.—Special first award. Spectacle and other lenses in all stages of manufacture—Special first award. Binoculars, microscopes, etc.—First award.
Evans, Lischer, and Webb, London. Capsules and patent medicine—First award. Coco wine—First award.
Gould, H. T., and Co., Hobart. Oil, extract, and various preparations of eucalyptus globulus—First award.
Johnston, J. D., Launceston. Articles for the toilet and proprietary medicines—Second award.
Jessop and Co., London. Chemicals—First award. Paints—First award. Oilmen's stores—First award.
Radman's Microbe Killer, Melbourne. Patent medicine—First award.
Spreadborough, John, Launceston. Mechanical dentistry—First award.
Timbury Eucalyptus Oil Company, Gladstone, Queensland. Essential oils distilled from the eucalyptus citriodora, the tea-tree, eucalypt lozenges—Special first award for collection. The essential oil distilled from the leaves of the eucalyptus melaleuca leucadendiam—First award.

Class XI.—Mathematical and Philosophical Instruments.

Gunn, W. R., and Co., Melbourne. Surgical instruments for the cure of various deformities, artificial limbs, trusses, belts, etc.—First award. Figure of child, showing appliances for every description of deformity fitted to it—First award.

Class XII.—Maps, Geographical and Cosmographical Apparatus.

Aikenhead, A., Malunnah, West Devonport. Map of Australia, done while at Horton College—Commended.
Williams, H. W., Geelong, Victoria. Specimen of phonography—Commended.
Maurice, F., Melbourne. Relief plan of Tasmania, showing, by scale, rivers, mountains, railways, roads, etc.—Special first award.
Williams, A. C., Launceston. Map of Australia—Commended.
Wilson, W. D., State School, Pyengana, George's Bay. Map of Tasmania—Commended.
Nicholson, G. G., Launceston. Map of Tasmania—Special first award.
Mabin, R. D., Old Beach, Tasmania. Map of Tasmania—Commended.

Fenton, James, Launceston. Pen and ink sketch showing the rise and progress of Tasmania—First award.

Davies, Joseph, Beaconsfield. Geological maps of the Beaconsfield district—Commended.

Robinson, Edgar, Melbourne. Shorthand—Special first award.

Mines Department of Victoria. Geological maps of various mining districts, geological map of Australia—Special first award.

Lands Department of Victoria—Map of Victoria (divisional)—Special first award.

Kuhn, A. A., East St. Kilda, Victoria. Map of Tasmania—Very highly commended.

Midland Railway Company Limited, New Zealand. Map of Canterbury and Westland—Highly commended.

Bardou, J., Perpignan, France. Cigarette papers—Special first award.

Brickhill, James, Launceston. Map showing chromo-lithographic work—First award.

Government Printer, New South Wales. Books, bookbinding, printing, etc.—Special first award.

GROUP C.—FURNITURE AND ACCESSORIES.

This may be looked upon as the most elastic group in the whole of the Exhibition, inasmuch as it comprises almost every article of art or manufacture used in the household.

The first class deals with cheap and fancy furniture, which was fairly represented by some of the local manufacturers, who displayed to the very best advantage the artistic taste of their workmen, not only in the carving and tastefully ornamented woodwork, but also in the upholstering and decorative work which comes under Class 14.

In Class 15 (Crystal Glass and Stained Glass) Tasmania had to make room for other and older countries—Bohemia, Austria, Germany, and France being well to the fore, Victoria showing some artistic church windows of great merit. The wonderful collection of Bohemian glass exhibited by Mr. Bossomaier, Mr. Singer, and Mr. Moser was, throughout the whole period of the Exhibition, one of the main attractions, and caused many visitors to wend their way through the Avenue of Nations to the spot allotted to these enterprising exhibitors.

In Class 16 our local manufacturers again took a leading part. Mr. Campbell showed some excellent and most promising potteryware from the Sandhill kilns: the bricks, drain pipes, and ordinary potteryware could not be excelled, whilst his attempts at superior work are most encouraging; indeed, some specimens of Mr. Campbell's work would hold their place in any part of the world. McHugh Bros. also exhibit first-class drain pipes and other ironstone ware.

In Class 24 some creditable exhibits were shown in the British and Foreign courts, Colonial productions being mostly confined to household soaps, perfumery, and essences, made here from imported materials.

Class 25 embraced a multitude of fancy articles, needlework, embroidery, etc., which occupied a large space, and from its endless variety attracted much attention, not only from the exhibitors, but from their friends. The long list of awards made in that class will show that the competition was keen, and the labour of the jury was taxed to the utmost to deal fairly with the articles they had to adjudicate upon.

CLASSES XIII., XIV., and XVII.—Cheap and Fancy Furniture, Upholsterers' and Decorators' Work, Carpets, Tapestry, and other stuffs for Furniture.

Alcock and Co., Melbourne. Billiard tables—Special first award. Billiard cues—First award. Patent automatic billiard marker and indicator—First award. Pool and pyramid marker—First award.

Dempsters, Launceston. Dining-room furniture, manufactured by the exhibitors from specially-selected Tasmanian blackwood, velvet pile carpet, medicine cupboard in oak, oil paintings, landscapes, and festooned decorotions of silk tapestry and Roman satin—Special first award for collective exhibit.

Lawrance, G. R., Launceston. Ceiling decoration for dining-room—Special first award.

Lawrie and Bishop, Birmingham. Patent wire meat safes, rat traps. birdcages, door mats, etc , in wire, also wove wire for mining and sewing purposes—Special first award for collective exhibit.

Tear, Henry, and Co., Sydney. Cheap fancy drawing-room and dining-room suites—Second award.

Perry, John, Melbourne. Furniture turnery—First award.

McLean Bros. and Rigg Limited, Sydney. Patent theatre and opera house seats—First award.

Rawson, C., Launceston. Mantelpieces and hall stand—First award.

Fallshaw Bros., North Melbourne. Billiard table and accessories—First award.

The Midland Perambulator Company, Birmingham. Perambulators and patent safety mail or go-cart on rubber wheels—First award for collective exhibit.

Colonial Architects' Department, New South Wales. Carved golden fleece, coat of arms, busts of Nelson and Justice Windeyer—First award.

Miller, James, and Co., Melbourne. Cocoanut matting, fibre mats, fibre, and wool mats—Special first award.

M'Caw, Stevenson, and Orr, Belfast, Ireland. "Glacier" for window decoration—Commended.

Kennerley, Thomas J., Sydney. Patent pipe (anti-nicotine)—First award.

David Storrer, Launceston. Drawing-room suite—First award. Sideboard of oak grown in Tasmania (first sideboard made of oak grown in Australasia)—First award.

Warrington, S. V. and E. A., Launceston. Photo frames, doll tables, dressing table, three pairs oxhorns, one cabinet of foreign coins—Commended.

French, G. J., Launceston. Woods in various grainings and various marbles ; embossed, stained, and ornamental glass work ; ainter's and decorator's work, paperhangings, etc.—Special first award for collective exhibit.

Chatteris, Mrs. Henry, Sydney. "Left at home," a picture worked by hand in silk—Highly commended.

Clegg, J., Christchurch, New Zealand. Rubber tyre perambulators with steel bodies—First award for workmanship and finish.

Catley, R. W., New Town, near Hobart. Table and workbox to match of Tasmanian wood—Commended.

Coombe, Joseph, Campbell Town. Fancy table—Highly commended.

Hall, James, Hobart. Music cabinet made of old fruit cases, original design—First award.

Gagel, Conrad, Coburg, Germany. Basketware—First award.

Forsyth, Richard, Sandhill, Launceston. Collection of picture frames made by the exhibitor of Tasmanian clays—First award.

Polglase, J. H. P., North Melbourne. Eider-down and kapok ventilated patent bed quilts—First award.

Sharman, Howard, Launceston. Hearthrug—Commended.

Beadle, Joseph, Trevallyn, Launceston. Picture frame made of glass —Second award.

Munnew, A., Launceston. Ottoman music stools in Tasmanian blackwood, with patent raising movement—First award.

Class XV.—Crystal and Stained Glass.

Webb, Thomas and Son, Limited, Stourbridge, England. Ornamental glass—Special first award for chaste design and high finish.

Friebner, Ens, and Eckert, Volkstedt, Germany. Dresden biscuit china—Special first award.

Walsh, Walsh John, Birmingham. English flint glass and delicate colouring and cutting, cut table glass and fancy glass—Special first award.

Brooks, Robinson, and Co., Melbourne. Stained glass window, "The calling of St. Matthew," designed and executed for Christ Church, Launceston—Special first award. Embossed decorative glass for halls, etc. —First award. Embossed staircase window—First award.

Von Fischer, J., Buda-Pesth, Hungary. Artistic china and majolica ware—Special first award for high finish and artistic ornamentation.

Holmes, John, Bagshot, Surrey. Glass and china engraving—First award for general household glass engraving.

Hughes, Rogers, and Co., Melbourne. Stained glass window for church ("St. Agnes"), and domestic mosaic and leaded work—First award.

Moser, Ludwig, Carlsbad, Austria. Carlsbad jewel glass, with solid gold decorations and raised enamel figures—Special first award for jewelled glass and enamelled glass, artistic ware of the highest finish.

Kister, A. W. Fr., Scheibe. Ivory glass—Special first award for ivory glass, beautifully embellished and artistically ornamented.

Montgomery, William, Melbourne. Two panels, "Bowling" and "Hunting," and one panel, "Parable of the talents"—Second award.

Rachmann, B., Berlin. Handpainted Bohemian glass—Special first award for speciality in handpainted placques.

Spitzer, C., Paris. Handpainted Bohemian glass—Special first award for delicate colour and ornamentation.

Singer, Maurice, Haide, Bohemia. Bohemian glass—Special first award for collective exhibit.

Webb, Frank, South Melbourne. Engraving on glass and photo-engraving on glass—Special first award.
Zeckert, Johann, and Sohn, Meisterdorf, Bohemia. Brass-mounted glass goods—First award.
Bay, G., Paris. Triplicate mirror—First award.
Schmid, Er., Vannes-C-Chatel, France. Ordinary glass—Hon. mention.
Boussard, Paris. China flowers—Special first award.

Class XVI.—Pottery, including Bricks, Tiles, Drain and other Pipes.

Webb, Thomas, and Sons, Stourbridge, England. Artistic white china—Special first award.
Price's Patent Candle Co., Limited, London. Earthenware china for holding nightlights—Hon. mention.
Doulton and Co., Lambeth Pottery, London. Artistic pottery—Special first award for collective exhibit.
Whitfield, Mabel, Carrick. Handpainted drain tile—Hon. mention.
Whitfield, Eveline, Carrick. Handpainted jar containing pot with ferns—Hon. mention.
Jory and Campbell, Launceston. Plain and ornamental bricks, fire bricks, white enamelled bricks, and terra cotta—First award.
Hall, W., Yokohama, Japan. Handpainted china—First award for collective exhibit of Japanese art china.
Elton, Sir E. B., Bart., Clevedon Court, England. Elton ware art pottery—Special first award.
Campbell, John, Launceston. Handpainted earthenware, majolica and decorated ware, made by exhibitor—Special first award for collective exhibit of colonial-made china, majolica, and decorated ware, showing great progress, and deserving every encouragement. Bristol, cane, and Rockingham ware—First award.
Campbell and Jory, Sandhill. Machine-made bricks, moulded bricks, terra-cotta panels—Special first award.
Cosgrove, Bros., Punchbowl. Hand-made bricks—Hon. mention.
Innocent, T. B., Glen Dhu. Hand-made, machine-pressed bricks, hand-made and machine-made bricks—First award.
Sheriff and Jarvis, Latrobe. Hand-made bricks—Hon. mention.
Campbell, John, Potteries, Launceston. Collective exhibit of every description of earthenware made by exhibitor—Special first award for collective exhibit. Sanitary ware, drainpipes, tiles, and terra cotta, including flower-pots and art ware—First award. Dripstone filters—Special first award.
Fulham Pottery and Cheavin Filter Company Limited, Fulham. Rapid water filters and pocket filters—First award.
Newey, R., and Sons, George Street, Launceston. Collection of garden pottery, flower-pots and saucers, seed pans (round and square), orchid pots and pans, fancy garden potteryware—First award.
Doulton and Co., Lambeth, England. Filters—First award.
McHugh Bros. and Jackson. General assortment of drainpipes, bends, junctions, traps, and other connections for sanitary arrangements; also drain, garden, and gutter tiles, and agricultural pipes for farm drainage—First award.

Adams, R. T., City Road, Melbourne. Improved patent carbon filters—First award. Syphon and high pressure filter—First award.

Classes XX., XXI., and XXII.—Gold and Silver Smiths' Work, Bronzes, Art Castings, Repoussé Work, Clocks and Watches.

Stewart, F. and W., Launceston. Sterling silver cradle—Special first award. Exact copy of wager boat in silver and gold—Special first award. Model of old Tamar Rowing Shed in sterling silver—First award. Horse's hoof mounted in sterling silver as inkstand—First award.

Addis, G., Launceston. Jewelry in process of manufacture, and manufactured watches, clocks, etc.—Highly commended.

Hart, W., and Sons, Launceston. One case platedware—Second award.

Stenning and Seaton, London. The patent pickle fork and other similar articles, and Alpha pickle fork holders—Special first award. [For ingenious and useful requisites, and superior workmanship and finish, these goods command attention.]

Lange, M., Berlin. Simili diamonds set in gold and silver—Special first award. [Best imitation diamonds and pearls, and setting in sterling metal.]

Barclay, James, Launceston. Plated goods—Special first award.

Hahn and Weiss, Vienna. White-metal goods—First award.

Robottom, H. J., Prahran, Victoria. Embossing on silver and copper by chasing punches—Special first award.

Fr. Kister, A. W., Schiebe, Germany. Biscuit figures and china and gold decorations—Special first award.

Hawley, John, and Sons, Coventry. Silver watches—Second award; Gold watches—First award.

Lohmann, C., London. Clocks and bells—First award for best collective exhibit.

Macfarlane Bros. and Co., Hobart (agents for the Rockford Watch Manufacturing Co., Rockford, Illinois, US.A.). Speciality in railroad watches, also works ot the same—Special first award for best commercial value and collective exhibit for silver watches.

Lang, Martin, Berlin. Imitation jewelry, set in gold—First award.

Curtis, Frank, Dunedin. Lion brand non-mercurial plate powder, for cleaning silver and electroplated ware—Special first award.

Walker and Hall, Sheffield. Silver-plated goods, spoons and forks, table cutlery, and Sonora silver spoons and forks—Special first award for collective exhibit; first award for spoons, forks, table cutlery, and Sonora silver spoons and forks.

Bay, Gustav, Paris. Wire cutter—First award. Spoons—Commended.

Class XXIII.—Apparatus and Processes for Heating and Lighting, Matches, etc.

Webb, Thomas, and Sons, Limited, Stourbridge, England. Lamps—Special first award.

Smith-Harvey Patent Lighting Company, 453 Collins Street, Melbourne. Patent gas-making apparatus—First award. Portable gas

lamps—First award. Smith-Harvey patent kerosene burner—Special first award.
Wright and Butler, Limited, Birmingham. Table lamps—First award. Hanging lamps—First award. Hand lamps—First award. Brass hall or stand lamps—Special first award. Stable, police, railway, and ship lanterns (collectively)—Special first award.
Dowling, George, and Co., South Melbourne, Victoria. Hot water cylinder—Special first award.
Alsing and Co., Limited, 27 Leadenhall Street, London. Matches—First award.
Brandwood, Joseph, Brisbane Street, Launceston. Portable copper—Special first award. Fire and burglar proof safes—Special first award. Ovens—First award.
Cook, J., and Sons, Birmingham. Patent mining lamps—Special first award. Mine lamps—First award.
Launceston Gas Company. Apparatus used in the manufacture, distribution, and use of gas, gasaliers, globes, burners, gas engines, cooking and heating stoves, etc.—First award for the collection; and Special first award for "Shamrock" cooking stove.
Worsnop, C. H., Halifax. Patent oil stoves—Special first award. Patent oil lamps—First award.

Class XXIV.—Perfumery, Toilet and other Soaps.

Price's Patent Candle Company Limited, London. Toilet soap—First award.
Styant-Browne, F., and Co., Launceston. Case of perfumes manufactured by exhibitors; also samples of Fluide d'Hiver, Floraline, Vegetable Dentifrice, and other toilet articles—Highly commended as a collective exhibit. Bouquet perfumes—Second award.
Hatton and Laws, Launceston. Perfumery (Corra Linn, Telingha, Imperial Bouquet)—Highly commended.
Australian Perfume Company, Sydney. Assorted perfumes and essences—Second award.
Sardon, H., and Co., London. High class perfumes, speciality, Fragrant Ozone—Highly commended.
Ant Adamck, Vienna. Fancy perfumery—First award for exhibit in artistic imitation of natural fruits.
Moll, F. S., London. Toilet soap of all kinds—Highly commended.
Warrick Bros., London. Perfumed lozenges—First award.
Hinks, Underwood, and Co., Bournemouth. Rock plate powder, royal metal polishing paste, Stainaline—First award. Furniture polish—First award.
Crown Perfumery Co., London. Perfumery and toilet soaps. Speciality, Crab Apple Blossom and Lavender Salts—First award for Crab Apple Blossom and Lavender Salts, and Special first award for collective exhibit.
Wilson, A., London. Preparations for the teeth, Bunter's Nervine, Dentine—First award for Bunter's Nervine and Dentine.
Gosnell, John, and Co., London. Cherry tooth paste—First award. Cherry Blossom perfume—First award. Cherry Blossom powder—Highly commended.

Burroughs, Welcome, and Co. Pinol soap, Pinol—First award. Lanoline soap and other toilet preparations—Special first award. Eucalyptus soap—First award.

Manola Perfume Company, London. Manola perfume—First award.

CLASS XXV.—Leather and Basket Work and Fancy Articles, including Pipes, Ivory and Tortoiseshell, Bone, and Wood Work.

Mariner, Ethel, Launceston. Plush cushion with roses and wattle.—Highly commended.

Brickhill, Frank L., Launceston. Macrame bracket drape—Highly commended.

Venus, May, Launceston. Crotchet wool tea cosey—Highly commended.

Pascoe, Ella, Launceston. Child's shirt—Highly commended.

Vincent, Miss, Launceston. Fancy and plain needlework by children under 13 years of age—First award.

Hutchinson, May, Hobart. Child's dress and hat—First award.

Hutchinson, Eva J., Hobart. Two knitted guernseys and a crotchet tea cosey—First award.

Barton, Mary, Ravenswood. Lady's set of handsewn underlinen.—Special first award.

Styant-Browne, Mrs. Emma, Launceston. Woolwork picture from painting by Landseer—First award.

Dunning, Mrs., sen., Launceston. Handworked quilt—First award.

Fletcher, Clara Kate, Launceston. Gum and wattle mantel drape on plush—First award.

Murrell, Mrs. Winifred, Launceston, Cone frame—First award.

Penneyston, Mrs., Beaconsfield. Two patchwork counterpanes—First award.

Pagan, Mrs. Alicia, Launceston. Picture needlework, blue gumtree blossom—First award. Picture needlework, wattle blossom—Highly commended.

Shearn, Mrs. M. A., Launceston. Tablecover knitted in one piece without seam or join—First award. Knitted curtain made with crotchet cotton—First award. Knitted counterpane without seam or join—Second award.

Tapp, Katie Venetia, Oatlands. Embroidered handkerchief mounted on yellow cushion—First award.

Percy, Amy L., Scottsdale. Necklace made of vertebræ of Tasmanian black snake—Highly commended.

Knight, Olive May, King's Road, Chelsea, England. Hospital scripture text quilt—First award.

Gill, H. H., Hobart. Electric body belts for therapeutic purposes—Special first award.

McDonald, Mrs. J. T., Launceston. Berlin woolwork, " Rebecca at the Well," and " The Huguenots "—Highly commended.

Price, Mary, Launceston. Crazy patchwork counterpane and afternoon tea cosey—Special first award.

Stabb, Alma, Hobart. Worked fan pockets, cushion, and mantel drape—First award.

Beadle, J. Glass picture frame, showing the art of making an ornamental frame from coloured glass—First award. [The jurors in Class A. awarding a commendation for the picture, a group of flowers, whereas the exhibitor intended the frame only to be adjudicated.]

Chatteris, Mrs. Henry, Paddington, Sydney. "Left at home," a picture worked by hand in silk—First award.

John Earle and Jas. Billings, Hobart. Group of horns and hoofs—First award.

Whitfeld, Mabel. Handpainted (draped) gipsy table, variegated blackberry leaves and views—Commended.

Badcock, Kate, Glenore. Crochet antimacassar—First award.

Earle, John, Hobart. Stag's head—First award.

Robertson, C. E., Carrick. "Abraham offering Isaac," on satin—Hon. mention.

Matthews, Miss, Melbourne. Embroidered handkerchief—Commended.

Marchant, A. E., Mole Creek. Model of a lady's boot carved in coal with a penknife; cork model of the Clifton Rocks, England—Highly commended.

Twomey, J., Melbourne. Christmas, New Year, and other cards, made of Australian and New Zealand ferns—First award.

Stewart, Mrs. James, Scottsdale. Crazy patchwork quilt—First award.

Wellwisher, H., Carrick. Birdcage—Highly commended.

Jones, Esther T., George Town. Fancy work—First award.

Marsh, W. R., Launceston. Specimens of silk weaving, "Exhibition, 1851," "Portrait of the Duke of Wellington"—First award.

Devall, M. F., Launceston. Collection of shells arranged as a picture frame—First award. Group of waterlilies and foliage worked in arascene—Highly commended.

Symons, Mrs., Victoria. Artificial flowers in wax and paper—First award.

Gow, David, Sydney. Dairy utensils, butter prints (designs carved by hand), butter pats, etc.—Special first award.

Davies, Ann Jane, Launceston. Knitted counterpane—Special first award.

Room, Mrs. D., Mayfield. Wax flowers—Special first award. Ornamental shells and seaweed—First award for collective exhibit. Macrame mantel drape—Highly commended.

Drewery, Annie L., General Hospital, Launceston. Cotton crochet bed quilt—First award.

Dobson, Mrs. A., Deloraine. Crochet work—First award.

Webb, Mrs. Nina, South Melbourne. Machine work, embroidery—Special first award. Lace making—Special first award. Crewel work—Special first award. Writing on handkerchiefs—Special first award. [The judges make special reference to embossing on net, also to speed attained by the exhibitor in performing allotted task, viz., 59 seconds, and to her excellent writing.]

Nichols, Mabel C. B., Blackwood Park, Castra. Patchwork quilt—First award.

Mansell, Hunt, Catty, and Co., London. Paper table decorations, lace papers, dish collars, ice cups, bottle caps, etc.—Special first award.

Webb, Thomas, and Sons, Stourbridge, England. Lamp shades made of the new pleated paper—Special first award.

Howard, Mary Flora, Launceston. Arascene sunflower cushion—First award.

Warland, Ruth M., Mount Stewart Road, Hobart. Plain and fancy knitting—First award.

Whitfeld, Septima, Silwood, Carrick. Drawing-room ornament covered with moss and stones—Highly commended.

Evans, Isaac, Birmingham. Registered designs in ladies' belts made of best English leather, men's belts, rug straps, cigar and cigarette cases, purses, etc.—Special first award.

Kirkby, Beard, and Co., Birmingham. Needles, hairpins, pins (speciality, the self-threading needle and the scientific hairpin)—Special first award.

Hudson, Kate, Launceston. Handpainted vases—First award.

Mitchell, Mrs. Mary, Deloraine. Knitted counterpanes, antimacassars, pillowcases, and sachets to match—First award.

Kenworthy, Rosina, Launceston. Raised wattle blossom, worked in wool and silk on velvet—First award.

Irvine, Mrs. C. J., Launceston. Collection of shells, seaweed, and pebbles from Tamar Heads and East Beach; group of seaweed and wild flowers from Tamar Heads; group of ferns from Hokitika, New Zealand; group of wild flowers from Brighton, Victoria—Special first award.

Frost, L. M., Launceston. Patchwork counterpane of silk, containing 1050 pieces—Special first award.

Koch, Julius, Melbourne. Embroidery by machine—First award for moss embroidery.

Cutler, M. S. and E., Hamilton-on-Forth. Writing on pocket handkerchief by embroidery machine—First award. Embroidery crazy cover (outlining in colours on net) by embroidery machine—Special first award.

Zech, A. J., Fitzroy, Victoria. Embroidery-writing on handkerchiefs, executed by Miss Eldred, 16 years of age—Second award.

Holmes, Miss, Melbourne. Writing on handkerchiefs by embroidery machine—Highly commended.

Paton, R. P., Hobart. Beadwork pockets—First award.

Paton, S., Hobart. Gum and wattle cushion top—First award.

Potts, Dorothy, Launceston. Wool cushions, plush bracket, satin bracket, tea cosey (beaded)—Hon. mention.

Hunt, Mrs., Launceston. A bead vase—First award.

GROUP D.—TEXTILE FABRICS, CLOTHING, Etc.

The entries in this Group were not as numerous as they might have been.

In Class 26 Clark and Co., of Paisley, Scotland, had the monopoly, showing, as they do at all International Exhibitions, a most complete collection of sewing cottons of every possible kind, whether for hand or machine work.

Messrs. Farrelly, Stewart, and Co., of Brisbane Street, Launceston, and Messrs. R. F. Forster and Co., of Birmingham, exhibited trunks, portmanteaus, hat boxes, and a variety of travelling appliances.

Victoria contributed some excellent exhibits in tents, tarpaulins, water bags, canvas hose, and well-finished oilskin clothing.

A grand show of ready-made clothing from Sargood, Butler, and Co., of Melbourne, and another from Dodgshun, Sons, and Co., of Launceston, have taken high-class awards.

In boots and shoes Mr. Coutts, of Brisbane Street, displayed a collection showing that there are workmen in Tasmania capable of turning out first-class articles, quite equal in finish or style to any of the imported goods.

Class XXVI.—Cotton, Cotton Fabrics, pure and mixed.

Clark and Co., Paisley, Scotland. Sewing cotton for hand or machine use, knitting, crochet, embroidery, macrame, darning, and every variety of cotton thread—First award.

Class XXVIII. — Wool, and all Woollen Fabrics, Flannels, Tweeds, etc.

Bulman, Peter, Launceston. Collection of woollen goods, blankets, twilled and plain flannels, tweeds, shawls, etc.—Special first award.

Hamlyn Bros., England. Serges and estamenes—Special first award.

Appleby, Curtis, and Co., England. Woollen and worsted suitings—Special first award.

MERINO WOOL, UNWASHED.

Section 1.—Six Fleeces, Unskirted, Ewes of any age.

Lewis, William, Stoneleigh, Beaufort, Victoria. Wool from sheep bred from the Studley stud flock, bred by exhibitor; 368 days growth, paddocked; age of sheep, 2 years and 3 months—Special first award.

Russell, Philip, Carngham, Victoria. Wool from pure Merinos bred by exhibitor; 371 days growth; housed 6 months; age of sheep, over 1½ years—First award for Victoria.

Clarke, George C., East Talgai, Hendon, Queensland. Wool from pure Merinos bred by exhibitor from pure Tasmanian blood, principally from the St. Johnstone and Mona Vale studs; about 360 days growth; mixed ages—First award for Queensland.

Gibson, James, Belle Vue, Epping, Tasmania. Wool from sheep descended from German sheep imported about 50 years back, and improved by selection ever since; bred by exhibitor; 370 days growth; about 15 months old; paddocked—Special first award for Tasmania.

Archer, Joseph, Panshanger, Longford, Tasmania. Wool from sheep in Panshanger stud flock; 365 days growth; age of sheep, 2 years and 2 months; paddocked, housed from September 24, 1891; bred by exhibitor—First award for Tasmania.

Section 2.—Six Fleeces, Unskirted, from two-toothed Ewes which have been shorn as lambs.

Clarke, George C., East Talgai, Hendon, Queensland. Wool from pure Merino sheep bred from pure Tasmanian blood, principally from St. Johnstone and Mona Vale studs; about 360 days growth; mixed ages—Hon. mention for Queensland.

Gatenby, Herbert, Rhodes, Longford, Tasmania. Wool from sheep by pure Merino rams and pure Merino ewes; 371 days growth; 15 months old; paddocked; bred by exhibitor—First award for Tasmania.

Gatenby, Herbert, Rhodes, Longford, Tasmania. Wool from sheep by pure Merino rams and pure Merino ewes; 371 days growth; 15 months old; paddocked; bred by exhibitor—Honourable mention for Tasmania.

Gibson, James, Belle Vue, Epping, Tasmania. Wool from sheep descended from German sheep imported about 50 years back, and improved by selection ever since; bred by exhibitor; 370 days growth; about 15 months old; paddocked—Special first award for Tasmania.

Gibson, James, Belle Vue, Epping, Tasmania. Wool from sheep descended from German sheep imported about 50 years back, and improved by selection ever since; bred by exhibitor; 370 days growth; age of sheep, about 15 months; paddocked—Second award for Tasmania.

Lewis, William, Stoneleigh, Beaufort, Victoria. Wool from sheep bred from the Studleigh stud flock; bred by exhibitor; 369 days growth; paddocked; age of sheep, 1 year and 7 months—Special first award for Victoria.

Section 3.—Six Fleeces of Rams' Wool, Unskirted.

Russell, P., Carngham, Victoria. Wool from pure Merino sheep bred by exhibitor; 371 days growth; age of sheep, over 1½ years; housed six months—Special first award for Victoria.

Lewis, William, Stoneleigh, Beaufort, Victoria—Champion Prize for all the Colonies.

Younghusband and Co. Limited, Melbourne. 30 samples of wool, season 1891-92; collective exhibit—Special first award.

CLASS XXX.—Hosiery and Underclothing.

Thompson, W. S., and Co., Limited, London. Corsets, busks, and hosiery—First award.

CLASS XXXI.—Clothing for both sexes, Boots and Shoes, Artificial Flowers, Hair, Wigs, etc.

India-rubber and Gutta-percha Telegraph Works, Melbourne. General collection of india-rubber goods—First award.

Farrelly, Stewart, and Co., Launceston. Two complete suits of livery —Second award.

Sargood, Butler, and Nichol, Melbourne. Men's and boys' manufactured clothing, shirts, hats, and ties—Special first award.

Newton, E. E., and Sons, Cressy, Tasmania. Boots, leather, leggings, etc.—Highly commended for imported and colonial goods.

Dempster and Co., Launceston. Bridal costume—First award.

McLaren and Co., Melbourne. Waterproof oilskin clothing—First award.

Dodgshun, Sons, and Co., Launceston. Clothing—First award.

Coutts, George, Launceston. Boots and shoes—First award.

Weingott and Sons, Sydney. Waterproof clothing, cloaks, and leggings—Special first award.

CLASS XXXII.—Jewelry, other than Gold and Silver, Platedware, Jet, Amber, Coral, Mother-of-Pearl, Steel, Precious Stones (real and imitation).

Angelo, Santamaria, and Co. (of Rome), London. Cameo shells—First award.
Koch, Julius, Melbourne. Agate jewelry—First award.
Thuriet and Bardach, Vienna. Imitation jewelry—First award.
Zech, A. T., Victoria. Amber jewelry—First award. Patent revolving pins—Special first award.
Collard and Renon, Paris. Gold jewelry—First award.
Lazard, Paris. Watch chains—First award.
Plumet, Paris. Jewelry mounted in imitation, diamonds, enamel flowers, bracelets, lockets—First award.
Caron, P., Paris. Jewelry mounted in imitation, precious stones, etc.—First award.
Regad, A., Fils, Paris. Imitations of all known precious stones—First award.

CLASS XXXIII.—Portable Weapons (Guns, Pistols, Sidearms); Hunting and Sporting Equipments.

Ferguson, J. C., and Co., Brisbane Street, Launceston. Case of guns by W. W. Scott and Co.—First award. Case of guns and rifles by W. W. Greener—First award for breechloaders.
Joyce, F., and Co. Limited, Waltham Abbey Works, London. Sporting ammunition—Special first award.
Ward and Sons, Birmingham. Sporting rifles—First award.
Ferguson, John C., and Co., Launceston. One case guns and revolvers made by William Cashmore, Birmingham, showing variety of grade in breechloading hammer and hammerless guns—Special first award. [The jurors draw attention to the excellence of workmanship in these guns.]

CLASS XXXIV.—Travelling and Camp Equipage, Tents, etc.

Farrelly, Stewart, and Co., Launceston. Travelling bags, portmanteaus, trunks, etc.—First award.
Hall, A. J., Launceston. Opossum rugs—Second award.
Hart Cycle Company Limited, Wolverhampton. Bicycles—First award for cheapness of exhibit.
Foster, R., and Co., Birmingham. Trunks and safes—First award. Bicycles—Special first award.
McLaren and Co., Melbourne. Tarpaulins, canvas hose, and water bags—First award.
Morgan, Wm., Melbourne. Tents, camp equipments, and flags—First award.
Cook, J., and Sons, Limited, Glenorchy. Furs and rugs—First award.

Class XXXV.—Toys, Dolls, Playthings, etc.

Perry, John, Limited, Melbourne. Indian clubs of colonial woods—First award.
    Crouiser Aine, Paris. Animal toys—First award.
    Martin Oreste, Paris. Musical balloons—First award.
    Barre, M., Paris. Toys—First award.
    White, R. P., Fitzroy, Victoria. Tops, etc.—First award.
    Zech, A. J., Fitzroy, Victoria. Patent tops, etc.—First award.

GROUP E.—MINERALS, ORES: CRUDE AND SMELTED.

This portion of the Exhibition presented a thoroughly representative collection, both as regards quality and the quantity of the various forms in which metallic minerals occur in this island. The intention from the first was to make it essentially of an economic character, so that the public at large could appreciate the stability of our mining industry. With this object in view, elaborate scientific detail in the classification of the various exhibits was looked upon as of secondary importance. The court, as a whole, clearly establishes the extensive and varied auriferous resources of the colony; and there is every reason to believe that a vast amount of good has already resulted from the display it presented in the Exhibition. It is certainly gratifying to know that the large amount of attention paid to it both by the local public and visitors from the other colonies clearly indicated the interest it created. The massive exhibits shown must have resulted in permanent benefit to Tasmania, whilst those of a scientific character were critically examined by many educated people who were comparative strangers to the colony, including a number of visitors to the Science Congress which was held in Hobart in the early part of the year. The high praise so generally bestowed clearly proves that the Commissioners acted wisely in proportioning so large an extent of space for this important display.

A thoroughly qualified mining authority was in constant attendance (at the expense of the companies exhibiting), and he furnished valuable information to enquirers in regard to the extent as well as the values of the ores exhibited. It is satisfactory to think that in all cases the awards were given with justice and discretion, and met with the approval of the various companies and private individuals exhibiting. They were considered purely on their merits, so that a fairly equitable arrangement was adopted, and where an exhibit was not of really first-class character as regards display, bulk, and apparent intrinsic value, the record of the claim and locality from which it was obtained were not taken into consideration.

GOLD.

Unfortunately but few of our companies were fairly represented, but the display made by the leading company—the Tasmania—was of a comprehensive character. The exhibit comprised a large gilded obelisk representing the bulk amount of gold obtained from the mine since its commencement. This was erected on a base on which was displayed a varied assortment of the auriferous matrix, such as is the average derived from the mine; whilst there were also shown cards giving full statistics of the returns from this our most important gold mine. Close by was shown a large bulk sample of the same material, much of which gave abundant evidence of its rich character. The New Golden Gate Company, Mathinna, exhibited lode stuff, and the New Castray Company, Whyte River, showed an instructive series, displaying the peculiar auriferous tufaceous rock and alluvial drift overcapping the same, and also an ingot of retorted gold. The New Pinafore Company, Lefroy, exhibited from time to time ingots of gold produced from the mine, the last of which represented the bulk weight of 1,020 tons of quartz, being an average of 19 dwts. 15 grs. to the ton. The Volunteer, Lefroy, one of the most recent additions to the long list of mining companies in this island, exhibited some interesting samples from their property, being portions of a bulk quantity taken out of the claim, 33 tons of which gave a return of 241 ozs. 8 dwts., or an average of 7 oz. 6 dwt. 1 gr. to the ton. It is to be regretted that many other prominent companies were not represented, and that a few of those which were did not display anything like the exhibits that the occasion warranted. At the same time, sufficient examples were shown, and satisfactory information was diffused, to prove beyond all doubt that Tasmania is richly endowed with the precious metal.

SILVER.

In this division a display worthy of the marvellous developments of the last three years was shown, and a great many companies, at considerable trouble and expense, combined and made an impressive exhibit of their argentiferous wealth; and where such general unanimity existed, it would be invidious to particularise that of any one company. It was considered advisable to erect a large massive trophy, so that, simultaneously, solid bulk samples, as well as the diverse nature of the ore, could be displayed, and this was so satisfactorily carried out that the conjoint effort of the companies presented a huge mass weighing considerably over 80 tons. This was made the more valuable by being flanked with elaborate glass cases displaying an educational series of the more valuable and associated minerals peculiar to a silver field. A large quantity of the ore thus shown, and the cases just referred to, were provided at the expense of the Department of Mines, and the thanks of the community are due to that branch of the Civil Service for the valuable assistance rendered, both in this special feature and in other portions of the Tasmanian Mineral Court. An interesting feature in the Court was a very neat and instructive display, of a somewhat novel nature, made by the Bank of Australasia. The happy idea occurred to Mr. O. C. Williams, manager of the Launceston branch of the institution, that corresponding collections from the Broken Hill and Tasmanian silver fields, if shown in juxtaposition, would be interesting. This was acted upon, and the public verdict has been that a more thoughtful arrangement could scarcely have been made; whilst many visitors were impressed with the peculiar similitude of the silver-bearing samples from Broken Hill and those of the silver field on the west coast of this island. Messrs. Stitt and Collingsworth, of Zeehan, at some considerable amount of trouble and pecuniary outlay, got together an elaborate series of all the mineral species hitherto discovered in that portion of the colony, and with commendable generosity presented it to the Mines Department.

TIN.

The display made in this section was individually small, but the world-famed Mount Bischoff Company made a representation which was in every way worthy of its wealth and position as the foremost mining company in Tasmania. The exhibit was highly interesting to the general public, and instructive to more studious visitors. The display consisted of a huge pyramidal structure, adorned with splashings of frondose metallic tin, around the base of which was arranged a wall-like mass of ingots, and on the top of these were glass cases showing the various grades of dressed black tin and crushed lode stuff. There was a further display of the peculiar forms of lode stuff occurring at Mount Bischoff. The mineral associates and country rocks were exhibited in huge bulk samples, of great scientific importance, many of which, in a few years time, will become most difficult to duplicate. The company also exhibited ingeniously-constructed models of the ore-crushing and tin-dressing appliances used at the mine, and excellent portraits of Mr. F. W. Kayser, the manager, and Mr. James Smith, the discoverer, of the mine. The Great Republic Company, Ben Lomond, made a nice display, which at a glance gave a clear idea of the tin-bearing lode stuff —crude, dressed, and prepared for market, with an illustrative series of lode associations peculiar to the district in which the mine is situated. Displays of a creditable character were also made by the Granite Bar, Great Western, Lone Hand, Fly-by-Night, and other companies, but it is to be regretted that many prominent properties were not represented. To Mr. H. Grant, of St. Helens, thanks are due for procuring what was termed the Portland Mineral Trophy. This really valuable display comprised samples from many lode and alluvial mining companies working in the north-eastern portion of the colony, systematically and neatly arranged, so as to form an instructive whole. Had it not been for the foresight of this gentleman, many interesting features in our tin mining industry would have been wanting in the Exhibition.

CLASS XXXVI.—Collection of Rocks, Mineral Ores, Stones, Refractory Substances, Earths and Clays, Rock Salt, Mineral Fuels, Asphalt, Bitumen, Mineral Tar, Petroleum, etc.; Process of Washing and Extracting Precious Metals; Metals in Crude as well as Manufactured; Tools, and all kinds of Hardware.

Castray Gold Mining Company, Launceston. Gold matrix in lode and alluvial, with samples of gold extracted therefrom—Highly commended.

Tasmania Gold Mining Company Limited, Launceston. Trophy, specimens of ore, gold, etc., from the Company's lode at Beaconsfield —Special first award.

Tasmanian Gold and Bismuth Association. Native bismuth, hornblendic matrix—Highly commended.

Petterd, W. F., Launceston. Tasmanian gems, cut and in the rough native condition—Special first award. General collection of minerals, principally Tasmanian—First award.

Bank of Australasia, Launceston. Collection of Broken Hill (N.S.W.) and West Coast (Tasmania) mineral specimens—Second award.

Comet Prospecting Association. Samples of argentiferous ores from the Company's claim at Dundas—First award.

Heazlewood Silver Mining Company, Burnie. Silver-lead ore from the Company's sections—Third award.

New Silver Stream Silver Mining Company, Zeehan. Fine grained galena ore from the Company's mine—Second award.

North Grubb Silver Mining Company, Zeehan. Ore from the Company's mine—Second award.

North Silver Stream Silver Mining Company, Zeehan. Ore from the Company's mine—Second award.

Oceana Silver Mining Company, Zeehan. Mineral specimens from the Company's claim—Commended.

Silver Queen Prospecting Association, Zeehan. Silver-lead ore from the mine—Second award.

Western Silver Mining Company. Argentiferous galena and associated minerals—First award.

Success Extended Silver Mining Company, Dundas. Silver ore in galena—Third award.

Sylvester Silver Mining Company, Zeehan. Silver-bearing ore——First award.

Whyte River Silver Mining Company. Samples of argentiferous ores—First award.

Grant, Henry, St. Helens. Specimens representative of the tin deposits of the Blue Tier—First award.

Great Republic Tin Mining Company. Cabinet containing stone from the lode, dressed ore, and metal—First award.

Lone Hand Tin Mining Company. Blocks of lode from the Company's mine at Ringarooma—Commended.

Mount Bischoff Tin Mining Company. Trophy—Special first award.

Cornwall Coal Company, Launceston. Coal pyramid—Second award.

Wickham and Bullock Island Coal Company Limited, Newcastle, N.S.W. Two sections of coal, weight four tons—First award.

Blackman, J. T., Launceston. Collection of paints, pigments, chrome, etc., purely Tasmanian products—First award. Hematite iron ore—Hon. mention.

Glenarnock Iron and Steel Company, Glenarnock. Pig iron, steel, etc.—First award.

Purified Coal and Coke Company, N.S.W. Purified or washed coal and coke—Second award.

Kalsomine and Metallic Paint Company, N.S.W. Paint, ochres, and disinfecting kalsomine—Third award.

Australian Kerosene Oil and Mineral Company, N.S.W. Kerosene shale and stearine retorted from the shale—First award.

Minister of Mines, Sydney. General collection of economic minerals and collection of alluvial and reef gold—Special first award.

Carter, Robert, Launceston. Specimens of silver from Balstrup's Manganese Silver Mining Company—Second award.

Price, Robert H., Launceston. Collection of mineral specimens—Third award.

Whittle, B. H., Evandale. Collection of ores and minerals—Third award.

Bernacchi, Signor, Spring Bay. Natural Portland cement, crude and prepared—First award.

Edgell, B. H. and L. V., Launceston. Mineral and geological specimens—Commended.

Mintaro Slate Quarry Company, Melbourne. South Australian slate—Highly commended.

Mudgee Sharpening Stone Company, Sydney. Carpenters' sharpening stones, slip stones, shearing and grinding wheels, etc.—First award.

United Asbestos Company, London. Italian asbestos and all kinds of asbestos goods—First award.

Keen, Robinson, and Bellville, London. Keen's Oxford blue, A.D. 1742—First award.

Patent Borax Company, Birmingham. Borax crystals, prepared Californian borax, borax starch glaze, borax sanitary powder—First award.

Clausen, Chr., Hamburg. Patent asphalt—Highly commended.

Stokes's Patent Nail Company, N.S.W. Nails—First award.

Executive Commissioner for N.S.W. Cheap tools for carpenters and bushmen—Highly commended.

Sybry, Searls, and Co., Sheffield. Steel and steel goods—First award.

Webster, A. G., and Son, Hobart (agents for T. and W. Smith). Wire ropes and cables for hauling, winding, and other purposes—First award.

Melbourne Glass Bottle Company, Spottiswoode. Glass bottles—First award.

Jackson, F., Launceston. Brass locks, tills, cupboards, iron safes, padlocks, etc.—First award.

Bernacchi, Signor, Maria Island. White freestone—First award.

Blenkhorn, James, Railton. Lime—First award.

Fysh Bros., Oatlands. Brown freestone—Hon. mention.

Walker, J., Ross. White freestone—Hon. mention.

Launceston City Corporation. Bluestone—Hon. mention.

Blackman, James Thomas. Hematite iron or oxide of iron—First award.

Kalsomine Metallic Paint Company, Sydney, N.S.W. Kalsomine—First award for New South Wales.

Purified Coal and Coke Company, N.S.W. Coke—Special first award. [The jurors beg to note the excellent quality of this coke, as being well adapted for smelting purposes.]

The Mole Creek and Zeehan Mineral Prospecting and Exploration Company Limited. Blocks of cannel coal or mineral oil shale from the Company's claim, Barn Bluff, near Mount Pelion—Special first award for Tasmania.

Mahony, Myles, Westbury. One ton of copper ore from the Pandora Company, Frankford—Highly commended.

CLASS XXXVII.—Products of Forestry, Specimens of Timber; Wood for Cabinet-work, for Building and other purposes; Colouring and Resinous Substances, Charcoal, Dried Wood, Potash, Turnery, Straw Work, etc.

Trustees Tasmanian Museum, Hobart. Tasmanian Timber Trophy, designed by G. S. Perrin, F.L.S., Conservator of Forests of Victoria, late Conservator of Forests of Tasmania—Special first award.
Von Mueller, Baron F., P.H. and M.D., Phytologic Museum, Victoria. Samples of woods—Special first award. [The jurors desire to place on record the excellent manner in which the various woods of the Colonies have been exhibited by Baron Von Mueller.]
New Zealand Midland Railway, New Zealand. Marketable timbers, rough and polished, veneering woods, picture frames, Venetian blinds, bent timbers, etc.—Special first award.
Skinner, J. T. H., and Co., East Dereham. Fretwork materials, three-ply wood—First award.
Cotton, A. B., Riversdale, Tasmania. Bark for tanning purposes, 1 sack—First award.
Cotton, Joseph, Glen Heroit, Cranbrook, Tasmania. Black wattle bark for tanning purposes—Hon. mention.
Sidebottom, W., Launceston. Wattle bark samples—Special first award.

CLASS XXXVIII.—Products of Hunting, Fishing, etc.; Collections or Drawings of Terrestrial and Amphibious Animals, Birds' Eggs, Fishes, Mollusca, and Crustacea; Furs and Skins, Undressed Feathers, Horn, Teeth, Ivory, Tortoiseshell, Sponges; Guns, Traps, Snares, Fishing Nets, Lines, Hooks, etc.

Bartleet and Son, Abbey Mills, Redditch, England. Fishing tackle, needles, etc.—Special first award.
New South Wales Executive Commissioner, Sydney. Cockatoos, cockatoo parrots, Blue Mountain and other New South Wales live birds, exhibited in aviary of New South Wales Court—First award.
Rohn, A. T., Sydney. Two glass cases of New South Wales birds, rug made of 145 opossum tails, white kangaroo, rock wallaby, two stuffed diamond snakes, native bear and young, kangaroo rat, twenty-three pieces assorted curios—Special first award.
New South Wales Government Fisheries Department, Sydney. Photographs of New South Wales fish, set of paintings of New South Wales food fishes, prepared maps showing the oyster fisheries of New South Wales, collection of New South Wales fish preserved in spirits (to be judged as a collective exhibit)—Special first award.
Carr, Thomas, Brisbane Street, Launceston. Trout from Great Lake —Hon. mention. Collective exhibit, stuffed fish and birds—First award.

CLASS XXXIX.—Agricultural Products not used for food; raw Cotton, Flax, Hemp, and other Fibres; Wool, washed and greasy; Pharmaceutical substances; Tobacco, raw and manufactured; Tanning and Dyeing substances; Preserved Fodder, and substances for Feeding Cattle, Sheep, Dogs, etc.

Miller, James, and Co., Melbourne. Manilla rope, rope from N.Z. flax, shop twine, mats and matting, hemp, jute—First award. Tarred rope, coir—Second award. Reaper and binder twine—First award.

Donaghy, M., and Sons, Geelong. Manilla rope, rope from N.Z. flax—Second award. Reaper and binder twine—First award. Coir rope, bolb rope, halyard line, and deep sea line—First award.

Cleghorn, W., jun., Dundee. Jute and oakum—First award. Engine-cleaning waste—First award.

Brain, E., Tunbridge. Rope halters made from N.Z. rope—Second award.

M'Connaghy, Michael, Invalid Depot, Launceston. Rope halters—First award for excellence of workmanship.

Tasmanian Soap and Candle Company Limited, Launceston and Hobart. "Acme" stearine candles, "R. D." stearine candles, finest stearine especially made for miners' use—Special first award for quality and cheapness. Fluted and plain "Owl" wax candles, composite candles ("Emu" brand, made of wax and stearine)—First award. Soda crystals (washing soda)—Second award. Laundry soap, "Marvel" soap, "Gold Medal" soap, blue mottled soap—First award.

Immanuel and Duswald, Frankfort. Perfumery and toilet soaps in artistic designs—First award.

Alsing and Co., Limited, London. Paper made from wood pulp—Special first award.

Clarkson, A., and Co., West Cowes, England. Ointment and cattle medicine—First award. Patent medicine, "Painkiller"—First award.

Moslem Cigarette Company Limited, London. Turkish cigarettes—Special first award. Cut tobacco, Turkish tobacco—Special first award. Cigars—First award.

Ness and Co., Darlington. Disinfectant powder—First award. Hemo-Cresol, the universal purifier—First award.

Nicholls, William, and Co., Chippenham. Fluid extract of annatto—First award.

Solomon, Cox, and Co., Melbourne. Solution for horses, cattle, and dogs; also for human application—First award.

Rosenthal, Aronson, and Co., Launceston. Olfato cigars—First award.

McLaren and Co., Melbourne. Canvas—Special first award.

Morgan and Co., Melbourne. Canvas—First award.

Price's Patent Candle Company, Battersea, London. Cloth oils, machinery oils—First award. Stearine, paraffine, ceratine—First award for collective exhibit. Candles in all forms and qualities, hand-painted candles, nightlights—Special first award for collective exhibit.

Lloyd, Frank, and Co., New South Wales. Horse and cattle food—First award.

Walden, J., Launceston. Naphthaline—First award. Samples of oils—First award.

Gould, H. T., and Co., Hobart. Eucalyptus globulus (blue gum) distilled from Tasmanian trees, and various preparations of E. globulus—Special first award for Tasmania. [The jurors are pleased to call special attention to the above exhibit as being a new industry in Tasmania, calculated to be of general service in medicine, and a valuable item of export.]

Bosisto, J., and Co., Richmond, Victoria. Acacia mollissima catechu for tanners—First award. [The jury are of opinion that if the above could be supplied at a reasonable price it would be most advantageous to tanners.] Eucalyptus balsam, for veterinary purposes—First award.

Bigg, Mr. Sheep dip, specific for scab—Second award.

Draper and Jones, Melbourne. Hakeman's sheep dip—Hon. mention.

Walden, J., Launceston. Grass-tree gum, exuded from the tree, habitat Northern Tasmania, soluble in alcohol, and then forms a polish for furniture—First award.

Hart, W., and Sons, Launceston. Quibell's sheep dip—Special first award.

Ness and Co., Darlington. Sheep dip—Second award.

CLASS XL.—Leather and Skins: Tanned, Curried, Dressed, and Dyed Leather; Varnished or Patent Leather; Morocco and Sheepskins; Skins Grained, Chamoyed, Tanned, Dressed, or Dyed.

Walden, James, Launceston. Collection of skins, raw and manufactured—First award for collection of skins, pelts, etc.

Cook, J., and Sons Limited, Glenorchy. Leather in various branches—tanned, dressed, and dyed—Special first award for the varied and excellent collection of leather, from the hide to the finished basils.

Dale, John T., London. Dubbin for softening and preserving leather—First award. Kid reviver for boots and shoes—First award. High preservative for leather bags, trunks, etc.—First award.

Arnold's Compressed Leather Company, N.S.W. Compressed leather—First award for an excellent process for utilising refuse leather.

Radke, A. W., near Sydney. Leather mill belting, wire and hemp stitched or lace sewn, belt leather, and lace leather—Special first award for mill belting only.

Ludowici, J. C., and Son Limited, Sydney. General collection of belting—Special first award for collective exhibit of leather work of all descriptions.

GROUP F.—MACHINERY, Etc.

This section of the Tasmanian International Exhibition, which occupied the large transversal annexe at the end of the Avenue of Nations, was undeniably the most complete and most attractive part of the whole.

In this Group Great Britain and the Australian Colonies occupied a large space; here, also, some local firms made a most creditable display.

Messrs. Davey, Paxman, and Co., of Colchester, Tangye and Co., Hornsby, Ransomes and Sims, and other British firms, were duly and largely represented. Victoria, South Australia, and New Zealand held their own in agricultural as well as mining machinery. In that line there was a grand display made by Messrs. A. G. Webster and Co., of Hobart, Messrs. Ferguson and Co. and Hart and Sons, of Launceston.

Canada had a separate court for the display of agricultural implements, which took high honours.

In ploughs, Tasmania ran a close race with some Victorian exhibitors.

In conclusion, a special notice must be taken of the exhibits from Mr. W. H. Knight, of the Phœnix Foundry, Launceston, who had a collection of locally-made engines of various descriptions, as well as first-rate specimens of castings, which deservedly won Special first class awards.

One of the most interesting collections of useful machinery was that exhibited by Joseph Baker and Sons, of Flinders Lane, Melbourne, which was, during the whole period of the Exhibition, shown in full operation at Mr. Russen's Model Bakery. The Bailey-Baker patent continuous oven and the complete plant of biscuit-making machinery and baking appliances was one of the attractions of the Exhibition. Both the exhibitor of the machinery and the enterprising manufacturer who kept it at work for nearly four months deserved all the awards they have received.

CLASS XLI.—Mining and metallurgy; Boring Machines (Artesian, Diamond Drills, etc., for cutting Coal, Rocks, etc., for working Mines or Quarries; appliances for Lowering and Hoisting Miners, Pumping Water, Ventilating Shafts, etc.; Safety Lamps, Apparatus for Saving Life, Apparatus for the Mechanical Dressing of Ores, Fuel for Metal Work of all kinds.

Hornsby, Richard, and Sons Limited, Grantham, England. New Colonial winding and hauling engine—Special first award for excellence of workmanship, strength, and quality of material.

Knight, W. H., Launceston. One 4 h.p. vertical engine and steel boiler, with patent high speed governor and new and improved injector

—First award. One 4-h.p. horizontal steam engine and steel boiler—First award. One 14-h.p. horizontal steam engine "Phœnix"—Special first award.

Cradock, George, and Co., Wakefield, England. Steel and iron wire ropes—Special first award.

McLaren and Co., Melbourne. Canvas buckets with valve at bottom, for mining purposes—First award.

Wallbridge and Co., Launceston. Water engine manufactured by A. T. Burt, Dunedin, New Zealand—First award.

Thompson and Co., Castlemaine, Victoria. Patent safety mining cage—First award. Winding gear—First award.

Tangyes Limited, Melbourne. Tangye's improved patent sight-feed lubricator—Special first award. Tangye's Tool holder—First award. Amateur's lathe—Highly commended. Engine for electric lighting, vertical engine with reversing gear, "Archer" engine coupled to centrifugal pump, centrifugal pump coupled to a Floyd's engine, circular saw, 4-h.p. Soho engine (used for dairying purposes), two duplex pumps —First award. Special pump with Holman's valves, Mark's double-purchase winch, single and double purchase winch, tripod jack, bottle jack, ratchet jack, bottle traverse jack—Highly commended. Radial drilling machine, portable drilling machine, bench drilling machine, hydraulic jacks, and punching bear—First award.

Davey, Paxman, and Co., Colchester. Winding engine and winding drums—Special first award.

Smith, F. and W., Newcastle-on-Tyne. Wire ropes and cables for hauling and other purposes, ensilage stack press—First award.

Rand Drill and Rackarock Company, Melbourne. Little Giant rock drill—Special first award. Acrobat Drill and stand for popping, No. 3 Slugger mounted on column, pulveriser—First award each.

Fulton, G. E., and Co. Limited, Adelaide. Two 8-h.p. hoisting engines with double drums, fitted complete on cast-iron bed-plate. (Engines of this type are made up to 25-h.p.)—First award for compactness of design and stability.

Flood, Frederick, Melbourne. Patent waterlift and self-acting windmill sail—First award.

Evans, Joseph, and Sons, Wolverhampton. Steam pumps and hand pumps—First award.

Davidson and Brown, Hobart. Grinding and amalgamating pans. The tailings being crushed to a fine powder, all gold is saved and amalgamated—First award for wet grinding.

Clarkson-Stanfield Concentrators, Limited, London. Clarkson-Stanfield dry ore concentrator and classifier, with working model of same—First award.

Bickford, Smith, and Co., Tucking Mill, Cornwall, England, and Sandhurst, Victoria. Bickford's patent safety fuse for use in all blasting operations, Bickford's patent ignitors and instantaneous fuse for firing simultaneously any number of holes—Special first award.

CLASS XLII.—Agricultural Implements, Tools, Machines, used in the Cultivation of Fields and Forests, in all branches of Husbandry (Sowing, Planting, or Harvesting), whether worked by Hand, Horse, or Steam power; Carts and other rural means of transport; Manures, Organic or Mineral.

Webster, A. G., and Son, Hobart (agents for Reid and Gray, Dunedin). Chaffcutter—First award. Disc harrow—First award. Seed drill—Special first award. Ploughs and harrows—Special first award for collection.

Webster, A. G., and Son, Hobart (agents for Pulsometer Engineering Company. Pulsometer—First award.

Webster, A. G., and Son, Hobart (agents for Bickle rock drill). Rock drill—First award.

Webster, A. G., and Son, Hobart (agents for R. Hornsby and Sons, Limited). Collection of single and double furrow ploughs—First award as a collective exhibit. Strawsoniser—First award. Traction engine—First award. Portable engine—First award. Colonial engine—First award. Reaper and binder—First award. Mowers—Second award. Reapers and mowers—Second award.

Webster, A. G., and Son, Hobart (agents for S. L. Allan and Co., Philadelphia, U.S.A.) Planet Junior implements for field and garden—First award.

Webster, A. G., and Son, Hobart (agents for Barnard and Lake, England). Thatchmaker—First award.

Webster, A. G., and Son, Hobart (agents for the Aspinwall Manufacturing Company, U.S.A.) Potato planter and fertiliser—Special first award.

Webster, A. G., and Son, Hobart (agents for Murray and Co., Scotland). Crown threshing machines—Highly commended.

Harrap, Alfred, and Son, Launceston (agents for Booth, McDonald, and Co., New Zealand). Disc seed harrows—First award. Iron windmill, built entirely of iron and steel—Special first award. Deering all steel chain drive reaper and binder—First award for durability and lightness of construction in steel and special bearings, with improved binder. Booth-McDonald double-furrow plough—First award. Deering mower—Special first award

Ferguson, Mephan, Carlton, Victoria. Iron gates—Highly commended. Water supply and irrigation pipes—Special first award for collective exhibit.

Beal, G. W., Melbourne. Automatic railway carriage lock—Special first award.

Davey, Paxman, and Co., Colchester, England. Portable single cylinder steam engine, with patent antomatic governor—Special first award.

Trewhella Bros., Newbury, Victoria. Single and double purchase log jacks—First award.

Ross, E. W., and Co., New York. Chaff and fodder cutters—Highly commended.

Morgan and Co., Melbourne, Victoria. Canvas hose and couplings—Highly commended. Gymnasium fittings—Highly commended.

Titmus, L., Ulverstone. Iron plough—Special first award. Wooden plough—Excellent workmanship and high finish.

Garde and Crystal, North Melbourne. Three-furrow plough—First award. Double-furrow plough and single-furrow plough—Second award each.

Mitchell and Co., Melbourne. Double-furrow plough—First award.

Lennon, Hugh, Melbourne. Single-furrow plough for contractors' purposes—First award.

Ransomes, Sims, and Jeffries, Ipswich, England (Hinman and Wright, Launceston, agents). Lawn mowers—First award. New Australasian threshing drum—Special first award. Vertical engines—Special first award. Portable engine—Second award.

Andrews and Beaven, Christchurch, New Zealand. Patent travelling self-bagging chaffcutter, horse gear, corncrushers, cleaners—Special first award for collective exhibit.

Blackwell, Henry, Bishopsbourne. Iron swing plough, made by exhibitor—Highly commended.

Danks, John, and Sons, Limited, Melbourne. Pumps—First award. Sheet lead and pipes, engineers' and plumbers' brass-foundry—First award for collective exhibit. Engineers' and plumbers' brass work—First award. Sheet lead and pipes—First award. Bells—First award. Patent lawn sprinkler—First award.

Salisbury, Scott, and Co., Launceston. Fine perforated castings—Special first award. Heavy mine pump machinery—Special first award.

Mason, F., Sydney. Langley wool press—Special first award. Koerstz double acting pump—Special first award.

Hart, William, and Sons, Launceston. Walter A. Wood's reaper and binder—First award. W. A. Wood's enclosed gear mower with reaping attachments—Special first award.

Buckeye Harvesting Company, Launceston. Reaper and binder—First award for simplicity of construction and lightness of draught.

Ferguson, J. C., and Co., Launceston. McCormick reaper and binder—Special first award for construction and strength, coupled with simplicity. Harrison McGregor reaper and mower—First award. McCormick iron mowing machine—First award.

Massey Manufacturing Co., Melbourne. Reaper and binder—First award.

Allen, Thomas, Emu Bay. The "Bushman's Friend," being a model showing how the "Shoe" used for felling trees is fixed to trees—First award.

Gow, William, Sydney. Butter prints, dairy utensils, and general wood turnery—Special first award

Anglo-Continental Guano Company, London. Ohlendorff's guano and manures—First award for best collection of manures.

Turner, Thos., and Co., London. First award for chemical artificial manures.

Newey, R., and Sons, Launceston. Collection of manures and fertilisers—Highly commended for the collection of various patent horticultural manures.

Massey Manufacturing Company, Melbourne. Side delivery harvester—First award. Sharp's self-dumping horse hayrake—First award.

Lennon, Hugh, Spottiswoode, near Melbourne. Single-furrow plough, cast D shares, made by exhibitor—First award for excellent quality of material and manufacture. Double-furrow ploughs made by exhibitor—Highly commended, the share being of superior manufacture, ensuring durability.

CLASS XLIII.—Apparatus and Processes used in Agricultural Work, and used for the Preparation of Food, including Milling Flour, Kneading, Baking, Ice-making, and Refrigerating Machines.

Webster, A. G., and Son, Hobart (agents for R. A. Lister and Co., Dursley). "Alexandra" centrifugal cream separators, for hand, horse, or steam power—Special first award. "Triplex" horse gear for fast running machinery—First award.

Webster, A. G., and Son, Hobart. Cheese plant complete, by Lister and Co., Dursley, England—Special first award.

Jack Frost Freezing Company, Melbourne. Freezing machine for making ice, ice creams, fruit ices, etc.—First award.

Hunt, R., and Co., Earl's Colne, Essex. Atlas and Colonial chaffcutter, for hand, horse, and steam power; pony and horse gears, corn grinders, root slicers and graters—Special first award for collective exhibit.

Baker, J., and Sons, Flinders Lane, Melbourne. Bailey-Baker patent continuous oven—First award.

Russen, Charles, and Co., Wellington street, Launceston. Complete plant for biscuit manufacture, exhibited in motion and at work, from the mixing of the dough to the finish of the goods for market—Special first award.

Baker, Joseph, and Sons, Flinders Lane, Melbourne. Bailey-Baker patent plant of biscuit machinery, bread and cake machinery and bakery appliances, confectionery and ice cream machinery—First award.

Lempriere, W. J., and Co., Melbourne (agents for F. Selby and Co., Birmingham). Axles, springs, lamps, etc.—First award.

Buncle, John, and Son, North Melbourne. Combined crusher—First award. Chaffcutter and bagfiller combined—First award. Bark cutting machinery and disintegrator—First award. Corncrushing machinery—First award. Tobacco cutting machine—Highly commended. Circular saw (for timber) with patent teeth to economise time and labour in setting—Highly commended. Circular saw (for firewood) with patent teeth—Highly commended.

Andrews, Charles, Geelong. Patent cooking ranges—First award.

Cherry, E., Gisborne, Victoria. Concussion churn, butter worker, butter printer, and weigher (in Model Dairy)—First award.

Rice, Whiteacre, and Company, U.S.A. Steam generators for cooking food for stock, boiling water, heating rooms, and cleansing purposes—First award.

Class XLIV.—Machines and Tools in general not specified.

Walden, James, Launceston. Oils and skins—First award.

Knight, W. H., Launceston. One 1-h.p. horseworks of new design, made by exhibitor—Highly commended. One hand-power brick press for moulded and plain bricks—First award.

Jones and Co., Melbourne. Patent "Eureka" hot air oven—First award for cheapness.

Davey, Paxman, and Co., Colchester, England. One "Essex" patent vertical boiler—Special first award. Compound undertype engine, with automatic extension gear—Special first award.

Jackson, F., Launceston. Brass locks—Special first award.

Mundlos and Co., Madgeburg. Sewing machines—Special first award for collection from the same maker.

Funchen Bros., Aachen. Sewing machine needles—First award.

Melson and Griffin, London. "Bear" high pressure semi-metallic steam pump packing and jointing material—Special first award.

Kemp, R. V., Hobart. Working model vertical steam boiler—First award.

Winter, F. A., Sydney. Centrifugal dish washer—First award.

Pitman, W., Rushcutters' Bay, New South Wales. Horse shoes—Special first award for excellent display of collective exhibits, the workmanship being exquisite.

Taylor Limited, Liverpool. Disinfectant—First award. Automatic disinfector—First award.

Salisbury, Scott, and Co., Launceston. Compound marine engine in motion—Special first award.

Paton, John, Launceston. Model lathe—Special first award.

Osborn, J. Lee, Sydney. Pooley's patent weighing machines—First award.

Stewart, F. and W., Launceston. Dies, die-sinking, and general medal striking—First award.

Moran, A. W., Melbourne. Medal presses, die-sinking, and medal making—First award for collective exhibit.

Lamson Service Limited, Sydney. Cash railways—Special first award. Lamson cash check and self-adding cash register—Special first award.

Dainton, George, and Co., Melbourne. Fancy and plain brass and copper work—Special first award. Baths—Highly commended. Ventilators—Highly commended. Portable copper and range boilers—Highly commended.

Dowling, George, and Co., South Melbourne. Refrigerators for milk and beer—First award.

Cashel, Barter, and Co., Melbourne. Lubricating machine oil—Special first award.

Butler, W. H., Melbourne. Portable coppers—Highly commended. Colonial ovens—Highly commended.

Brierly, John A., and Co., Melbourne. "Victory" gas engines—First award.

Bain, Williams, and Co., Coatbridge, Scotland. Bain's winder for wire fencing—First award.

Ferguson, J. C., and Co., Launceston. Implements for field and garden—First award.

Stott and Hoare, Melbourne. Remington typewriter—First award for durability, easy manipulation, simplicity, ahd workmanship.

Lamson Store Service Company, Limited, Sydney. The English typewriter—Second award for simplicity of parts and for working in view of the operator.

Cunningham, J. E., Sydney. No. 2 and 3 Caligraph writing machine —Special first award, gold medal. Edison's Mimeograph copying machine—Highly commended.

Saunders, H., London. Neo-Cyclostyle—First award for great simplicity and perfect reproduction. Yost typewriter—Special first award for mechanical construction, quality of material, durability, and effective working.

Knight, W. H., Launceston. Wrought-iron double riveted high pressure navigation tubes—Special first award.

Danks, John, and Son, Melbourne. Patent pickling pump—Special first award. Patent spray pump—First award.

Grigor, D., Melbourne. Fancy bandsawing woodwork—Special first award.

United Horseshoe and Nail Company, Cubit Town, London. Machine-made horseshoes and nails—First award.

Class XLV.—Carriages and Wheelwrights' Work.

Webster, A. G., and Son, Hobart. Tire benders, to bend tires up to 16 in. x 1 in.—First award.

Adams, Griffiths, and Dudley, Launceston. Bent wood for carriage work, manufactured from Tasmanian blue gum, blackwood, and other woods—Special first award for collective exhibit.

Burton and Knox, Burwood Road, Hawthorn, Victoria. Goddard buggy and lady's pony carriage—Special first award. [The jurors express their thorough satisfaction at the excellence of the workmanship and machines.]

Perry, John, Melbourne. Bent timber, shafts, poles, etc., turnery work, spokes, felloes, hubs, pickhandles, etc.—Special first award for bent wood ; First award for shafts and poles.

Selby, Frederick, and Co., Birmingham. Carriage axles, lamps, etc. —First award.

Class XLVI.—Harness and Saddlery.

Pride, William, Geelong. Set carriage harness, gent's saddle and bridle, lady's saddle and bridle, stock saddle and bridle—First award.

Power, T. P., Melbourne. Collection of saddlery and harness— Special first award for excellent workmanship and superiority of the material used.

Newton, E. E., and Sons, Cressy. Harness and saddlery—Second award.

TASMANIAN EXHIBITION, 1891-92.   97

CLASS XLVII.—Railway Apparatus, Engines, Carriages, etc.

Hart, William, and Sons, Launceston. Traction engine—Special first award.

Bloomfield Brothers, Melbourne. Patent portable tramway and rolling stock (Bochum Union)—Special first award.

Ferguson, J. C., and Co., Launceston (agents Patent Nut and Bolt Company, Birmingham, England). One case, containing samples of this company's manufactures, from raw material to finished goods—First award for collection.

CLASS XLVIII.—Telegraphic Appliances, Electric and all appertaining to Electricity.

Bates, William, Gasworks, Hobart. Electric battery—Hon. mention. [The jurors regret that owing to the unfinished manner in which this exhibit is presented they are unable to give it a first-class certificate.]

The Crompton Electric Supply Company, New South Wales. 1 110-volt 65-amp. compound dynamo, 120-light machine (16 candle power); 1 110-volt 45-amp. compound dynamo, 80-light machine; 1 2-h.p. motor, 1 table motor for ventilation: cables, wires, pendants, brackets, etc.; instruments for electrical purposes, viz., 2 volt meters, 2 ammeters, 1 galvanometer, switches, main, branch, etc.; fuses, main, branch, etc.; lamp holders, shades, carbons, and petty material connected with electrical work; medical battery, indicator, and bell, with samples of pushes, cells, etc.—Special first award.

Spencer-Canning, W. E., Melbourne. Electric lighting dynamos, 24 lights each 16 candle power—First award.

India-rubber, Gutta-percha Telegraphic Company, Silvertown, London. Rubber goods for telegraphic, electrical, and telephone engineers—Special first award. Rubber goods for hospital purposes—Special first award. Rubber goods for ironmongers, gasfitters, plumbers, and household purposes—Special first award. India-rubber, gutta-percha, ebonite, and vulcanised fibre goods, etc.—Special first award. English oak-tanned Avonside and Hepburn's pump leather—First award. Submarine cables and torpedo-firing apparatus, also artistic tiling—Special first award. Rubber goods for athletic clubs—Special first award. Diving dress and apparatus for under-water work—Special first award. Collective exhibit—Special first award.

CLASS XLIX.—Building Materials of all kinds; Drawings, Models, etc., of Public Buildings, Mansions, Cottages, Lighthouses, Industrial Dwellings, etc.

Draper and Sons, Melbourne. Patent automatic flap-action earth closet, and microbine disinfectant, deodoriser, and antiseptic, fluid, powder, and soaps, non-poisonous and stainless—First award. [Special notice given to the exhibitors' patent sealed pans.]

Faija, Henry, London. Cement testing plant—First award for tensile tests.

H

Gunn, J. and T., Launceston. Building requisites—Special first award for first-class joiners' work, and first award for imported building requisites.

Knight, William Henry, Phœnix Works, Launceston. Iron verandah and balcony posts, panels, brackets, frieze, balcony chairs and seats, and ornamental castings, made by exhibitor—First award for chairs and iron furniture, and second award for balcony and verandah castings.

Lysaght, John, and Co. Limited, Bristol and London. Galvanised iron, galvanised wire netting (colonial made)—First award.

Matthews and Yates, Manchester. Air propellers for ventilation—Special first award for simplicity, cheapness, and efficiency.

Saupe and Busch, Dresden, Radebeul. Patent embossed metal plates for advertising—Special first award.

Lempriere, W. and J., Melbourne (agents for St. Pancras Iron Company, London). Model of stable fitted up—First award.

Wallbridge and Co., Launceston. Sanitary appliances, specimens of plumbers' work, plumbers' fittings—First award.

Gunn, J. and T., Launceston. Samples of timbers, mantelpieces, etc.—Special first award. The "Invincible" open and close fire range—First award. Panelled blackwood dado bookcase—Special first award. Staircase of Tasmanian blackwood and Huon pine, also one of kauri pine and Tasmanian blackwood—Special first award.

CLASS L.—Navigation : Drawings or Models of Ships, Boats, Steamers, Floating Docks ; Materials for Rigging, Apparatus for Saving Life at Sea, Diving Bells, Rocket Apparatus, Flags and Signals.

Wyrill, Captain. Self-acting model yacht—Hon. mention.

Huddart, Parker, and Co., Limited. Model of s.s. *Burrumbeet*, *Corrangamite*, and *Elingamite*, fitted as armed steamers for Victorian Government—First award. Model of s.s. *Coogee*, running between Melbourne and Launceston—First award. Model of s.s. *Courier*, speed 21 knots an hour (in Geelong trade)—First award. Model of s.s. *Hygeia*, specially built for the Hobson's Bay excursion trade (beautifully fitted, and attaining a very high rate of speed)—Special first award. Model of modern cargo steamer for intercolonial trade—First award.

Dowling, George, and Co. Model of *Eagle* (tug), a very fast and powerful boat—Special first award.

Union Steam-Ship Company of New Zealand. Full model of s.s. *Rotomahana*—Special first award. Full model of s.s. *Mararoa*—First award. Full model of s.s. *Wakatipu*—Hon. mention. Half models of s.s. *Monowai* and *Takapuna*—Hon. mention. Chart table, showing position of fleet of 53 steamers—First award.

Edwards, F., Melbourne. Rob Roy canoe, built by exhibitor at the age of 17—Special first award.

Fraser, Alex. A., Inveresk, Tasmania. Model cutter yacht—First award.

Orient Steam Navigation Company, London. Half model of the new twin screw steamer *Ophir*—Special first award. Half model of the R.M.S. *Ormuz*—First award.

Horne, Louis, Launceston. Pearl cruising canoe—First award.

Launceston Marine Board, A. Evershed, secretary. Harbour boarding boat, length 28 ft., beam 6 ft. 4 in., built of Huon pine and other Tasmanian woods, copper fastened, built by H. T. Moore, Launceston—Special first award.

Phœnix Fireworks Company, Braybrook, England. Fancy fireworks and illumination lights, marine rockets, life-saving rockets, distress signals, light and fog signals—Special first award. Mortars for firing rockets—First award.

Ross and Duncan, Glasgow. Model of tug *Wybia*—First award.

Turk, R. J., Kingston-on-Thames. Model of double-sculling skiff—Special first award.

CLASS LI.—Military Clothing.

Jones, W., and Co., London, Government contractors. Helmets, outfits, official book, etc.—Special first award.

GROUP C.—ALIMENTARY PRODUCTS.

Cereals, flour, and meals made as much show as could be expected at a time when old grain was out of date and the new was still in the field: nevertheless, a fair collection was entered and filled a sufficient area of space. Our millers had well-fitted trophies, where flour and meal could be seen in great variety.

Grass and other seeds were also sent in to prevent the great firms from Great Britain taking all the honours. Sutton and Sons, of Reading, and James Carter and Co., of London, certainly exhibited wonderful trophies, and displayed the scores of medals awarded to their respective firms at all former exhibitions throughout the world. But if our own exhibitors had not so ostentatious a display, they took away well-deserved honours for their exhibits of Tasmanian seeds—for the variety as well as the utility of the goods shown.

The exhibits of aerated and self-raising flour caused some keen competition. The jurors were not satisfied with the ordinary tests, and even after many trials they were compelled to give an equal award to C. Russen and Co., of Launceston, and Swallow and Ariell, of Melbourne.

The two firms had a further contest for biscuits, cakes, and similar preparations, and here also the jurors have had a difficult task in arriving at a satisfactory conclusion.

The same difficulties arose in the judging of chocolates, cocoas, etc., where the well-known firms, Taylor, Symington, Fry, and Cadbury had entered the lists.

In preserved meats, fish, and other edibles, the entries were both numerous and varied.

Beers, cordials, and aerated waters were principally represented by Tasmanian exhibitors, and were of excellent quality.

Wines are dealt with separately by the Wine Jury, whose report follows.

CLASS LII.—Cereals, Farinaceous Products, Wheat, Rye, Barley, Rice, Maize, Millet, and other Cereals, in Grain and in Flour; Grain without husk, and Groats; Bread and Pastry, Biscuits, etc.

Keen, Robinson, and Bellville, London.   Pearl barley—First award. Robinson's patent groats—First award.   Robinson's patent barley—First award.   White groats—First award.   Oats—Special first award.

Birmingham Vinegar Brewery Co. (Holbrook and Co.), Birmingham. Blancmange powder, egg powder, baking powder, custard powder—First award.   Holbrook and Co.'s essence of coffee—First award.   Holbrook and Co.'s essence of coffee and chicory—First award.

Dean, T. B., York Street, Launceston.   Bread—First award.

Knaggs, J. B., Elizabeth Street, Launceston.   Wedding cake—First award.

Russen, C., and Co., Wellington Street, Launceston.   Biscuit trophy, fancy and plain biscuits, wedding, birthday, and christening cakes, confectionery, ice-creams, etc., showing the process of manufacture in their various branches—Special first award for collective exhibit, and the fact of the exhibits being manufactured at the Exhibition.   Special first award for Tasmanian made biscuits.

Swallow and Ariell Limited, Port Melbourne, Victoria.   Biscuits of every description, wedding and other cakes—Special first award for excellent quality of biscuits and cakes, and for their manufacture.

Wigram Bros., Christchurch, New Zealand.   Malt—Special first award. [The jury beg to note the excellent quality and high condition of this malt.]

Brunton and Co., Melbourne.   Flour—Championship of the colonies for highest points in manufacture, colour, and strength.   Victory steel roller flour—Special first award for Victoria.

Wood Bros., Christchurch, New Zealand.   Roller flour—First award for New Zealand.

T. W. Monds and Son, Carrick.   Roller flour—Highly commended. Pearl barley—First award.   Oatmeal—First award for Tasmania.   Milling oats—First award.   Flaked oats—First award.   Split peas—Commended. Wheat (winter)—First award.   Spring wheat—First award.

Luck, John, and Co., West Devonport.   Roller flour—Special first award for Tasmania.   Digestive meal—Highly commended.   Ruby digestive meal—Commended.   Wheat—Commended.

Newey, R., and Sons, Launceston.   Linseed meal—Highly commended.   English barley—First award.   Collection of cereals—First award.   Wheat (white)—First award.   Tuscan wheat—First award. Prolific wheat—First award.

Ritchie, David, and Son, Launceston.   Pearl barley—Commended. Digestive meal—Commended.   Flaked oats—Highly commended.   Split peas—Highly commended.   Oatmeal—Commended.

Swallow and Ariell Limited, Port Melbourne.   Digestive meal—First award for Victoria.

Affleck, Thomas, and Sons, Launceston.   Digestive meal—First award for Tasmania.

Farrar, H. W., and Co., Melbourne.   Duryeas' maizena—First award.

Scott, Jas., and Sons, River Forth, Tasmania. Oatmeal—Highly commended. Oats—Highly commended. Milling oats—Commended.

Roberts, James, Cootamundra, New South Wales. Wheat (purple straw)—Highly commended.

Fyansford Manufacturing Company, Geelong, Victoria. Snowflake crystal starch—Special first award.

Hurst and Son, London. Collection of cereals—First award.

Carter, London. Wheat—Highly commended as a collective exhibit

Moore Bros., New South Wales. Wheat—Commended.

Loiterton, Charles, New South Wales. Wheat—First award for New South Wales.

Wood Bros., Christchurch, New Zealand. Semolina grain (fine and coarse)—First award.

Maconochie Bros., Lowestoft. Oatmeal—First award.

Swallow and Ariell Limited, Port Melbourne. Beef biscuits—First award. Pilot bread—First award. Dog's bread—First award. Whole meal biscuits—First award. Aerated flour—First award.

CLASSES LIII., LV., LVI.—Fatty substances and Oils for food; Milk, fresh and preserved; Butter, fresh, salt, or tinned; Cheese; Vegetables and Fruit, fresh, dried, and preserved; Condiments, Sugar and Confectionery, including Jams, Sauces, etc.; Liqueurs, etc., etc.

Maconochie Bros., Lowestoft, England. Malt and other vinegars—First award. Sublime olive oil—First award. Curry powder—Hon. mention. Table salt—First award. Flavouring essences—First award. Lemon peel—First award. Salad cream—First award. Concentrated lemonades—First award. Seidlitz powder—First award. Sherbet—First award. Mixed pickles—First award. Golden Syrup—First award. Yorkshire sauce—First award. Baking powder—First award.

Australian Perfumery Company, Sydney. Essences of vanilla, lemon, and almond—Special first award.

Hinds and Co., Coventry. Phosphorzine, the great brain, nerve, and constitutional invigorator—Highly commended.

Evans, Sons, and Co., Liverpool. Compressed lime tablets and other medical sweets—First award. Montserrat sauce—First award. Montserrat lime juice—First award.

Bosisto, J., and Co., Richmond, Victoria. Essential oils from indigenous trees of Australia—Special first award. [The jurors have carefully tested the whole of the oils in this exhibit, and were greatly satisfied with the quality and excellence; they therefore have no hesitation in awarding a special first-class certificate for the collection.] Red gum lozenges—First award.

Lloyd, Frank, and Co., Sydney. Horse and cattle food—First award.

Birmingham Vinegar Brewery Company, Birmingham, England. Holbrook and Co.'s pure malt vinegar—First award. Holbrook and Co.'s Worcestershire sauce, pickles, sauces, anchovy, etc.—Special first award. [The jurors desire to call special attention to the superior quality of the productions of this firm, and also to the manner in which they have been displayed and brought before the public.]

Swallow and Ariell Limited, Port Melbourne. Icing sugar—Special first award. Milk food—Special first award.

Champion and Co., Limited, London. Brown and crystal vinegar and genuine mustard—Special first award.

Gaylard, John C., Windsor Plantation, Bundaberg, Queensland. Collective exhibit of sugars of varieties (70 lbs. in each)—Special first award.

Irvine and McEachern, Launceston. Oilmen's stores and jams—Special first award.

Keen, Robinson, and Bellville, London. Keen's mustard, A.D. 1742 —Special first award.

Thrower, W. I., Launceston. Tomato sauce, Shamrock baking powder, egg powder, Klelum Bux and Co.'s curry powder—First award for mild sauce; second award for hot sauce; hon. mention for remainder of exhibit.

Tatlow, Charles J., Launceston. Genuine tomato sauce—First award. Mild sauce—Second award.

CLASS LIV.—Meat and Fish, preserved, smoked, and salted.

Higgins, Henry, Hobart. German sausages—First award. Hams and bacon—Special first award.

Castle Co-operative Salt Company, Adelaide. Salt—Special first award for collective exhibit. [This being a new Australian industry, the jurors desire to record their high opinion of the success achieved by the exhibitors.]

Coleman and Company, Norwich. "Winecarnis," Liebig's extract of meat and malt wine—First award.

Williams, F., Auckland, New Zealand. Tinned schnapper (smoked), tinned mullet (fresh)—Special first award.

Maconochie Bros., Lowestoft, England. Flake tapioca—First award. Macaroni—First award. Mushroom catsup—First award. Red herring —First award. Mock turtle and other soups—First award. Cod roes —First award. Digby chicks—First award. Dried sprats—First award. Haddock roes—First award. Bologna sausages—First award. Camp pie—First award. Scotch salmon—First award. White herrings and tinned herrings in sauce—First award. Bloater paste—First award. Mortadella sausage—First award. Ham, chicken, and tongue—First award. Devilled ham and tongue—First award. Rolled ox tongue—First award. Sweetbread—First award. Veal and ham—First award. Plum pudding—First award. Suffolk brawn—First award. Devilled tongue—First award. Russian caviare—First award. Oxford sausage —First award. Soles in cream, haddocks—First award. Anchovies—First award. Collective exhibit as above—Special first award. [The jurors desire to place on record the high opinion they have formed of the goods exhibited by this firm, and also to the high standard to which they have brought the art of preserving food for the million, and the low prices charged for the same.]

Skinner, B., Brisbane, Queensland. Turtle soup, beche-de-mer soup (preserved), potted dugong, preserved meats—Special first award for collective exhibit.

Swallow and Ariell Limited, Port Melbourne. Mince-meat, etc.—Special first award. [The jurors desire to direct attention to the superior quality of this exhibit, and feel assured that if more general attention were drawn to this class of goods housewives would economise and be able to place on their tables an article superior to the usual home-made mince-meat.]

Idris and Co., London. "Viking" food preparations for invalids—Special first award.

Class LVI.—Cocoas and Chocolate.

Fry, J. S., and Sons, Bristol (represented by Messrs. R. Green and Co., Launceston). Fry's homœopathic cocoa—Special first award. Fry's concentrated cocoa—Special first award. Fry's Ceylon chocolate—Special first award. Fry's Caraccas chocolate—Special first award. Exhibits of cocoas—Special first award for each variety exhibited. Collection of fancy chocolates—Special first award. A collective exhibit of cocoas and chocolates—Special first award.

Taylor Bros., London. A collective exhibit of cocoa and free restaurant—Special first award.

Symington, T., and Co., Edinburgh. Exhibit of coffee essence and free restaurant—Special first award. Essence of coffee and chicory—First award.

Farrar, H. W., and Co., Melbourne, Victoria. Taylor Bros.' soluble pure cocoa, condensed—First award.

Cadbury Bros., Bowinville, near Birmingham. Essence of cocoa—Special first award.

Smith, T. and H., and Co., Edinburgh and London. Essence of coffee with chicory, essence of coffee pure—Special first award. Chocolate and milk, cocoa and milk—Special first award

Maconochie Bros., Lowestoft. Cocoa, soluble—Special first award.

Macfarlane Bros. and Co., Hobart. Essence of coffee and chicory—Highly commended.

Class LVI.—Vegetables and Fruit, fresh, dried, and preserved, etc.

Saratoga Packing Company, Saratoga, U.S.A. Californian prunes—Special first award. [This exhibit is well worthy of the award, and there is no doubt in the minds of the jurors that the fruit which is now allowed to go to waste in this colony might, if judiciously treated, be made available for export.]

Maconochie Bros., Lowestoft, England. Dried herbs—First award. Spanish olives—First award. Bottled fruits—Special first award. Jams—First award.

Skinner, B. (Queensland Preserving Company), Brisbane. Queensland preserved pine-apple and Queensland preserved guava, etc.—Special first award.

Murrell, Mrs. Winifred, Launceston. Preserved jams and jellies—Special first award.

Newball and Mason, Nottingham, England. Dried herbs—Special first award.

Birmingham Vinegar Brewery Company, England. French olives—Special first award.

Maconochie Bros., Lowestoft, England. Fresh mackerel—First award. Potted venison—First award. Potted woodcock—First award. Scotch herring—First award. West India pickles—First award. Candied peel—First award.

Burroughs, Welcome, and Co., London. Kepler's extract of malt—Special first award.

CLASS LVII.—Wines.

"In handing over to the Commissioners the awards made in this section of the Tasmanian Exhibition, we desire to call their special attention to the footnotes we have appended to each colony or country represented. In addition to this, we deem it our duty to state that the whole of the wines submitted to us point to the great future of the vine-growing industry of Australia, more especially as regards its trade with Tasmania. The consumption of pure, wholesome, and non-intoxicating wines should be encouraged in a colony which cannot produce such an article. That a large trade could be opened for Australian wines in this island is beyond a doubt, provided the Government be prevailed upon to reduce the prohibitive rate of duty now in force. Steps have already been taken to bring this matter before the Tasmanian Government, and it is now under consideration. We would fail in our duty if we did not at this juncture express an opinion on so important a subject, which affects not only the trade of the country, but also the sobriety and morality of the people. It is beyond dispute that in all countries where pure wines are to be had at a low price intemperance is very much minimised. Wines such as we have had to judge—with an alcoholic standard varying from 15 to 21 per cent.—are being retailed in the Australian colonies at from 10s. to 15s. per dozen quarts. Such wines do not exceed 3s. to 4s. per gallon, if purchased in bulk from wholesale dealers, and even much less from the growers. All these wines are taxed indiscriminately in this colony 6s. per gallon in bulk and 8s. per gallon if bottled. Hence the small quantity imported. It is our opinion that if the duty were reduced to one fourth of the present rate the revenue would be benefited by the large increase in the consumption of such wines. We cannot conclude without congratulating the various colonies which have sent wines to this Exhibition for the careful selection of the samples forwarded. It is to be regretted that France has not competed in this group. Germany is represented by one exhibitor only, and this one has taken the highest award. Of Tasmanian wines we have had only one exhibitor, Mr. William Ricketts, who produces from fruit grown in the island a most creditable beverage, for which we have awarded a first-class prize."

NEW SOUTH WALES.

MEMO.—The jurors have much pleasure in recording their full appreciation of the whole of the wines submitted from New South Wales. Their character is totally distinct from the South Australian wines the jurors tasted last week. The wines from the Hunter River district are exceptionally good—some of them being quite equal to French or German vintages. The sweet wines are rich, full-flavoured, and in excellent condition.

Lindeman, H. J., Cawarra. Full-bodied wines (red): Shiraz—First award Burgundy—Special first award; Madeira—First award. Light wines (white): Hock—Special first award, and Champion prize for all the Colonies; Reisling—First award; Chablis—First award. Light wines (red): Hermitage—Second award; Claret—Special first award; Burgundy—First award. Sweet wines, or vin de liqueur (white): Muscat—First award; Verdeilho—Special first award; Tokay—First award. Sweet wines, or vin de liqueur (red): Madeira—Special first award; Lachrymæ Christi—First award; Port—Special first award.

Harbottle, Allsop, and Co., Sydney. Light wines (red): "Ettamogah"—Second award. Light wines (white): "Ettamogah"—First award; Reisling—First award.

Fallon, J. T., Albury. Light wines (red): Burgundy—First award.

VICTORIA.

MEMO.—The jurors regret that some of the wines were out of condition; as a whole, however, the samples submitted were first class. The Clarets, Burgundy, and Hermitage were excellent; the sweet wines were good, sound articles; some of the Sherry wines, with age, will make their mark in the English markets.

Braché and Co., Melbourne. Chasselas—First award. Reisling—Special first award. Hock—First award. Claret, '88 vintage—First award. Claret, '86 vintage—Special first award, and Champion prize for all the Colonies. Carbinet—First award. Burgundy—Special first award. Verdeilho—Second award. Port—Special first award. Frontignac—First award.

Greer, E., and Co., Melbourne. Madeira—Second award. Port—First award. Shiraz—First award.

The Australian Wine and Fruit Agency Company Limited, Melbourne. Hermitage (grower, J. Hamilton, of Rutherglen)—First award as a sweet wine. Pedro (J. Hamilton, grower)—First award. Pedro (J. Hamilton) —Special first award. Sherry (grower, J. Thompson, of Dookie)—Special first award.

Wodonga Winegrowers' Association. Muscat (Martin Kelly, grower) —Special first award. White, full-bodied (P. Adams, grower)—First award. Dry old (same grower)—First award as a dry sherry. Light Red (James Tenner, grower)—Highly commended. Light Red (A. Schlink, grower)—Highly commended. Red light dry (G. S. Manns, grower)—Highly commended. Red light dry (same grower)—First award. Red light (A. Schlink, grower)—Special first award. The following were each highly commended as young wines:—James Tenner, Red light dry; Robert Peoples, dry full-bodied; A. Schlink, Red sweet; Robert Peoples, dry full-bodied Red.

Weigel, A., and Co., Limited, Melbourne. Australian champagne—Special first award.

SOUTH AUSTRALIA.

MEMO.—The jurors wish to record the fact that all the wines forwarded by South Australia are of a high class, exceptionally sound, and that there is a great future before the wine industry of that colony.

Cleland, G. F., and Co. Limited, Adelaide. Old Port wine—Special Champion prize for all the Colonies. Chablis—Second award. Reisling —First award. Sauterne—Second award as Madeira. Tokay—First award. Madeira—First award. Frontignac—Special first award. Constantia—First award. Very old Port—Special first award.

Adelaide Wine Company. Collection of wines—Special first award.

Auld, W. P., Adelaide. Claret—Special first award.

Crozier, H. and E., Oaklands, Adelaide. Sherry—First award. Port—First award.

Dunstan, H., and Co., Stonyfell, Adelaide. Sherry—Second award. Old Port—Special first award. Muscat—First award.

Foureur, J. H., Hindmarsh, Adelaide. Champagne—Special first award.

Hardy, Thos., and Sons Limited, Adelaide. Chablis—First award. Claret—Special first award. Angaston Port—First award. Very old Port—First award. Muscat—Second award.

Sage, S. and W., Angaston, Adelaide. Chablis—Highly commended. Claret—First award. Frontignac—First award. Sweet Constantia—Special first award, a first-class liqueur wine.

Scott, H. J., and Co., Adelaide. Chablis—First award. Reisling—Second award. Madeira—Special first for Davenport's Madeira. Frontignac—Special first award. Constantia—First award. Stonyfell Muscat—Special first and Champion prize against all the Colonies.

Smith, S., and Son, Angaston, Adelaide. Chablis—Special first award. Reisling—Special first award. Claret—Second award. Very old Sherry—Special first award. Frontignac—First award. Constantia—Special first award. Family Port—Second award. Very old Port—First award. Muscatel—Highly commended.

Young, E. B., and Co., Adelaide. Hock—Second award.

Tasmania.

Ricketts, William, Big Oyster Cove. Fruit wines, Tasmanian Port, Black Currant wine, Sherry wine, Apple wine—Special first award for the excellence and high condition of the exhibits, which are most creditable, and deserve the highest commendation.

Foreign Wines.

Still Wines.—Braumeberger—Special first award; Josefshofer—First award.

Sparkling Wines.—Scharlachberger, sparkling Moselle—First award; Moigneau Père et Fils, Epernay, France, Champagne—Special first award.

Champion Prizes.

The Wine Jury asked for the Special Prized wines to be submitted again for a Champion award, when the following result was obtained:—

Class 1—Light White Wine, Lindeman's Hock, New South Wales.
Class 2—Light Red Claret, Braché's Claret, Victoria.
Class 3—Full-bodied Red Wine, G. F. Cleland and Co. Limited, South Australia.
Class 4—Liqueur Wine, H. J. Scott and Co., South Australia.

Liqueurs.

Duhr and Co., German Wine Company, Cologne. Benecalo Punch—Special first award.

Seide and Co., Breslau. Assortment of liqueurs—Special first award.

Class LVII.—Beer.

Boag, James, and Son, Esk Brewery, Launceston. Tasmanian ales and stout, draught beer—First award. Bottled ale—Special first award. Bottled stout—Special first award. Bulk ale—Special first award. Hops—Special first award. Malt—First award.

Fawns, J. G. S., Cornwall Brewery, Launceston. Bottled ale—Special first award. Bottled stout—Special first award. Bulk beer—Special first award. Bulk ale (full body)—First award. Malt—Special first award. Hops—First award.

Abbott, W. H., Phœnix Brewery, Launceston. Ale in bottle—First award. Light running beer on draught—Second award. Ale on draught (good bitter)—First award.

Lindsay Brewery Company Limited, Orange, New South Wales. Bulk stout—Special first award. Bulk ale—First award.

Button, Charles S., Ellesmere. Bottled ale, strong XXX, light body—Highly commended.

Younger and Son, George, Alloa, Scotland. Bottled ales and stout, Revolver brand—Special first award.

Pearson, George, Richmond, Victoria. Bottled Victorian stout—First award.

White, Edward, and Co., Dublin Brewery, Richmond, Victoria. Pale ale—First award. Lager beer—Special first award. Stout—Second award, not being in condition. The above are all Victorian manufacture.

Ehrenfried Bros., Auckland. Stout in bulk—Special first award. Light ale in bottle—First award. Stout in bottle—Special first award.

Australian Brewery and Wine and Spirit Company, Sydney. Beer and stout in bulk and bottle—Special first award as a collective exhibit.

Toohey, J. T. J., Sydney. Ales and porters—First award as a collective exhibit.

Champion Prizes.

Boag, James, and Son, Launceston. Stout in bottle and ale in bulk—Champion prize for Tasmania.

Fawns, J. G. S., Launceston. Ale in bottle—Champion prize for Tasmania.

White, Edward, and Co., Richmond, Victoria. Victorian lager beer in bottle—Champion prize.

Ehrenfried Bros., Thames, Auckland. Light running ale in bulk not exceeding 22lb. gravity, stout in bulk and bottle—Champion prize against the whole of the Colonies.

Class LVII.—Fermented Drinks: Wines (still and sparkling), Beer, Cider, Perry, Brandy, Whisky, Gin, Liqueurs, etc.

Button, C. S., Ellesmere. Ginger wine—Hon. mention.

Class LVII.—Whisky and Brandy.

M'Nab, Andrew, and Co., Leith, Scotland. Galley brand old Highland whisky, in bottle—Second award. Galley brand old Highland whisky, in bulk—Special first award.

Scott, H. J., South Australia. G. R. Scott and Co.'s old Highland whisky, in bottle—First award.

Farrar, H. W., and Co., Melbourne. Greenlees Bros.' Claymore whisky, in bottle—First award.

Dewar, John, and Sons, Perth, North Britain. Old Highland whisky—Special first award.

Saunders, Herbert, Yardley. Dawson and Co.'s Claich Mohr fine old Highland whisky—Highly commended.

Delaage and Fils and Co., Cognac, France. Brandy—Special first award.

Duhr and Co. (German Wine Company), Cologne. Brandy—First award.

Irvine and McEachern, Launceston. Wines and spirits and oilmen's stores—First award for collective exhibit.

Coleman's Irish whisky—First award.

Class LVII.—Cordials.

Bosisto, J., and Co., Richmond, Victoria. Liquor eucalypto, an aromatic tonic and stomachic rarity—Special first award.

Ferguson, George Alfred, Excelsior Cordial Words, Dubbo, New South Wales. Aromatic quinine wine—Special first award. Orange bitters—Special first award. Peppermint—First award. Lime juice cordial—Special first award. Staughton bitters—Special first award. Pine-apple cordial—Special first award. Cloves cordial—Special first award. Lemon syrup—Highly commended. Ginger wine—Special first award. Raspberry syrup—First award. Sarsaparilla—Highly commended. Hop bitters—Highly commended.

Newball and Mason, Nottingham, England. Ginger wine extract, etc.—Highly commended. Wine essences, hop beers, etc.—Highly commended.

Todd, J. W., and Co. Limited, Melbourne. Lime juice—First award for Victoria. Collection of oilmen's stores manufactured by the exhibitors—Highly commended as a collective exhibit.

Cornwall Company, per Hatton and Laws. Lime juice cordials, raspberry syrup, cherry syrup—Highly commended.

Hatton and Laws, Launceston. Collection of summer fruit drinks—Special first award.

Abbott, Mrs. M. E., Phœnix Cordial Factory, Launceston. Dark bitters (tonic)—Special first award. Hop bitters (tonic)—Special first award. Cloves cordial—First award. Quinine wine cordial—Special first award. Peppermint cordial—Special first award. Raspberry vinegar—Special first award. Ginger brandy cordial—Second award. Ginger wine cordial—First award. Lemon syrup cordial—Second award. Sarsaparilla cordial—First award. Lime juice cordial—First award for Tasmania. Aerated hop ale—Special first award. Aerated dandelion ale—Special first award. Aerated hop beer—First award. Orange bitters—Second award. Collective exhibit—Special first award.

Button, Charles S., Ellesmere. Cordials—Hon. mention for collective exhibit. Hop bitters—Second award. Peppermint—Second award. Orange bitters—First award. Ginger brandy—First award. Lemon syrup—Special first award. Raspberry vinegar—Second award. Lime juice—Second award. Square sarsaparilla—Special first award. Cloves

—Special first award. Hop tonic—First award. Lemon squash—Highly commended. Sodawater—Highly commended. Ginger ale—Highly commended. Lemonade—Highly commended.

Thrower, W. I., Launceston. Cordials—First award as a collective exhibit.

Maconochie Bros., Lowestoft, England. Lime juice cordial—Special first award for Great Britain.

CHAMPION FOR THE COLONIES.

Ferguson, G. A., Excelsior Cordial Works, Dubbo, N.S.W. Lime juice cordial.

Class LVII.—Aerated Waters.

Evans, Sons, and Co. Limited, Liverpool. Raspberry cordial—Highly commended. Sarsaparilla cordial—First award.

Birmingham Vinegar Brewery Company, England. Holbrook's ginger beer powder—Special first award.

Maconochie Bros., Lowestoft, England. Lime juice—Special first award for Great Britain.

Button, Charles S., Ellesmere. Aerated waters—Highly commended as a collective exhibit.

Ungar and Son, Buda-Pesth. Bitter natural mineral water—Special first award. Victoria natural mineral water—Special first award. [The jurors strongly recommend these natural mineral and bitter waters to the notice of the medical profession.]

Thrower, W. I., Launceston. Aerated waters—First award as a collective exhibit. Egyptian bitters—Special first award. Peppermint—First award. Orange bitters—Special first award. Ginger brandy—Special first award. Lemon syrup—First award. Raspberry vinegar—First award. Cherry brandy—Special first award. Square sarsaparilla—Second award. Cloves—Second award. Ginger wine—Second award. Hop bitters—First award. Lime juice—Special first award. Hop beer—Special first award. Lemonade dash—Highly commended. Montserrat—Highly commended. Tangerine—Highly commended. Templar ale—Highly commended. Cider—First award. Lemon squash—Highly commended. Ginger punch—First award. Orange champagne—First award. Jargonelle pear—Highly commended. Pine-apple champagne—Highly commended. Lemonade—Highly commended. Sodawater—First award. Ginger ale—First award.

Erp, John, and Sons, Hobart. White and brown vinegar—Special first award. [The jurors make special note of its excellent quality.]

Idris and Co., London. Kolozine—First award. Ginger beer—Special first award for Great Britain. Ginger ale—Special first award for Great Britain. Olympic waters—First award. Mammoth waters—First award. Seltzer water—First award. Sodawater—Special first award for Great Britain. Potash—Special first award. Lithia water—Special first award. Lemonade—Special first award. Quinine tonic water—Special first award. [The jurors make special mention of the high quality of this tonic.] Mineral waters—Hon. mention as a collective exhibit.

Birmingham Vinegar Brewery Company, England. Holbrook's fruit salt—Special first award.

Hinds and Co., Coventry, England. Aerated waters—Hon. mention as a collective exhibit. Seltzer water—First award. Kolozine—First award. Ginger ale—Second award. Ginger beer—First award. Lemon squash—Highly commended.

Abbott, Mrs. M. E., Launceston. Syphons sodawater—Special first award. Syphons kali water—Special first award. Lemonade—Special first award. Ginger ale—Special first award. Sodawater—Special first award. Sarsaparilla—First award. Fruit champagne—Special first award. Kali water—Special first award. Syphon seltzer water—Special first award. Syphons lithia water—Highly commended.

CHAMPION PRIZE.

Abbott, Mrs. M. E., Launceston. Champion prize for sodawater against all other samples submitted.

CLASS LVIII.—Horticulture, Floriculture, Arboriculture, Flowers, etc.

Hurst Bros., Houndsditch, London. Vegetable seeds in glass bottles—Hon. mention. Grasses (natural) mounted—Hon. mention. Agricultural seeds in glass bottles—Hon. mention. Flower seeds in glass bottles—Hon. mention.

Newey, R., and Sons, Launceston. Collection of preserved vegetable models—Hon. mention. Collection of floral decorations—Hon. mention. Collection of garden syringes or pumps—Hon. mention.

Carter, Jas., and Co., High Holborn, London. Collection of English seeds, collection of preserved vegetables, roots, etc.—First award.

Newey, R., and Sons, Launceston. Collection of agricultural seeds, fertilisers, heating apparatus, handlights, preserved vegetables, roots, etc.—First award. Collection of grass and clover seeds—First award.

Hurst and Son, London. Collection of flower, vegetable, and agricultural seeds and garden requisites—Second award.

Sutton and Sons, Queen's seedsmen, Reading, England. Collection of horticultural seeds—Special first award. Collection of vegetables and roots, modelled from nature—First award. Collection of vegetable and flower seeds, showing the purity of the samples as supplied to the exhibitors' customers throughout the world—First award. Collection of agricultural seeds as exhibited in educational cabinet—First award. Sutton's seed germinators, literature, educational cabinet of grasses, flax in its various stages, knives and garden cutlery, hygrometer, fumigator, etc.—First award. Sutton's concentrated manure—First award. Natural grasses for permanent and temporary pastures—First award. Three cabinets of garden requisites—First award. Cabinet of garden cappers, including the Averruncator for pruning all trees—First award. Spray diffuser—First award. Garden syringes—First award. Garden tools—First award. Sutton's lawn mower—First award.

Keen, Robinson, and Bellville, London. Mustard seed—First award.

Canterbury Seed Company, Christchurch, New Zealand. English rye grass seed—First award. Red clover—First award. Cow grass and meadow fescue—First award. Cocksfoot grass seed—First award. [The above seeds were all grown in Canterbury, New Zealand.]

Yates, Richard A., Launceston. Ladies' sprays, buttonhole bouquets—First award.

REPORT OF THE SPECIAL JURY.

Having been appointed by the Commissioners to deal with the protests entered by discontented exhibitors, and also to adjudicate on any exhibits which had not been judged, or had been entered in wrong classes, we beg to report that we have completed our task, and submit our decisions as under :—

1. In the case of protests, two only could be entertained, being duly entered in conformity with the Rules and Regulations (17 and 18, page 23 of Catalogue).

2. One protest was entered by Messrs. Munnew and Co. against the award of H.C. to Messrs. Broadwood and Sons for a pianoforte, which the protest alleges had not been properly examined. At our suggestion an expert—Mr. Thornthwaite—was called. In our presence he examined all the instruments entered for competition in the same Class, and at his recommendation we have raised Broadwood's piano from H.C. to a First Class Special. Mr. Thornthwaite certifies that this instrument is by far the best in the Exhibition.

3. The other protest was in the Type-writing Machine Class. In this case we referred to the jurors who made the awards, and finding that they declined to alter their decision, promised to examine the whole of the exhibits critically ; and we have, after mature consideration, decided to award to the Yost typewriter a First Class Special for its perfect construction and simplicity of action.

4. In the New South Wales Court, amongst the mineral exhibits, we have raised the classification of the New South Wales shale and oil, the coke and calcinium paints, which we considered had been seriously underrated.

5. In the matter of Mr. Farrant's indiarubber exhibits, over which there has been unnecessary friction owing to that gentleman having from the outset acted in contravention with the rules, we called upon the jury appointed to judge the waterproof clothing (Messrs. Petterd and Room) to deal separately with that exhibit. After close inspection they awarded a First Class certificate for that exhibit, leaving it for another set of jurors to deal with the other indiarubber goods belonging to the same firm. Mr. Farrant failing to attend a summons, the jurors declined to act. We, therefore, had to take the matter in hand, and awards in this instance were made with the utmost care, and we trust that they will end this long-pending grievance.

6. The judging of wrongly classed exhibits and articles omitted or passed by the jurors, occupied the whole of last week. We are, however, glad to be able to report that our labours are now at an

end; the awards have been handed over to the Secretary, and we trust that the Commissioners will approve of the manner in which we have dealt with both the protests as well as the complaints lodged in the Office either verbally or by letter.

In conclusion, we beg to state that in all cases in which we have given redress the exhibitors have expressed to us their entire satisfaction.

(Signed) W. R. MARSH
E. WHITFELD
JULES JOUBERT, Chairman.

March 9, 1892.

MISCELLANEOUS EXHIBITS.

Petterd, W. F., Launceston. Design and erection of united silver trophy, and general arrangement of Mineral Court—Special first award.

Technological Museum, Sydney (T. H. Maiden, F.R.S., Curator). Scientific collection of New South Wales wool samples—Special first award.

Price's Patent Candle Company Limited, Battersea, London. Collection of artistic show cards—Second award.

Monds, T. W., and Son, Carrick. Trophy as a collective exhibit—Special first award.

Walch Bros. and Birchall, Launceston. "Walch's Handbook of Gardening for Tasmania"—First award.

Clausen, C., Hamburg. Pavement of iron and asphalt, duly registered and patented—Hon. mention. [The special jury regret that in the absence of a practical test being made they cannot give a higher award.]

Government Astronomer of New South Wales. Publications of scientific and astronomical observations—Special first award.

Munnew, A., Launceston. Pavilion made of Tasmanian woods—Hon. mention.

Cross, W., Liverpool. Water-colour painting descriptive of a naturalist's business—Hon. mention.

The Australasian—Special first award.

Canterbury Times, New Zealand. Copy of that journal—First award.

Town and Country Journal—First award.

The Queenslander—First award.

Publisher of *Bell's Weekly Messenger*. Copy of that journal—First award for Great Britain.

Publisher of *Farm, Field, and Fireside*. Copy of that journal—Hon. mention for Great Britain.

Publisher of *Mark Lane Express*. Copy of that journal—First award for Great Britain.

Sergeant, J. S., Sydney. Stain eradicator—Hon. mention.

White, R. P., Melbourne. Eradicator for removing stains—Hon. mention.

Federal cement—Hon. mention.

Huddart, Parker, and Co., Melbourne. Photographs of steamboats and saloons of same—First award.

Wacksmuth, R., Launceston. Samples of red-skinned potatoes—First award.

Walch Bros. and Birchall, Launceston. "Fenton's History of Tasmania"—Special first award.

Price's Patent Candle Company, London. Model of the "Statue of Liberty" in stearine—First award.

Blackman, J. Thomas. Samples of paint, colours, etc.—Special first award.

Braché and Co., Melbourne. Trophy and collective exhibit—Special first award.

Binney, Catherine, Footscray. Portraits, etc., collective exhibit—Special first award.

Swallow and Ariell, Melbourne. Trophy and collective exhibit—Special first award.

Newton, E. E., and Sons, Launceston. Pegless clothes line—Hon. mention.

Adams, Griffiths, and Dudley, Launceston. Model of geometrical staircase for public buildings—First award.

Deane and Sons, Launceston. Samples of grainings—Special first award.

Munnew, Arthur, Launceston. For introducing into England native blackwoods of Tasmania in the construction of high-class pianofortes and music stools—Special first award.

Evans, Sons, and Co., Liverpool. Montserrat lime fruit juice cordial —First award for Britain.

Carter, Jas., and Co., London. Collection of seed grain and specimens of natural grasses—First award.

Edwards, A. E., Hobart. Working model of double cylinder steam engine—First award.

Butler, W. H., and Co., Melbourne. Portable selectors' oven—First award.

Mikolay, Gustav, Vienna. Pipes and cigarette holders—First award.

REPORT OF THE CHAIRMAN OF JURORS.

To the Commissioners of the Tasmanian Exhibition.

GENTLEMEN,

I have the honour to report that the judging and awards has been practically concluded.

At the beginning of our labours I submitted to the juries the rules passed by the Commissioners for their guidance, and throughout their work the juries have implicitly followed the wishes of the Commissioners.

The selection of jurors in some instances proved to be a work of time and patience, partly owing to the fact that many of the persons elected declined to act for various reasons.

The total number of juries appointed was 50, and the number of jurors 101. We commenced our work on the 25th January, and completed it on the 18th March.

The exhibits were grouped alphabetically from A to H, but there were 59 classes to be adjudicated upon.

The total number of awards made is 1451, of which 398 are Special, 672 First, 126 Second, and 255 Highly Commended.

There were only two protests against the decision of the juries. These have been carefully investigated and satisfactorily adjusted.

A Special Jury was appointed to deal with exhibits which had been erroneously classified. This jury also has dealt with complaints which were not actual protests, but merely slight errors in the awards. In all such cases this jury has dealt fairly with the complainants, and has given entire satisfaction.

At the request of the Commissioners I have solicited and obtained from the juries separate prefatory reports, which will be found at the head of each of the groups.

It would be invidious to mention any particular exbibit; in fact, it would be difficult to say which of the Courts deserved the greatest credit.

The number of awards may be taken as a criterion of the excellence of the exhibits, and a careful perusal of the award list will be the best guide in this matter.

The valuable assistance I have received from the members of the various Juries, more especially from Messrs. Marsh, Whitfeld, and D. F. Scott, have materially lessened my work and responsibility.

I have the honour, etc.,

JULES JOUBERT,
Chairman of Juries.

THE CLOSING CEREMONY

Was performed by His Excellency the Governor on March 22nd, in the presence of a brilliant assemblage, comprising Cabinet Ministers, the Speaker of the House of Assembly, delegates to the Postal Conference, the Commandant, the Sheriff of Tasmania, the leading residents of Launceston, and a number of visitors from Hobart and the country districts.

The arrangements made by Mr. Joubert were, like all that gentleman's work, exceedingly complete. A dais had been erected opposite to the main entrance to the Albert Hall for the accommodation of the vice-regal party, and space was reserved immediately in front of it for those ladies and gentlemen possessing the right of private *entrée*, the season ticket-holders being also provided for, whilst the general public were seated in the galleries. The choir occupied the stage, the tasteful dresses of the lady members adding materially to the attractiveness or the scene.

Punctually at three o'clock His Excellency the Governor, accompanied by Lady Hamilton and Mr. Harry Hamilton, the Mayor (Mr. S. J. Sutton) wearing his official chain and robes, and the Mayoress, arrived, and was received by the Commissioners and the leading Exhibition officials. A guard of honour, composed of members of the Launceston Rifle Regiment, under Captain Sadler, with Lieutenant Burrows as subaltern, were drawn up on either side of the passage leading from the main entrance to the dais, where seats were provided for them. The following members of the Postal Conference, with ladies, were also accommodated with chairs on the dais:—Hon. John Kidd, M.P., and Mrs. Kidd, New South Wales; Hon. J. Gavan Duffy, M.P., and Mrs. and Miss Duffy, Victoria; Hon. Theodore Unmack, M.P., and Mrs. Unmack, Queensland; Mr. and Mrs. J. Smibert, Melbourne; Hon. Wm. Copley, M.P., Adelaide; Hon. R. A. Sholl, West Australia; Mr. S. H. Lampton, New South Wales; and Mr. T. C. Just, Secretary to the Conference; also the members of the Tasmanian Ministry, Hons. B. S. Bird, Treasurer; A. T. Pillinger, Minister of Lands; and A. I. Clark, Attorney-General; the Commandant, Colonel Warner; and the Staff-Adjutant, Major Wallack.

The hall was crowded, there being over 2000 present, including the Mayor of Hobart, Mr. T. A. Reynolds, with Aldermen G. Hiddlestone, G. S. Crouch, J. Baily, W. Smith, and J. W. Johnson, with the Town Clerk, Mr. W. H. Smith; the Aldermen of Launceston, hon. Adye Douglas, M.L.C., Messrs. H. Edgell, D. Scott, E. H. Panton, P. Barrett,

M.H.A., W. I. Thrower, H. J. Dean, and R. H. Price, and the Town Clerk, Mr. C. W. Rocher; and many of the leading citizens of Hobart and Launceston.

The interior of the hall presented a very brilliant and animated appearance, this effect, of course, being due, to a considerable degree, to the large attendance of ladies, without whom the imposing ceremony would have lost much of its interest. The dais upon which the vice-regal party were seated was tastefully draped and furnished, the surroundings being in keeping with the occasion. The Exhibition orchestra and choir mustered in force, and the assemblage altogether may be said to have been —save for the absence of representatives of H.M. Navy—on a par with that of the opening ceremony.

Upon the arrival of His Excellency, the regimental band played the National Anthem, and this was taken up by the orchestra and choir, the solos being rendered by Misses Ida Cox and Alice Grant.

The Executive Commissioner (Mr. S. J. Sutton) opened the proceedings by offering the following prayer :—

" Almighty God, the Creator and Preserver of all things in heaven and earth, we, the creatures of Thine hand, desire to render in all humility the homage due to Thee. We thank Thee for the gifts of understanding and knowledge by which Thou hast taught us to search and apply the wondrous products of the arts and industries of men for the ultimate benefit of Thy creatures. Accept, we beseech Thee, our heartfelt thanks and gratitude, especially at this time when we are about closing this great gathering from all nations in the midst of the people of this island. Subdue in us all pride and vanity for the great success we have achieved, and teach us so to labour and use the knowledge we have acquired through this Exhibition of the work and handicraft of mankind that we may ever after benefit by the same, and in so doing work out the purposes of Thy holy will. Kindle our brotherly affection and gratitude towards all those who have assisted us in this great undertaking. Extend Thy blessing and Divine protection on all those who are about to leave our shores to return to their distant homes. We offer unto Thee our praise and prayer for a continuance of the further progress and advancement of that knowledge and wisdom which have led to the achievements in skill, handicraft, and discoveries which have been displayed within these walls—beseeching Thee to accept and bless them to our use. Through Jesus Christ, our Lord, who, with Thee and the Holy Spirit, liveth and reigneth ever one God, world without end. Amen."

The choir then rendered in a very impressive manner Mr. Brunton Stephens' Australasian National Anthem.

The Executive Commissioner read the following address :—

" To His Excellency Sir Robert George Crookshank Hamilton, K.C.M.G.

" YOUR EXCELLENCY,

"We, the Commissioners for the Tasmanian Exhibition, desire once again to welcome you within these walls, and repeat to you, as the representative of Her Most Gracious Majesty, the assurance of our devoted loyalty to Her Majesty's crown and person.

"On the 25th of November last your Excellency was pleased to declare this Exhibition open to the public.

"For the warm interest manifested by your Excellency from the inception of the undertaking we have to express to your Excellency our deep gratitude.

"The Commissioners have much pleasure in stating that universal satisfaction was expressed by the Press and the public with all the arrangements in connection with the opening ceremony, the general working of the Exhibition, the jury work, and, indeed, everything in connection with this great undertaking.

"The duties of the Commissioners have been made easy, owing to the willing co-operation of the official and other representatives from Great Britain, the Continent of Europe, and the sister colonies, as well as the exhibitors from our own island.

"We are glad of an opportunity to tender here publicly our thanks to those gentlemen with whom it has been our privilege to come in contact, and with whom we have become better acquainted since the opening of this Exhibition. We hope that they will, one and all, carry with them to their distant homes a pleasing recollection of their stay in Tasmania. We also trust that eommercially they will reap the benefit of the connections they may have formed in this colony.

"One of the attractions of this Exhibition has been the music in the Albert Hall. We would fail in our duty if we omitted to thank the ladies and gentlemen of the choir, who, under the conductorship of Mr. A. Wallace, have done such good service.

"We have to record our recognition of the arduous work of the jurors who have awarded prizes in the several groups, with so much care and attention that the protests have been so few and so readily adjusted that we may justly say that the awards have given universal and unanimous satisfaction.

"The attendance from the day of opening to the closing numbers 243,000, which, taken as compared with the total population of this city (17,248), or that of Tasmania (146,667), compares more than favourably with the records of previous Exhibitions in any part of the globe.

"It is gratifying to state that amongst the visitors a fair number came from Europe, and a very large proportion from the sister colonies.

"Thanks to the liberality of the Government and of the chief of the Railway Department, arrangements were made by the railway for a very large number of our fellow-colonists from almost every part of the island, and nearly all the State-school children have had an opportunity of visiting the Exhibition.

"Financially, we think that the Tasmanian Exhibition will prove an exception to the general rule, and leave a balance in the hands of the Commissioners.

"Prior to calling on your Excellency to declare the Exhibition closed we beg to hand you the following list of awards which have been made, as under:—

Country.	Special First.	First.	Second.	Hon. mention.	Total.
Great Britain	113	210	12	28	363
France	4	13	—	2	19
Germany	11	6	—	2	19
Austria	7	6	1	2	16
Italy	—	3	—	—	3
Switzerland	—	1	—	—	1
United States	5	5	—	—	10
Victoria	70	133	20	37	260
New South Wales	40	34	11	12	97
South Australia	17	18	8	3	46
Queensland	4	3	—	1	8
New Zealand	14	22	6	6	48
Tasmania	113	218	68	162	561
Total	398	672	126	255	1451

His Excellency, in reply, said:—Commissioners of the Tasmanian International Exhibition: Before declaring this Exhibition closed in accordance with your desire, I wish to express my high appreciation of the labours of those gentlemen upon whom the conduct of it has devolved, and to congratulate all concerned upon the wonderful success this Exhibition has attained. (Cheers.) Undertakings of this sort have become an important factor in this age of progress, and I join with you in the hope that the community of Tasmania will reap substantial benefit from the Tasmanian International Exhibition of 1891-92. (Cheers.) I rejoice to hear that everything connected with this Exhibition has been so satisfactory, and that such ready and efficient help has been afforded to the undertaking by all connected with it, as well as by the Press, who have given to its proceedings the prominence they deserve. Having regard to the population of Launceston and of Tasmania generally, the number of admissions is, I believe, unprecedentedly numerous, and your anticipation that this great undertaking will not only be accompanied by no financial loss, but that a substantial balance will remain in the hands of the Commissioners, is matter for the greatest congratulation. (Cheers.) I now declare this Exhibition closed.

His Excellency then resumed his seat amidst cheers.

The official representatives of the various countries exhibiting occupied seats on the left side of the dais, and at the conclusion of the addresses and reply they were called upon by His Excellency to receive the declaration of awards in the following order :—Great Britain, Mr. Arthur Day; France, M. Victor Laruelle; Germany, Austria, and Italy, Herr Bossomaier; Victoria, Mr. D. Fergus Scott; New South Wales, Mr. H. B. Hardt; South Australia, Mr. F. Notley Meadows; Queensland, Mr. Louis Saber; New Zealand, Mr. F. Notley Meadows; Tasmania, Mr. Alex. Morton. Switzerland and the United States were not represented.

As each representative stepped to the dais to receive the awards he was accorded a cordial round of applause, considerable enthusiasm being manifested at the appearance of Mr. Arthur Day and Mr. D. Fergus Scott.

"The Old Hundredth," sung by the choir, brought the proceedings to a close. It may be added that the singing was excellent throughout, and that Mr. A. Wallace as usual conducted, Miss Frost presiding at the organ.

THE BRITISH "AT HOME."

On the evening of the closing date Mr. Arthur Day, the Official Agent for Great Britain, gave an "At Home" in the building. The Court was closed to the public, and was adorned with choice flowers and fairy lights, whilst tables laden with light refreshments were placed in various parts of the room—for the space, with its nicely-grouped chairs and sparkling ornaments, really resembled a drawing-room. The names of the guests were announced as they entered the Court, and the guests were received by the genial host with that cordiality with which he always greets his visitors. The popularity of the Official Agent for Great Britain was testified to by the number of ladies and gentlemen who accepted his invitation, amongst whom were His Excellency the Governor and Lady Hamilton, Cabinet Ministers of Tasmania and the Colonies, the Executive Commissioner, the Official Agents for Austria, Germany, France, Victoria, New South Wales, and New Zealand, Mr. Ford (representing the New South Wales Department of Mines), and the leading citizens of Launceeton. A string band played musical selections in the early part of the evening, and later on the services of St. Joseph's Band were engaged. The "At Home" was in every respect a thorough success. It opened with a hearty British welcome, and closed with a cordial greeting from one who has made many friends in this city.

At the termination of the "At Home," the Mayor called for three cheers for Mr. Day, which were very heartily given, the building echoing again and again with the tribute of respect and warm feeling shown to the British representative. After this the good old chorus "He's a jolly good fellow" was given.

Mr. Arthur Day, in acknowledging the compliment, said that he was exceedingly glad to have been present at the Tasmanian International Exhibition. He had made many new friends while he had been in Launceston, and he had renewed his acquaintance with many he had met in Melbourne, Sydney, Adelaide, and Dunedin. To all those friends he extended his most hearty thanks for the kindly courteousness they had displayed towards him. He had spent a pleasant time while in Tasmania. There might be some people here who considered he "pushed" Great Britain too much—(cries of "No, no! It is our mother country!")—but he would, wherever he was, endeavour to forward the interests of that dear land, and unless he in his position as its representative came first in connection with exhibitions he would not go at all. England was justly proud of the little colony in which he was at present representing her. She knew that the resources of the island were great, and that her people were right loyal subjects of Her Majesty the Queen. Some insignificant and ill-advised people in the Colonies endeavoured to raise the cry of separation from the mother land—(interjections of "No, never!")—but that could never be, for if they ever seriously attempted such a course they must sink. He would like all to be unanimous in wishing to keep Great Britain and her dependencies united as one whole nation, with the same sympathies and destiny. The standard of Great Britain could not be lowered, and they, as subjects, should do all in their power to maintain its historic glory. In conclusion, he again thanked those from whom he had received so many kindnesses in Launceston.

THE MAYORAL PICNIC.

The official closing of the Tasmanian International Exhibition formed the occasion of an exceedingly pleasant picnic at Denison Gorge on March 23rd, when 161 guests assembled at the invitation of the Mayor, Mr. S. J. Sutton, M.H.A. A special train left the Launceston railway station at eleven o'clock, and arrived at its destination a couple of hours later, having made a short stay at one of the wayside stations, where the fragrant weed was distributed to smokers amongst the party. A large marquee had been erected at the Gorge, and was tastefully decorated with flags and evergreens, whilst a *recherche* luncheon was spread beneath its shelter. Denison Gorge is a romantic spot, and the minds of those present could not but contrast the present with the past, and speculate upon the surprise which the pioneer residents of the district would have experienced at seeing tables laden with choice viands at the Denison Gorge. The catering was all that could be desired; indeed, it was in keeping with the reputation for princely hospitality which Mayor Sutton has acquired. His Worship was untiring in his endeavours to promote the pleasure and comfort of his guests, and was ably assisted by the Town Clerk, Mr. C. W. Rocher, to whose excellent arrangements much of the success of the gathering must be attributed.

Very soon after the arrival of the train the guests sat down to partake of the good things provided.

The chair was occupied by Mayor Sutton, who had on his right the Treasurer (Hon. B. S. Bird), Attorney-General (Hon. A. I. Clark), Minister of Lands (Hon. A. T. Pillinger), Mr. P. Barrett, M.H.A., and Mr. Henry Button; and on his left the Mayor of Hobart (Mr. Reynolds), the Speaker of the House of Assembly (Hon. N. J. Brown), Hon. Adye Douglas, and Hon. W. Dodery, M.L.C.

After ample justice had been done to the viands,

The Mayor proposed the usual loyal toasts, "The Queen," "The Prince and Princess of Wales," and "His Excellency the Governor"—who was unavoidably absent—and made feeling reference to the recent royal bereavement. The toasts were loyally honoured.

Mr. H. Button proposed "The Ministry." In doing so he said under the British Constitution the Sovereign, the Lords, and the Commons had to form the laws; but Gladstone had told them that a fourth estate had grown up, and that was the Ministry, who were charged with the responsibility of seeing that the laws were duly carried out, that the subordinate departments were worked properly, and to endeavour by every possible means to advance the interests of the country, and to advise measures for the achievement of these advantages. In some of the British Colonies lately—Canada especially—there had been an amount of corruption that had brought discredit upon some of their institutions; certainly upon the Administration in Canada; but it had never been the misfortune of Tasmania, throughout all the changes of Administration, to record anything approaching what had occurred there; and he thought that they could all give the Government of the day credit ¦for having acted according to the best of their judgment. (Cheers.) It was necessary that opinions should differ, for a conflict of opinion generally led to bringing out the truth—(hear)—and Tasmania had had the good fortune to have a succession of Ministries who had certainly not brought disgrace upon the colony. (Cheers.) There were very often outside influences which were prejudicial to the administration of the law. Personal interests were sometimes antagonistic to the general interests of the community, and it was possible to take advantage of the "powers that be" to carry them out; but he thought they had very little to complain of in that respect, and he was quite sure that their population would continue to maintain that vigilance in regard to the administration of the affairs of the country which, he believed, had had a great deal to do with their present position. (Cheers.) Mill said "The price of liberty is eternal vigilance." Whatever confidence they might have in the Ministry, however they might admire them, they must watch them—(a voice: "We do")—and watch others outside as well. (Hear.) He thought the present Ministry had really played a very important and successful part in our little politics, and at any rate in the great event which had brought them together to-day—the celebration of the close of the Tasmanian International Exhibition, which owed a considerable amount of its success to the assistance afforded by the Ministry of the day. They had required a little pressure, no doubt—(Hear, hear, and laughter)—but it was their duty to require pressure. If every project that human ingenuity could devise were to receive aid from the Treasury by merely proposing it they would be involved in endless expenditure. Holding these views he had great pleasure in proposing "The health of the Ministry."

The toast was enthusiastically drunk, the company singing "For they are jolly good fellows."

The Treasurer (Hon. B. S. Bird), who was received with loud and continued cheering, in responding to the toast, expressed regret that his hon. colleague the Premier (Hon. P. O. Pysh) was not present, for, knowing the flights of eloquence into which he could rise, he (Mr. Bird) felt at a disadvantage. However, he had to thank them, and he did thank them, on behalf of the Ministry, very heartily for the very kind way in which the toast had been received, and would endeavour to cut his remarks, as his colleague, the Premier, always did, very short. (Laughter.) They were supposed to be celebrating the funeral of the Tasmanian International Exhibition. (Cries of "No, there is a big kick in it yet.") Well, there were evidently believers in resurrection, but in what form the Exhibition was going to live after its closing he did not know. However, they were celebrating the official closing, and they all felt that it had been prosperous. Many in Hobart had looked forward with a large amount of interest to the opening, and many doubted whether it would be a success, but all were gratified to see that the attendance had been good, and the efforts of the Commissioners had been so successful, and the show what it ought to have been. (Cheers.) Indeed, they all felt that it had exceeded their most sanguine anticipations. He was wondering what the Commissioners were going to do with the surplus. (A voice: "Give it to the Treasurer.") He was trying to remember whether the Government had paid over the whole of the £4000 that Parliament had so generously voted for the Exhibition. There was to be a surplus of some £2000—(a voice: "£3000")—and the Mayor was very reticent about this sum. But he had been giving him some advice concerning it. There was a lot of depression in some of the colonies at the present time, and he could hardly hope, sanguine as he was in most things, to do without "putting on the screw," as Treasurer, and a thousand or two would be acceptable from the surplus —(a voice: "Don't you wish you may get it?" and laughter)—if the Mayor, with his well-known generosity, would hand it over. (Laughter.) For the very kind things that had been said of the Ministry he—and he was sure he spoke for his colleagues—was very grateful. He thought it might be said that all the Ministries who had held office in the colony had endeavoured honestly and earnestly to do their best for the colony, and trusted that the time was far distant when men would hold office who would be actuated by any other motives. (Cheers.) As for the present Ministry, they all knew that they administered the laws so well that nothing was ever said against them; they did all things so well, —even down to the minor details of customs in relation to customs. (Laughter.) It was a good thing that the Ministry had a watchful Opposition, both in the Parliament and the Press, and he always tried to profit by fair criticism, and tried to show it up if it was not fair. (Hear, hear.) He concluded by expressing the hope that the Government would profit by past experience, and that in the present Ministry the people of this colony had a Government in whom they might worthily place their confidence. (Cheers.)

Mr. Alex. Webster (one of the Commissioners) proposed the toast of "The Parliament of Tasmania." As treasurer of the Exhibition, he said he would know pretty clearly where the money was going before he signed a cheque. (Laughter.) He thought the Parliament of Tasmania would bear very favourable comparison with those of the adjoining colonies. They had their "ins and outs," and those who were out did all they possibly could to change places with those who were fortunate enough to be in, and so Parliament ran on. There were many who criticised their Parliament, and sometimes the criticism was deserved, but he thought members were entitled to their thanks for the services they had rendered to the colony. Alluding to the Exhibition, he paid a tribute to the Mayor, who had taken so active a part in it, and to all those who had assisted in making it the most successful Exhibition in the colonies. He was sure that the Government would be recouped for the amount of money they had advanced, and that the country generally would derive immense benefit from the Exhibition. (Cheers.)

The Hon. Wm. Dodery briefly responded on behalf of the Legislative Council.

The Hon. Nicholas Brown (Speaker of the House of Assembly) in responding on behalf of that body expressed his thanks for the manner in which the toast had been received. They had often been told, he said, that Parliament was what the people made it; but while that was pertectly true, it was only a half truth, for Parliament was very much what members themselves made it. (Hear, hear.) So long, however, as they recognised the truths and doctrines which underlaid the constitution, then Parliamentary institutions would be a success, and as far as Tasmania was concerned, it would, as Mr. Webster had said, bear favourable comparison with other colonies. Where they had failed it was owing to a want of recognition of the laws of the foundation of the Constitution. He alluded to the work done by the present Ministry, and passing on to the Exhibition expressed the opinion that its good results would be felt for many years. One of the results, it was hoped, would be the removal of the restrictions which had been gradually built up against each other's commerce. With regard to the Mayor of Launceston, when the future historian of Tasmania recorded the events of 1891-92, amongst the names of those who had done good service to the country would be that of Samuel J. Sutton. (Loud and continued cheering.) He again thanked them for the way in which the toast had been honoured, and wished the Exhibition a successful issue. (Cheers.)

The Hon. Adye Douglas proposed "The Municipal Institutions throughout Tasmania," and in doing so alluded to the great amount of good derived by the people from Municipal government, and the assistance the various Councils, Trusts, and Boards were to the Parliament. At the same time he would like to see the system extended in Tasmania, so that the people would better understand the power they possessed having a voice in the election of members of Parliament. The toast was enthusiastically drunk.

The Mayor of Hobart (Mr. T. A. Reynolds), in responding, alluded to the criticisms to which members of Municipal Institutions and Parliament were subjected, and expressed the opinion that although complaints were made of the taxies levied, the results of the Corporation expenditure were sufficient return for the money paid by the citizens in this form.

Hon. A. I. Clark (Attorney-General) proposed the health of the Commissioners of the Tasmanian International Exhibition. He had not the pleasure of being present at the opening, but was pleased at witnessing the ceremony which took place at the close of a career of success. He believed the Commissioners had done the whole colony good—a good which would be felt outside the colony. The Exhibition had effectually removed the slur cast upon Tasmania by people who called it "Sleepy Hollow," for it had shown that its people could do as well as any others, and perhaps better. (Cheers.) One particular feature of the Exhibition was that the Commissioners exactly measured what could be done—they had not fallen into contempt by making it too small, nor had they brought about a *fiasco* by attempting too much. The Exhibition would be long remembered in the history of the colony, and the Commissioners also, who had rendered a national service.

The Mayor, who was received with cheers, in responding, said the Commissioners had adapted themselves to circumstances. But they owed a very great debt to several factors—the principal of which was the Municipal Council, who had built the Albert Hall, without which the Exhibition could not have succeeded—(hear)—the next was the fact that the Tasmanian Government had contributed £4000 towards the object, and he believed that from the Premier downwards the Parliament were satisfied with the result of their liberality, for the Commissioners had done their best, and the result financially and otherwise was good. (Hear.) He was one of those who expected great results from the Exhibition, both in this and the other colonies—(cheers)—and, moreover, it would stimulate the southern capital to hold a similar Exhibition in future years. (Hear.) The results of the Exhibition would not only be enjoyed by themselves, for some of them would soon shuffle off this mortal coil, but by their children, who would reap the full advantage. His brother Commissioners had also been stimulated by the same idea. They had played their little game, and let them hope there were better things to follow. If there were any dissatisfied people in the community let them ask themselves if it was possible that a body of less than a quarter of a million of people could carry out such an institution without good results following? (Cheers.)

Mr. Jules Joubert (General Manager) who, in rising to respond, was received with loud and continued cheering, said he had been nine or ten months in Launceston, having come at the solicitation of his friend Mr. Sutton, and at the suggestion, when he was in Dunedin, of his friend Mr. A. Barrett. He had always been told that Tasmania was a little paradise, and after ten months residence he must tell them that he had travelled the world over and never was in a country more charming, both in regard to climate and people. Certainly the people were sometimes slow to move, but when they did move it was for a good purpose. It was a matter for wonder how warmly the Commissioners had plunged into the project for the Exhibition. They did not join the eight hours movement, but had worked many hours a day; and though he had been connected with forty-seven exhibitions, he had never seen one so successful as that which had just closed. (Cheers.) It was successful, in the first instance, because wisdom had selected for it a site which, geographically, was the most acceptable in the colony, being easily accessible to the larger sister colonies; and then it was carried out by earnest men whose hearts were in the right place. (Cheers.) As the chairman had told them, the Corporation had erected a magnificent building, which for years to come would be an ornament to the city;

and as for the money they had borrowed—for it was really borrowing—it had been returned, for the Treasurer would find that the increase of traffic on the railways and the increase of revenue from the Customs duties would amply repay the Government. (Hear, hear.) Moreover, the extension of the trade of the colony with the world at large would be a great benefit to the Treasurer. They knew that a great many visitors had taken an interest in the mining industry, and he believed that nine-tenths of the money realised by some of those who were connected with the Exhibition had been invested in mining in the colony. The views of the people had been expanded, and the results of the Exhibition, far from dying out, would remain a permanent benefit to the colony. As for himself, he had not benefited pecuniarily largely, but he had benefited in having made a large number of staunch friends, and when he left Tasmania the list of his friends would be largely increased. There were some people could regret him, and he asked whom on earth the statesman—he meant the *Democrat*, and all democrats thought they were statesmen—would have to abuse when he had gone. That was not a *lapsus linguæ*, and he would like to have the *Democrat* sent to him after he left the colony, because *qui bene amat bene castigat*—if it did not like him it would not chastise him. (Laughter and cheers.)

The Hon. A.T. Pillinger (Minister of Lands), in an appropriate speech, proposed the health of the Mayor, alluding in happy terms to the fact that much of the success of the Exhibition was due to that gentleman's energy.

The Mayor briefly returned thanks.

Mr. Peter Barrett proposed the toast of "The Exhibitors and Visitors," and in doing so alluded in flattering terms to the visiting representatives, and to the excellent taste which had been displayed in the arrangement of the products of the various countries. He referred to the difficulty which had existed in the primary negotiations in connection with the Exhibition, and said when the Ministry were approached first they were the most unbelieving set that he had ever met with. (Laughter). However, they had redeemed their reputation, and he was glad that all had ended well.

The toast was cordially honoured.

Mr. D. Fergus Scott responded, and regretted that Mr. Arthur Day and the representatives of foreign countries, South Australia, New Zealand, and New South Wales were absent. On behalf of Victoria he returned hearty thanks for the manner in which the company had honoured the toast, and in a few happy remarks referred to the pleasant relations which had always existed between the exhibitors and the Commissioners, and hoped that the Exhibition would more closely federate the colonies.

Mr. H. Nicholls (editor of the Hobart *Mercury*) also responded, and referred to the fact that when he was approached by the Executive Commissioner to give his support to the Exhibition he had consented to do so, and done so without any jealousy as to North and South. (Cheers.) He was present to offer his congratulations upon the success of the Exhibition, and not to speak paltry nonsense of North or South. The success of the Exhibition had been splendid; they had accomplished more than he could have believed possible under the most favourable circumstances, and he congratulated them heartily upon it. (Cheers.)

Mr. A. Barrett proposed the toast "The Ladies," and in doing so accorded a graceful and happy tribute to the Lady Mayoress (Mrs. S. J. Sutton).

Hon. H. I. Rooke appropriately responded.

The remaining toasts were "The Press," proposed by Mr. John Henry, M.H.A., responded to by Mr. Ronald W. Smith (*Launceston Examiner*), Mr. J. W. McWilliams (*Daily Telegraph*), Mr. H. Nicholls (Hobart *Mercury*), and Mr. Sharpe (*Democrat*), and "The Host" (Mayor Sutton).

Luncheon over, the visitors divided themselves into parties, and strolled up the Gorge until the bell sounded for the return trip, but before taking their seats in the train their thoughtful host had provided tea and biscuits for their delectation. The weather, which was somewhat threatening in the morning, did not fulfil the apprehensions which were entertained, the clerk, no doubt, feeling that when the sun of prosperity had beamed so continuously on the Tasmanian International Exhibition it would be bad taste on his part to throw a damper on its concluding incident. The special left the Gorge at 5·15 p.m., and reached the terminal station at 7 p.m., and the hearty cheers which the guests, when they alighted upon the platform, tendered to the ·Mayor and Mayoress constituted a compliment as well deserved as it was hearty and spontaneous.

AGRICULTURAL & HORTICULTURAL SHOW.

On April 1 and 2 an Inter-Tasmanian Agricultural and Horticultural Show was held in the Exhibition building, which resulted in the best and most comprehensive display yet made in the colony. The southern societies and residents, notably Mr. C. E. Davies, Secretary to the Tasmanian Pastoral and Agricultural Association, entered heartily into the project, and contributed largely to the success which fittingly crowned the career of the Exhibition.

The following were the judges :—

GROUPS A. and B.—CEREALS, GRASS and OTHER FARM SEEDS.—Messrs. S. J. Sutton, E. Gaunt, G. P. Hudson.

GROUP C.—ROOTS.—Messrs. E. H. Sutton, sen., D. Burke, James Lamont.

GROUPS D., E., and G.—VEGETABLES, FRUIT, HOPS, and HORTICULTURAL.—Messrs. Box, Stewart, T. Wade, Robertson, M. E. Robinson, E. Whitfeld.

DAIRY PRODUCE.—Messrs. — Johnston, sen. (Hobart), R. Douglas Harris, W. R. Marsh.

POULTRY.—Messrs. George Padman, W. McElwee, H. Heald.

DOGS.—Messrs. T. H. Bosworth, T. Carr, H. Weedon.

GROUP I.—MACHINERY.—Messrs. A. Webster, Wm. Luck, Jas. Scott.

APICULTURE.—Messrs. W. Smith and S. Bendall.

TASMANIAN EXHIBITION, 1891-92. 127

PRIZE LIST.

Group A.—CEREALS.

Winter Wheat—First prize, £2; second, £1. T. W. Monds and Son, Carrick, 2½ bushels, grown by John Friend, Glenore, 67¼lb., 1; W. H. D. Archer, Brickendon, Longford, Braemar Velvet, 65½lb., 2; York, Schmidt, and Company, Sheffield, Kentishbury, Boutcher's Velvet, grown by George Morris, 64½lb., H.C.

Spring Wheat—First prize, £2; second, £1. T. W. Monds and Son, 3½ bushels, grown by John Hall, Blshopsbourne, 69½lb., 1; R. Newey and Sons, Launceston, 1 bag, 68lb., 2.

Wheat in sheaf, 6 sheaves—First prize, £1. York, Schmidt, and Co., Boutcher's Velvet, grown by Messrs. C. and W. Banfield, 68lb., 1.

Chevalier Barley—First prize, £1. W. F. B. French, Glenore, 60lb.

English Barley—First prize, £1. R. Newey and Sons.

Cape Barley—First prize, £1; second, medal. R. Newey and Sons, 1 bag, 1; W. H. D. Archer, from half an acre of land, yield 32 bushels, 2.

Tartarian Oats—First prize, £1. R. Newey and Sons.

Milling Oats, any variety, name of oats to be stated—First prize, £1; second, medal. T. W. Monds and Son, 54½lb., 1; J. Scott and Son, Leith Mill, River Forth, 52½lb., 2; York, Schmidt, and Co., Sheffield, Kentishbury, grown by Mr. A. G. Peart, 53¾lb., H.C.

Oats in sheaf, 6 sheaves—First prize, £1; second, certificate of merit. York, Schmidt, and Company, Sheffield, Kentishbury, grown by David Hope.

Rye—Prize, medal. R. Newey and Sons, 2.

Golden Tares—Prize, medal. R. Newey and Sons, 1; A. Harrap and Son, Cameron Street, 2.

Grey Tares—Prize, medal. R. Newey and Sons.

Grey Peas—Prize, medal. W. F. B. French, Glenore, 1; York, Schmidt, and Co., grown by John Hope, 2; R. Newey and Sons, H.C.

Dun Peas—Prize, medal. R. Newey and Sons, 1; A. Harrap and Son, 2.

' Any other Cereal, not otherwise enumerated—Prize, medal. Henry Williams, Hillside, Ulverstone, 1 bag white peas, 1; F. W. Briggs, Scottsdale, bag of Johnson's Wonderful beans, 1 and 2; R. Newey and Sons, bag blue peas, H.C.

Flour (Roller), 1 sack, from Tasmanian wheat—First prize, £2; second, £1. John Luck and Co., West Devonport, 1; T. W. Monds and Son, 2; Thomas Affleck and Son, Longford, H.C.

Oatmeal, 1 cwt.—First prize, £1; second, medal. T. W. Monds and Son, 1; J. Scott and Son, 2.

Rolled Oats, 1 cwt.—First prize, £1. T. W. Monds and Son.

Pearl Barley, 1 cwt.—First prize, £1. T. W. Monds and Son.

Milling Wheat, 1 sack.—Special prize by Daniel Archer, Esq., Longford Hall, £1 1s.—W. H. D. Archer.

1 bushel White Wheat, 1 bushel Tartarian Oats, 1 bushel Cape Barley, 1 bushel Italian Grass Seed—shown collectively, and grown in Tasmania—Special prize, by George F. Thirkell, Esq., Darlington Park, £1 1s. R. Newey and Son, Launceston.

Extra.—A. Harrap and Son, Cameron Street, Launceston, blue peas.

Group B.—GRASS SEEDS AND OTHER FARM SEEDS.

English Rye Grass Seed—First prize, 10s.; second, medal. R. Newey and Sons, 1; A. Harrap and Son, 2.

Italian Rye Grass Seed—First prize, 10s.; second, medal. John Langdon, Eskavillaton, King's Meadows, 1 and 2.

Cocksfoot Grass Seed—First prize, 10s.; second, medal. R. Newey and Sons, 1; F. W. Briggs, 2.

Meadow Fescue Grass Seed—First prize, 10s. R. Newey and Sons.

Timothy Grass Seed—First prize, 10s. R. Newey and Sons.

Prairie Grass Seed—First prize, 10s.; second, medal. A. Harrap and Son, 1; R. Newey and Sons, 2.

Rib Grass Seed—First prize, 10s. R. Newey and Sons, 1 and 2.

White Clover Seed—First prize, 10s.; second, medal. R. Newey and Sons, 1 and 2.

Red Clover Seed—First prize, 10s.; second, medal. R. Newey and Sons, 1 and 2.

Hop Clover Seed—First prize, 10s.; second, medal. R. Newey and Sons.

Lucerne Seed—First prize, 10s. R. Newey and Sons.

Trefoil—First prize, 10s.; second, medal. R. Newey and Sons.

Any species of grass or Clover Seed not otherwise enumerated—First prize, 10s.; second, medal. R. Newey and Sons, 1 bag Cow Grass Clover, English, 1; R. Newey and Sons, 1 bag Hungarian Forage Grass, 2; R. Newey and Sons, 1 bag Alsyke Clover, English, H.C.

Canary Seed—First prize; 10s. R. Newey and Sons.

Hemp Seed—First prize, 10s. R. Newey and Sons.

Rape Seed—First prize, 10s. R. Newey and Sons.

Linseed—First prize, 10s.; second, medal. Hatton and Laws, 1 and 2; R. Newey and Sons, H.C.

Meadow Soft Grass. R. Newey and Sons.

Collection of Agricultural Seeds—Prize, £1. R. Newey and Sons.

Extra.—Thomas Affleck and Son, Longford, Digestive Meal.

Group C.—ROOTS.

Long Mangolds, 6—First prize, 10s.; second, medal. W. E. Shoobridge, 1; J. Marshall, Strath, Hagley, 2.

Yellow Globe Mangolds, 6—First prize, 10s.; second, medal. R. Newey and Sons, 1 and 2; W. E. Shoobridge, H.C.

Swede Turnips, 6—First prize, 10s.; second, medal. J. Woolnough, Evandale Junction, 1; York, Schmidt, and Co., grown by Joseph Cox, area under crop 2 acres, average yield 10 tons, 2.

Field Carrots, 1 sack—First prize, 10s.; second, medal. W. E. Shoobridge, 1; R. Newey and Sons, 2.

Garden Carrots, 1 sack—First prize, 10s.; second, medal. W. E. Shoobridge, 1; W. Ling, 2 and H.C.

Parsnips, 1 sack—First prize, 10s.; second, medal. W. E. Shoobridge, 1; J. Marshall, 2; J. H. Huett, Harbourne, near Elizabeth Town, H.C.

Onions, 1 sack—First prize, 10s.; second, medal. W. Ling, 1 and 2; R. Hall, H.C.

Potatoes, 1 sack—First prize, 10s.; second medal. James A. Fogg, Ulverstone, 1 bag "Redskin," grown on 12 acres, digging 6 tons of marketable potatoes, 1; John Lade, St. Mary's, H.C.

Potatoes, collection 3 varieties, 1 sack of each—First prize, £1; second, 10s. York, Schmidt, and Co., Kentishbury, grown by E. Sullivan, 2; F. Rees, H.C.

Turnips and Chicory—First prize, 10s.; second, medal. W. E. Shoobridge.

Collection or Trophy of Roots, not less than 6 sorts—First prize, £1. W. E. Shoobridge.

Group D.—VEGETABLES AND HOPS.

Cabbage, 3 heads—First prize, 5s.; second, Certificate of Merit. W. E. Shoobridge, 1; F. Walker, 2.

Red Cabbage, 3 heads—First prize, 5s.; second, Certificate of Merit, W. E. Shoobridge, 1; W. McOrmond, 2.

Cauliflower, 3 heads—First prize, 5s. W. E. Shoobridge.

Peas, half peck—First prize, 5s. Frank Walker and Co., H.C.

French Beans, 3lb.—First prize, 5s. F. Walker, 2.

Runner Beans, 3lb.—First prize, 5s. W. Ling.

Celery, 3 heads—First prize, 5s.; second, Certificate of Merit. W. Ling, 1; Frank Walker and Co., 2.

Vegetable Marrows, 3—First prize, 5s.; second, Certificate of Merit. Frank Walker, 1; W. Ling, 2; Charles Wathen, H.C.

Pumpkin, 1—First prize, 5s.; second, Certificate of Merit. Robert Headlam, Vaucluse, Conara, 1; Frank Walker, 2; W. E. Shoobridge, H.C.

Lettuce, 3—First prize, 5s.; second, Certificate of Merit. Frank Walker, 1; W. E. Shoobridge, 2.

Tomatoes, 3lb.—First prize, 5s.; second, Certificate of Merit. Wm. Ling, 1 and 2.

Spinach, half peck—First prize, 5s.; second, Certificate of Merit. Frank Walker.

Any other Culinary Vegetable not otherwise enumerated—First prize, 5s.; second, Certificate of Merit. R. Newey and Sons, 1 and 2.

Collection of Vegetables, 8 sorts—First prize, £1; second, 10s. W. E. Shoobridge, 1; Wm. Ling, 2; Frank Walker, V.H.C.; Sutton and Son's collective exhibit, First-class Certificate of Merit; F. Abbot, Hobart, Certificate of Merit.

Hops, 1 bale—First prize, £2; second, £1. C. E. Knight and Co., Dunn Street, Hobart (1892, H. Nicholson), 1; T. Nicholson, jun., 2; Rufus Jeffry, 3.

Group E.—FRUIT.

Apples, Culinary, soft, 1 plate of 5 Apples—First prize, 10s.; second, medal. Frank Walker, 1; George Wm. Salier, Vine Grove, Scottsdale, 2; J. N. Palmer, Bagdad, Com.

Apples, Culinary, keeping, 1 plate of 5 apples—First prize, 10s.; second, medal. Dr. Benjafield, Hobart, 1; C. G. H. Lloyd, Bryn Estyn, New Norfolk, 2; F. W. Briggs, Scottsdale, 3.

Apples, Dessert, soft, 1 plate of 5 apples—First prize, 10s.; second, medal. Robert C. Gatenby, Stewarton, 1; Frank Walker, 2; F. W. Briggs, H.C.

Apples, Dessert, keeping, 1 plate of 5 apples—First prize, 10s.; second, medal. N. Turner, Lilydale, 1; Dr. Benjnfield, 2; C. G. H. Lloyd, Bryn Estyn, New Norfolk, H.C.

Pears, Culinary, 1 plate of 5 pears—First prize, 10s.; second, medal. Alex. W. Millar, Glen Hope, Carrick, 1 and 2; J. McLennan and Sons, H.C.

Pears, Dessert, 1 plate of 5 pears—First prize, 10s.; second, medal. Dr. Benjafield, 1; J. McLennan and Sons, 2; W. Ling, H.C.

Quinces, 1 plate of 5 quinces—First prize, 10s.; second, medal. W. Bald, 1; C. B. Watchorn 2.

Damsons, 1 plate—First prize, 10s.; second, medal. Mary C. Dunning, Elphin Road, 1; R. Brooks, Longford, 2.

Plums, 1 plate—First prize, 10s.; second, medal. Wm. Ling, 1; Dr. Benjafield, 2.

Medlars, 1 plate—First prize, 10s.; second, medal. Mary C. Dunning, 1; Wm. Ling, 2.

Walnuts, 1 plate—First prize, 10s.; second, medal. Louis Horne, 1; J. McLennan and Sons, 2.

Almonds, 1 plate—First prize, 10s. Mary C. Dunning, 1.

Grapes, Tasmanian, 1 plate—Special prize of £1 1s., presented by Messrs. C. H. Smith and Co. Joseph Galvin, H.C.

Collection of Apples, 12 plates of 5 apples each—First prize, £1; second, 10s. J. N. Palmer, 1; W. E. Shoobridge, 2; Anthony D. Raymond, Ulverstone, H.C.

Case of Apples, any variety, packed for export—First prize, £1; second, 10s. Dr. Benjafield, 1; W. E. Shoobridge, 2.

Collection of Pears, 6 plates of 5 pears each. First prize, £1; second, 10s. Dr. Benjafield, 1; W. E. Shoobridge, 2.

Trophy of Apples, Pears, and other fruits—First prize, £5; second, £2. W. E. Shoobridge. Trophy of apples from Lilydale Fruit Board, Award of merit.

Any Fruit not otherwise specified—First prize, 10s.; second, medal. W. Ling, Preserving Melons, 1, 2, and 3; John Roberts, Bella Vista, Scottsdale West, 1 plate of Cape Gooseberries; F. Littler, Lyttelton Street, plate Peaches, 1, 2, and 3; Dr. C. J. Pike, Strawberries; C. S. Agnew, collective exhibit, Award of merit.

Collection of Jams, 6 varieties—First prize, 10s.; second, medal. Mrs. Winnifred Murrell, Cataract Hill, 1; Mrs. F. Littler, 2; Mary C. Dunning, H.C.

Collection of Jellies, 6 varieties—First prize, 10s.; second, medal. Mrs. C. W. Heyes.

Preserved Fruit, dry, 3 varieties—First prize, 10s.; second, medal. May Benjafield, Hobart.

Preserved Fruit, in syrup—First prize, 10s.; second, medal. Mrs. F. Littler, 1; May Benjafield, 2; R. Hall, H.C.

Preserved Fruit, Tart, 3 varieties—First prize, 10s.; second medal. Mary C. Dunning, 1; Mrs. F. Littler, 2 and H.C.

Wine, 3 bottles—First prize, 10s. C. Delger, Swansea.

GROUP F.—DAIRY PRODUCE.

Tub or crock of Butter—First prize, £1. W. Fair and Co., Dunorlan.

Fresh Butter, in plain pound rolls, made from hand-skimmed cream, 3lb.—First prize, 10s.; second, Certificate of Merit. Miss E. Phillips, Westbury, 1; F. W. Briggs, 2 Mrs. Donald McLennan, Cairn Brae, Scottsdale, H.C.

Fresh Butter, in plain pound rolls, made from machine-separated cream, 3lb.—First prize, 10s.; second, Certificate of Merit. A. Harra and Son, 1; W. E. Shoobridge, 2.

Fresh Butter, in plain pound rolls, made from hand-skimmed or machine-separated cream, 3lb.—First prize, 10s.; second, Certificate of Merit. Mrs. Donald McLennan, 1; F. W. Briggs, Scottsdale, 2.

Cheese, not less than 10lb.—First prize, £1; second, 10s. John Lade, St. Mary's, 1, 2, and H.C.

Bacon, 1 flitch—First prize, £1; second, 10s. Henry Higgins, Hobart, 1; Charles Bryant, Launceston, 2.

Ham, 1 ham—First prize, £1; second, 10s. Henry Higgins.

Hen Eggs—First prize, 5s.; second, Certificate of Merit. W. McOrmond, Campbell Town, 1; Henry Higgins, 2.

Round of Corned Beef—Special prize by R. Wacksmuth, Esq., 10s. 6d. Henry Higgins.

Butchers' Small Goods—First prize, £2. Henry Higgins.

Bread, home-made, not less than 2lb.—First prize, 5s.; second, Certificate of Merit. Mrs. C. W. Heyes, 1; Alex. W. Millar, 2.

Best Collection of home-made Pickles—First prize, £1; second, Certificate of Merit. Mrs. C. W. Heyes, 1; Mrs. Winnifred Murrell, 2; Mrs. Frank Williams, H.C.

Fowls, 1 pair, trussed—First prize, 5s.; second, medal. Henry Higgins, 1 and 2.

Ducks, 1 pair, trussed—First prize, 5s.; second, medal. Henry Higgins, 1 and 2.

Geese, 1 goose, trussed—First prize, 5s.; second, medal. Henry Higgins, 1 and 2.

Turkeys, 1 turkey, trussed—First prize, 5s.; second, medal. Henry Higgins, 1 and 2.

Group F.—Poultry.

Brahma, cockerel or pullet, any colour—First prize, 5s. and bronze medal; second, 2s. 6d. Wm. Pickford, Launceston, 1; J. A. Bain, Launceston, 2.

Cochin, cockerel, or pullet, any colour—First prize, 5s. and bronze medal; second, 2s. 6d. H. N. Hulme, Launceston, 1; Frank G. Cutts, Launceston, 2.

Game, cockerel or pullet, any colour (Wright's)—First prize, 5s. and bronze medal; second, 2s. 6d. R. Richardson, Launceston, 1; R. Brooks, Longford, 2.

Game, cockerel or pullet, any colour (Tegetmeier's)—First prize, 5s and bronze medal; second, 2s. 6d. R. Richardson.

Dorking, cockerel or pullet, any colour—First prize, 5s.; second, 2s. 6d. Richard Moore, Providence Valley, 1 and 2.

Plymouth Rock, cockerel or pullet, any colour. First prize, 5s. and bronze medal; second, 2s. 6d. W. McOrmond, Campbell Town, 1; John Hutchinson, Launceston, 2.

Andalusian, cockerel or pullet, any colour—First prize, 5s. and bronze medal; second, 2s. 6d. John Hutchinson, 1; Wallace and Jowett, Penquite, 2.

Minorca, cockerel or pullet, any colour—First prize, 5s. and bronze medal; second, 2s. 6d. W. McOrmond, 1; Wallace and Jowett, 2

Extra—Mrs. J. F. Irvine, blue bonnet parrot.

Leghorn, cockerel or pullet, any colour—First prize, 5s. and bronze medal; second, 2s. 6d. Wallace and Jowett, 1 and 2.

Houdan, cockerel or pullet, any colour—First prize, 5s.; second, 2s. 6d. O. S. Morrison, Invermay.

Crevecœur, cockerel or pullet, any colour—First prize, 5s.; second, 2s. 6d. J. W. Kerslake, Launceston, 1 ; Wallace and Jowett, 2.

Wyandotte, cockerel or pullet, any colour—First prize, 5s.; second, 2s. 6d. R. W. Stokell, Launceston, 1 and 2.

Malay, cockerel or pullet, any colour—First prize, 5s.; second, 2s 6d. Edmund Jewis, Launceston, 1 and 2.

Orpington, cockerel or pullet, any colour—First prize, 5s.; second, 2s. 6d. F. Mervin Littler, 1 and 2.

Hamburgh, cockerel or pullet, any colour—First prize, 5s.; second, 2s. 6d. George Shepherd, 1 ; W. McOrmond, 2.

Bantam, Game, cockerel or pullet, any colour—First prize, 5s. and bronze medal; second, 2s. 6d. R. Brooks.

Bantam, any other variety, cockerel or pullet, any colour—First prize, 5s. and bronze medal; second, 2s. 6d. J. Kerslake.

Turkey, any colour—First prize, 5s.; second, 2s. 6d. W. V. Field, Bishopsbourne, 1 ; R. Brooks, 2.

Geese, gander or goose, any colour—First prize, 5s.; second, 2s. 6d. R. Brooks.

Duck, duck or drake, any colour—First prize, 5s. and bronze medal; second, 2s. 6d. R. Brooks, 1 ; W. V. Field, 2.

Heaviest pair of Chickens, any variety—First prize, 10s.; second, 5s. Edmund Jewis, 2.

DOGS.

St. Bernard, dog or bitch—First prize, 10s. and bronze medal. Bosworth and Cato, Launceston, Lord Byron.

Newfoundland, dog or bitch—First prize, 5s.; second, 2s. 6d. Joseph Dodgshun, St. Leonards, 2.

Collie, dog or bitch—First prize, 10s. and bronze medal; second, 5s. R. B. Bidencope, Brisbane street, Launceston, 2 ; G. C. Gilmore's Gelert, H.C.

Greyhound, dog or bitch—First prize, 10s. and bronze medal; second, 5s. W. V. Field, 1 ; C. Bryant, 2 ; George Robinson, jun., Launceston, V.H.C.; J. McKinstry, V.H.C.

Pointer, dog or bitch—First prize, 5s. and bronze medal ; second, 2s. 6d. Hon. Thomas Reibey and J. Bracken, equal firsts.

English Setter, dog or bitch—First prize, 5s. and bronze medal; second, 2s. 6d. Thomas Carr, 1 ; George Scott, 2 ; Hon. Thomas Reibey, V.H.C.

Gordon Setter, dog or bitch—First prize, 5s. and bronze medal; second, 2s. 6d. William Russell, Perth, 1 ; Charles A. Stewart, St. Leonards, 2 ; James Lamont, H.C.

Irish Setter, dog or bitch—First prize, 5s. and bronze medal; second, 2s. 6d. C. E. Ritchie, 1 and 2.

Retriever, dog or bitch—First prize, 5s. and bronze medal; second, 2s. 6d. W. Collings, 2.

Field Spaniel, dog or bitch—First prize, 5s. and bronze medal; second, 2s. 6d. J. A. Bain, 1 ; W. R. Kilby, 2.

Water Spaniel, dog or bitch—First prize, 5s. and bronze medal; second, 2s. 6d. R. Brooks, 2.

Beagle, dog or bitch—First prize, 5s.; second, 2s. 6d. Hon. Thomas Reibey, 1.

Fox Terrier, dog—First prize, 10s. and bronze medal; second, 5s. George E. Harrap, 1; Edmund Jewis, 2; A. G. Cox, 3; R. Foster, V.H.C.

Fox Terrier, bitch—First prize, 10s. and bronze medal; second, 5s. J. Stuart Grange, 1; George Cox, 1 and 2; C. Bryant, V.H.C.

Irish Terrier, dog or bitch—First prize, 5s.; second, 2s. 6d. P. B. Banks, Waverley, Oatlands, 1 and 2; R. Cameron, Clairville, Evandale, 1; W. V. Field, Bishopsbourne, 2.

English Terrier, dog or bitch—First prize, 5s.; second, 2s. 6d. G. Searle, Clairville, Evandale, 2.

Rough-coated Terrier, dog or bitch—First prize, 5s. and bronze medal; second, 2s. 6d. F. Littler, 1; A. Scott, 2; J. McKinstry, 3.

Toy Spaniel, dog or bitch—First prize, 5s.; second, 2s. 6d. H. Crocker, jun.

Staghound, dog or bitch—First prize, 10s.; second, 5s. Richard Graves, 1; Robert J. Ellis, 2.

Extra—J. Herbert Cato, 2 St. Bernard pups, 1; Mrs. J. F. Irvine, lady's lapdog, 1; J. W. Emms, Cocker Spaniel slut, 1; P. B. Banks, Irish Terrier pups, 1 and 2.

GROUP G—HORTICULTURE.

POT PLANTS.

Stove or Greenhouse Plants, 12—First prize, £2. Frank Walker.

Tuberous-rooted Begonias, in flower, 24—First prize, £3. J. McLennan and Sons.

Fibrous-rooted Begonias, in flower, 4—First prize, 10s.; second, medal. Frank Walker, 1 and 2.

Fibrous-rooted Begonias, foliage only, 4—First prize, 10s.; second, medal. Frank Walker, 1; J. McLennan and Sons, 2.

Fuchsias, Double, 4—First prize, 10s. J. McLennan and Sons.

Fuchsias, Single, 4—First prize, 10s. J. McLennan and Sons.

Ornamental Foliage Plants, 4—First prize, 10s. Frank Walker.

Ferns, 4—First prize, 10s.; second, medal. Frank Walker, 1 and 2.

Lycopods, 4—First prize, 10s.; second, medal. Frank Walker, 1 and 2.

Palms, 4—First prize, 10s.; second, medal. Frank Walker, 1 and 2.

Collection of Pot Plants—First prize, £1. Frank Walker.

CUT FLOWERS.

Dahlias, 24—First prize, 10s. J. McLennan and Sons.

Dahlias, 12—First prize, 5s. J. McLennan and Sons.

Pinks, Carnations, and Picotees, 6—First prize, 5s. C. F. Pitt, Campbell Town.

Miscellaneous Garden Flowers, 6 species—First prize, 5s.; second, Certificate of merit. Frank Walker, 1; W. Ling, 2.

Phlox Drummondi, 6—First prize, 5s. W. McOrmond, Campbell Town.

Chrysanthemums, 6—First prize, 5s. J. McLennan and Sons.

Any Flower not otherwise specified, 6 blooms—First prize, 5s.; second, Certificate of merit. W. Ling, Zinnias, 1; C. F. Pitt, Campbell Town, specimen Cosmos Bipinnatus, 2.

Bridal Bouquet—First prize, 5s. Frank Walker.
Hand Bouquet—First prize, 5s. Frank Walker.
Table Bouquet—First prize, 5s. Frank Walker.
Flower, Fruit, and Vegetable Seeds—First prize, £1. R. Newey and Sons.
Forest Seeds—First prize, 10s. R. Newey and Sons.
Models of Edible Roots—First prize, 5s. R. Newey and Sons.
Collection of Garden Requisites—First prize, 5s. R. Newey and Sons.
Any other exhibit relating to Horticulture, not otherwise specified—First prize, 5s. R. Newey and Sons.
Extra.—James Lamont, Boronia, Invermay (for exhibition only), growing plant of native Sweet-scented Vernal Grass, the original plant being found and brought from the Western Tiers, H.C.

GROUP I.—IMPLEMENTS, MACHINERY, ETC.

Buggy—First prize, £1; second, 10s. John C. Ferguson and Co., built by A. W. Marshall and Co., Latrobe.
Pagnal—First prize, £1; second, 10s. John C. Ferguson and Co., built by H. W. Marshall and Co.
Iron Plough—First prize, £1; second, 10s. Levi Titmus, Leven, 1; H. Blackwell, Bishopsbourne, 2; John Drake, Evandale, H.C.
Wooden Plough—First prize, £1; second, 10s. Wright and Waddington, Hagley, 1; Levi Titmus, 2; John Drake, H.C.
Double-furrow Plough—First prize, £1; second, 10s. John C. Ferguson and Co., H.C.; A. Harrap and Son, H.C.
Subsoil Plough—First prize, £1. Levi Titmus.
Set Heavy Harrows—First prize, 10s. John Drake.
Set Light Harrows—First prize, 10s. John Drake.
Extra—John C. Fergusou and Co., Launceston, Farmer's Favourite Forced Feed and Manure and Seed Drill.

GROUP K.—APICULTURE.

Bee-keeping appliances—W. and T. Newman, George street, Launceston, collection of apiarian requisites.
Honey—W. and T. Newman, honey and comb honey, 1; Alfred Mornington, Bitteswell, Burnie, honey, 2.

EXTRAS.

Home-made Cake—Mrs. C. W. Heyes, Evandale.
Tomato Sauce—Mrs. C. W. Heyes, 1; R. H. Ingamells, Longford, 2; Mrs. F. Williams, 3.
Plum Sauce—Mrs. C. W. Heyes.
Swiss Roll—Mrs. Frank Williams.
Tomato Chutney—Mrs. F. Williams.
Preserved Fruits—R. Miller and Co.

TASMANIAN INTERNATIONAL EXHIBITION, 1891-2.
Revenue Account to July 19, 1892.

Dr.

	£	s.	d.
To Buildings and Grounds	4550	11	11
,, Lighting	1238	19	9
,, Laying on Water	33	15	11
,, Wages and Salaries	2050	12	4
,, Firemen and Sundry Labour	178	10	10
,, Customs Overtime	139	6	0
,, Music, Entertainment, Sports, etc.	1485	7	10
,, Printing, Stationery, and Advertising	754	1	4
,, Official Agents	620	10	9
,, Depreciation of Furniture and Plant	269	17	8
,, Medals and Prizes	651	7	0
,, Freight and Cartage	139	5	7
,, Photographs for Season Tickets	119	18	0
,, Power for Machinery in motion	138	3	1
,, Cablegrams, Cleaning Offices, and Petty Cash	87	8	11
,, Insurance of Pictures	76	0	1
,, Sundries	90	9	5
,, Travelling Expenses	30	10	9
,, Interest and Exchange	14	14	0
,, Legal Expenses	14	12	8
,, Loss on Model Dairy	182	17	7
,, Wine Duties	271	18	9
,, Official Record	135	0	0
,, Agent-General on account of Certificates	50	0	0
,, Launceston Municipal Council—value of articles handed over	955	16	3
,, Accountants' Fees	10	10	0
,, Auditors' Fees	10	10	0
	14,300	16	5
,, Balance Revenue to Balance Sheet	180	2	8
	£14,480	19	1

Cr.

	£	s.	d.	£	s.	d.
By Government Subsidy—Parliamentary Votes	4000	0	0			
,, Wine Duties	271	18	9			
,, Printing Official Record	85	0	0			
,, Cabled to Agent-General	50	0	0			
,, Fancy Fair	247	9	8			
,, T. W. Monds, Esq.—Special Prize	10	0	0			
				4664	8	5
Less Wine Duties				271	18	9
				4392	9	8
,, Gate Receipts				6427	3	2
,, Space				1804	14	5
,, Season Tickets				851	3	6
,, Catering Privilege				475	0	0
,, Advertising Privilege				240	5	6
,, Photographing Privilege				105	0	0
,, Side Shows				88	19	6
,, Other Privileges—Medals and Cartage				25	0	0
,, Hire of Show Cases				37	10	0
,, Cloak Rooms and Lavatories				26	18	10
,, Sundry Revenues				6	14	6
				£14,480	19	1

W. H. TWELVETREES,
ACCOUNTANT.

Audited and found correct.

28th July, 1892.

HENRY EDGELL, } AUDITORS.
T. GLADMAN,

TASMANIAN INTERNATIONAL EXHIBITION, 1891-2.

Balance Sheet, July 19, 1892.

Dr.

LIABILITIES.

	£ s. d.	£ s. d.
To *Sundry Creditors*:		
" Henry Button	85 0 0	
" F. and W. Stewart	75 12 0	
" Ronald W. Smith	40 0 0	
" Secretary	8 0 0	
" Auditors	10 10 0	
" Accountant	10 10 0	
" Launceston City and Suburbs Improvement Association	21 18 9	
" Owners of Pictures sold	85 16 1	
		337 6 10
" Balance from Revenue account		180 2 8
		£517 9 6

W. H. TWELVETREES,
ACCOUNTANT.

Cr.

ASSETS.

	£ s. d.	£ s. d.
By Cash in National Bank		339 16 1
" Stamps		1 2 0
" *Sundry Debtors*:		
Government of Tasmania	85 0 0	
Agent-General for Tasmania	88 7 11	
Launceston Bank for Savings	3 3 6	
		176 11 5
		£517 9 6

Audited and found correct.

T. GLADMAN, } AUDITORS.
HENRY EDGELL,

28th July, 1892.

Explanatory of the above accounts, the item Government Subsidy comprises the parliamentary votes of £1000 and £3000 respectively, to which is also added the sum of £271 18s. 9d., being the amount claimed by the Treasury for Wine Duties (£250 of which has been paid to the Launceston City and Suburbs Improvement Association), together with £85, the cost of printing the Official Record and £50 cabled to the Agent-General.

In the Revenue account is a sum of £955 16s. 3d.; this represents the book value of articles which have been handed over to the Launceston Municipal Council in satisfaction of all claims against the Commissioners in respect to buildings and grounds erected at a cost of fourteen thousand pounds and occupied by them during the period of the Exhibition.

The credit balance of £180 2s. 8d., less expenses and some possible charges not yet ascertained, is available for a *pro rata* distribution amongst exhibitors in accordance with the provisions of Rule 6. The consent of exhibitors is being solicited to the appropriation of their shares to the Launceston City and Suburbs Improvement Association for the purposes of the Exhibition Park. As soon as all have signified their wishes in regard to this matter the sums in question will be handed over.

The sum of £1500 subscribed by the citizens of Launceston as a guarantee fund does not appear in the balance sheet, the Commissioners deeming it advisable, as the guarantee was not required, to return the same to the several guarantors.

               (*Signed*)   SAMUEL J. SUTTON,
                                            Executive Commissioner.

August 2, 1892.

PRINTED BY H. BUTTON, "LAUNCESTON EXAMINER" OFFICE.

www.ingramcontent.com/pod-product-compliance
Lightning Source LLC
Chambersburg PA
CBHW030333170426
43202CB00010B/1108